Classical Sparta
Techniques Behind Her Success

Oklahoma Series in Classical Culture

Oklahoma Series in Classical Culture

Series Editor
A. J. Heisserer, University of Oklahoma

Advisory Board

Ernst Badian, Harvard University
David F. Bright, University of Illinois at Urbana-Champaign
Nancy Demand, Indiana University
Elaine Fantham, Princeton University
R. M. Frazer, Tulane University
Ronald J. Leprohon, University of Toronto
Robert A. Moysey, University of Mississippi
Helen F. North, Swarthmore College
Robert J. Smutny, University of the Pacific
Eva Stehle, University of Maryland at College Park
A. Geoffrey Woodhead, Corpus Christi College, Cambridge/
   Ohio State University
John Wright, Northwestern University

Classical Sparta
Techniques Behind Her Success

Edited by
Anton Powell

Foreword by Paul Cartledge

University of Oklahoma Press : Norman and London

Library of Congress Cataloging-in-Publication Data

Classical Sparta

  (Oklahoma series in classical culture ; # 1)
  1. Sparta (Ancient city) I. Powell, Anton.
II. Series.
DF261.S8C58   1989   938'.9   88–20748
ISBN 0–8061–2177–7

Classical Sparta: Techniques Behind Her Success is Volume 1 in the Oklahoma Series in Classical Culture.

Contents

List of Contributors

Paul Cartledge is a University Lecturer in Ancient History and Fellow of Clare College, Cambridge. In addition to two books, *Sparta and Lakonia 1300–362 BC* (Routledge & Kegan Paul, 1979) and *Agesilaos and the Crisis of Sparta* (Duckworth & Johns Hopkins, 1987), he has published almost a hundred articles and reviews on ancient Greek and Roman history, one fifth of them specifically on Sparta.

Ephraim David, born in 1945, is Associate Professor of Ancient History and Head of the Department of History at the University of Haifa in Israel. Author of *Sparta between Empire and Revolution* and *Aristophanes and Athenian Society of the Early Fourth Century*, he has also written a number of articles on Greek history and political theory.

N.R.E. Fisher, born in 1944, is Lecturer in Classics at University College, Cardiff. His publications include *Social Values in Classical Athens* (1976), and articles on '*Hybris* and Dishonour', *Greece and Rome* 23 (1976) and 26 (1979) and on Greek and Roman Associations, Symposia and Clubs in *Civilizations of the Mediterranean* (M. Grant and R. Kitzinger, eds, 1988).

Alan Griffiths is a Lecturer in Greek and Latin at University College London, with a special interest in all forms of ancient narrative and in the uses to which Greek myth was put in art, literature and thought.

Stephen Hodkinson is Lecturer in Ancient History at the University of Manchester. He is author of several articles on Spartan society and economy, as well as on settlement and animal husbandry in ancient Greece.

James Hooker is Reader in Greek and Latin in the University of London. Among other writings on the history, language and literature of ancient Greece, he has published *The Ancient Spartans* (Dent, 1980), which later appeared in a German edition (*Sparta, Geschichte und Kultur*, Reclam, 1982) and an Italian edition (*Gli Spartani*, Bompiani, 1984).

List of Contributors

Robert Parker, born in 1950, is a Lecturer in Greek and Latin Languages and Literature, and Fellow of Oriel College, Oxford. He has written *Miasma: Pollution and Purification in Early Greek Religion* (1983), and several articles, including 'Greek States and Greek Oracles' in *Crux. Studies presented to G.E.M. de Ste. Croix* (1985), and 'Myths of Early Athens' in J. Bremmer (ed.), *Interpretations of Greek Mythology* (Barnes & Noble, 1987).

Anton Powell is a professional writer. Born in 1947, he has published articles on Athenian and Spartan politics in various academic journals. He is the author of the undergraduate textbook *Athens and Sparta* (Routledge, 1988). He has also written several books on Greece for children. Since 1985 he has been organiser of the London Classical Society.

Introduction

Lakonian studies were effectively refounded by Geoffrey de Ste. Croix, whose *Origins of the Peloponnesian War* not only stated unforgettably Sparta's problem with the helots but also set an example in the deriving of fresh and convincing interpretations of classical literary texts. Since the appearance of his book, important progress has been made by others (among them several contributors to this volume) in exploring permanent problems within Sparta's own citizen body. Arising from these developments, the argument which engendered the present volume was briefly this: since Sparta's enduring difficulties were great, and yet her success (considering her size) was extraordinary, unusual and effective procedures among the Spartans are worth looking for.

All the papers now forming this book have been presented orally to a seminar of the revived London Classical Society. When counsels were initially divided on the suitability of the seminar format for the Society, it was intervention by James Hooker and Norma Miller which secured the seminar's future. To them the organiser of the seminar, the editor of this volume, acknowledges a great debt.

The Society is indebted also to the University of London's Institute of Classical Studies. The Institute has housed most of our meetings; its secretariat has provided our most important publicity; its library and other facilities provide an indispensable focus. We remember with especial gratitude the vision and energy of the late Victor Ehrenberg, who helped to create not only the London Classical Society but also the Institute itself.

Finally, the editor records his debt to Ephraim David and David Harvey, for the learning and the goodwill which they brought to discussion of papers at the seminar; and to Paul Cartledge, whose direct contribution to this book has gone far beyond the writing of the Foreword.

A. Powell

Foreword

Paul Cartledge

The subject of Sparta is surprisingly apt to provoke powerful passions within the professionally dispassionate academic sodality. 'Narrow-minded jealousy' and 'utter inhumanity' were the collective Spartan characteristics that obtruded on one recent historian's sombre vision, whereas another could almost simultaneously observe that Sparta 'with all its obvious faults' was yet 'a mystery and an inspiration to generations of intelligent men'.[1] This apparent contradiction is as flagrant as the often-noted contrast between the terrible beauty of 'the magnificent Laconian landscape'[2] and the terrifying abstention from artistic cultivation of the beautiful habitually practised by, or at any rate ascribed to, its ancient inhabitants.

Perhaps the only truly satisfying way of resolving these and other seeming paradoxes of the ancient Spartan experience is to work them through in a novel or play.[3] Denied that luxury, scholars wrestle with them under more commonplace conditions. The sheer quantity of scholarship on Sparta since the pioneering work of J.C.F. Manso (1800–5) is therefore a tribute to the enduring immediacy and fascination as well as intractability of the many basic issues of society, economy, politics and ideology posed by Spartan history.[4] There is plenty of space for another volume of essays by divers hands on problems of Spartan history and culture.[5]

The question rather is one of approach and framework. In the long run ancient Sparta failed, both as a power-unit and as a social system. Yet, however comforting that may be to a fatalist in the mould of Herodotus (I.5.3–4), Sparta's run was a very long one indeed, and even after the collapse of the fourth century BC the state possessed a remarkable capacity for regeneration as

x

late as the second century AD. Moreover, the idea of Sparta — or rather a multiple legacy of often very disparate ideas — has outlived antiquity to be a formative influence still in many societies to this day.[6] It is therefore entirely appropriate that this volume should be devoted to explaining the varieties and techniques of Spartan success, if only to complement the equally necessary historiographical task of accounting for that two-fold failure.[7]

Spartan success can usefully be located on two broadly distinguishable planes: the ideological and the institutional. Straddling these two, and partaking both of propaganda and myth (in the broadest sense)[8] and of social structure, is Spartan religion. Much has been written on individual Spartan cults and festivals and on Spartan religious iconography,[9] but little or nothing on Spartan religion as a system of ideas and practices or its location within Spartan society as a whole. And this is in spite of the telling evidence provided by observant non-Spartans who knew Sparta and Spartans well at first hand: for instance, the understated remark of Herodotus (V.63.2) that the Spartans 'rank the things of heaven more highly than the things of men', or Xenophon's comment on the daily pre-dawn sacrifice conducted by the commanding king on a campaign that, 'could you witness it, you would consider all other people to be mere improvisers in military matters and the Spartans the only real technicians of warfare' (*Lak. Pol.* XIII.5). Parker's essay (pp. 142–72), which gives *multum in parvo*, thus fills a real gap. By isolating and emphasising what he takes to be the distinctive features of Spartan ritual life and identifying the role of religion in Spartan public affairs generally, he is able to show how the gods were, as he puts it (in suitably military language), 'at the top of the chain of command that ran down through Spartan society'.

It was precisely to forge and strengthen that chain that the Spartan elite went to such pains to get their ideology right. Hoplite warfare was by no means the only kind in which they were technically expert. As has been well noted by a French scholar who has contributed greatly to our understanding of Spartan mentality, 'one of the most striking characteristics of Spartan society is the effectiveness with which ideological pressure was exerted by the dominant group' — whether that group was the nobles (pressuring the commons), the men (putting pressure on the women), the adults (on the young), or the master class (oppressing the helots).[10] It is perfectly proper therefore that half the essays in this volume address themselves to broadly ideological issues, while all of the remainder touch on ideology in some significant way or other.

Hooker (pp. 122–41) examines in chronological order a series of examples of Spartan propaganda designed for both domestic and foreign consumption. The operational distinction he draws between 'state' (that is, officially sponsored by a dominant political grouping) and unofficial or private, 'non-state' propaganda can be applied usefully to Griffiths's enquiry into the mental health of King Kleomenes I (pp. 51–78). Both kinds were clearly deployed inside and outside Sparta to provide Herodotus with the raw materials for his brilliantly retouched picture of Kleomenes as an unstable and unscrupulous religious deviant bearing more than a passing resemblance to his older Persian contemporary Cambyses.

Finally on the ideological plane there is Powell's wide-ranging exploration of Sparta's exploitation of the lie, with special reference to visual techniques of deception (pp. 173–92). This has the perhaps rather paradoxical effect of rehabilitating Sparta against a crescendo of denunciations of Spartan stupidity and near-sighted obtuseness. But whatever we may think privately of the morality of the Spartan regime at home or of its contribution to the greater glory of ancient Greece at large, informed appreciation of the mental basis of that regime's longevity and spiritual power is nothing less than its historiographical due.

The three remaining essays treat of a deep tranche of Sparta's most important social and economic institutions. Yet Fisher's analysis of Spartan social drinking (pp. 26–50) rightly begins with a basic point of method:

> as so often with Sparta, it is convenient to start with the 'mirage', or the 'ideal type', before proceeding to considera-tion of the degree of contradictions and tensions in the system, and of the extent to which the operations of these rules and laws began to break down through the classical period.

Both the functions and the dysfunctions of the consumption of wine (properly mixed with water, of course, in contrast to Kleomenes' outlandish habit of taking it neat) within the controlled environment of the common messes are admirably teased out here. But for a fuller appreciation of the systems collapse that engulfed Sparta in the fourth century and brought down the finely balanced mess-organisation in the process, it is necessary to turn to Hodkinson's sophisticated exercise in historical demography (pp. 79–121).

Employing a heavy battery of analytical techniques, including computer simulation to eke out critical scrutiny of the ambiguous army-figures provided by the notoriously unstatistical ancient literary sources, Hodkinson concludes that Sparta's critical *oliganthrōpia* in the early fourth century was the result of a significant combination of social, economic, cultural and genetic factors and of the decisively deleterious conjunction of long-term trends and short-term developments. Differential property-ownership within the Spartan citizen estate is rightly seen as the key variable. The new social order elaborated in the seventh century was predicated upon a common lifestyle, expressed and symbolised through participation in a common mess, member-ship of which was a condition of citizenship. But as long as there was anomalous distribution of landed property, peer-group equality among the *homoioi* was at best a pious aspiration kept alive by a spirit of compromise. In the course of the fifth and fourth centuries that spirit was battered into oblivion. In this and Hodkinson's two previous essays on the crisis of classical Sparta, the modern student will, I believe, find the best short explanation of the processes whereby Sparta's failure was bred of Sparta's very success.[11]

After that rather sobering passage it would be pleasant to end on a note of jocular hilarity. But as David's grimly realistic account demonstrates, not least by its generously comparative approach, Spartan cachinnation was for the most part no laughing matter (pp. 1–25). Even laughter was an integral part of the *étatisme* of Sparta's closed society, in which it was an affair of state where, when, why and how one did — or did not — laugh. It comes as no surprise to learn that laughter was exploited in Sparta as yet one more channel of propaganda, a suitable reminder with which to close that the ideological and insti-tutional planes are separable only in theory, not in living actuality.

August 1987

Clare College,
Cambridge

Notes

1. W.G. Forrest, *A history of Sparta c.950–192 BC* (1968; 2nd edn, London, 1980), 152. E. Badian, 'Agis III', *Hermes* 95 (1967), 170–92, at 179.
2. A.J. Toynbee, 'Greek light on world history', *ABSA* 45 (1950), 1–10, at 7, in a characteristically Toynbee-esque meditation on alleged historical 'recurrences' prompted by the situation of the Menelaion and Mistra on opposite sides of the Spartan basin.
3. Many such works of imaginative literature are dealt with perceptively, if inevitably all too briefly, in E. Rawson, *The Spartan tradition in European thought* (Oxford, 1969); I would mention in dispatches Naomi Mitchison's gargantuan novel of the third-century BC Spartan revolution, *The Corn King and the Spring Queen* (1931), with Rawson, 365.
4. Full bibliographical references up to 1983 may be found in the works cited in my *Agesilaos and the crisis of Sparta* (London & Baltimore, 1987), vii.
5. See most recently E. Lanzilotta (ed.), *Problemi di storia e cultura spartana* (Rome, 1984), where happily religion features prominently.
6. In addition to Rawson (n. 3, above) see *Agesilaos* ch. 22 with the bibliography there cited.
7. For very different recent attempts to fulfil the latter task see, on one hand, G.L. Cawkwell, 'The decline of Sparta', *CQ* 33 (1983), 385–400, and on the other my *Agesilaos* and the works of Hodkinson (n. 11, below).
8. For myths as culturally coded messages informing a community's daily life and culture see e.g. Gilbert Adair, *Myths & Memories* (Glasgow, 1986).
9. For instance, S. Wide, *Lakonische Kulte* (Leipzig, 1893); E.-L.I. Marangou, *Lakonische Elfenbein- und Beinschnitzereien* (Tübingen, 1969); and most recently M. Pipili, *Laconian iconography of the sixth century BC* (Oxford, 1987).
10. J. Ducat, 'Aspects de l'hilotisme', *Anc. Society* 9 (1978), 5–46, at 30 n. 86.
11. S. Hodkinson, 'Social order and the conflict of values in Classical Sparta', *Chiron* 13 (1983), 239–81; 'Land tenure and inheritance in Classical Sparta', *CQ* 36 (1986), 378–406.

1

Laughter in Spartan Society

Ephraim David

Aristotle presented man not only as a political animal but also as a laughing animal.[1] These characteristics of mankind are closely interconnected: both of them stem from the sociable nature of the human being. Laughter is an aspect of human behaviour closely associated with many realms of social life, a social phenomenon *par excellence*. The French philosopher Henri Bergson aptly remarked that, in order to understand laughter, we must examine it in its natural environment, which is society.[2] It may be justifiable to invert Bergson's remark (or rather to complete it) and to assert that, in order to understand a certain society, it is important to examine its laughter. The purpose of this paper is to analyse the various aspects and functions of laughter in Spartan society.

Austerity and sobriety are among the most notorious traits of classical Sparta, the cornerstones of its peculiar system as well as of the mirage it engendered. It is therefore at first glance surprising to discover within the pantheon of austere Sparta a divinity personifying such a 'luxury reflex'[3] as laughter. What appears to be even more surprising is to find Lycurgus, the mysterious lawgiver who became the very symbol of austerity, credited with the initiative of erecting a statue of Laughter. Plutarch tried to elucidate his hero's interest in the matter:

> For not even Lycurgus himself was immoderately austere; indeed, Sosibius relates that he actually dedicated a little statue of Laughter and introduced seasonable jesting into their drinking parties [*symposia*] and similar places of common entertainment, *to sweeten*, as it were, their hardships and austere way of life.[4]

Sosibius, the source quoted by Plutarch here, was the first Laconian scholar, an antiquarian of the late third century BC, who had a special interest in the local cults of Laconia.[5] The cult of Laughter is rationalistically interpreted in the above passage as a by-product of the lawgiver's intention of providing a sort of compensation for the stress and austerity of the Spartan *diaita*. Relaxation, relief from tension, has often been regarded by various theoreticians of laughter (from Aristotle to modern gelotologists)[6] as one of its vital functions, and in Sparta this function may well have been even more necessary than elsewhere.

The cult of Laughter is mentioned once more by Plutarch, in his biography of Cleomenes (9.1): 'The Lacedaemonians have not only sanctuaries of Fear but also of Death, Laughter and other similar things that may befall them [*kai toioutōn allōn pathēmatōn*].' This is the opening sentence of a digression dealing with the cult of Fear in Sparta. Here Plutarch does not mention his source.[7] In his biographies of Agis and Cleomenes he usually follows Phylarchus as far as the narrative is concerned, but these biographies contain also a certain amount of non-Phylarchean material, particularly in the digressions. The digression concerning the cult of Fear and especially the remark on the cult of similar '*pathēmata*' can most plausibly be traced back once more to Sosibius in view of his well known interest in Laconian cults in general and the mention of the Laughter cult in particular.[8] The cult of these divinities at Sparta implied an awareness of their mysterious power[9] but not a submission to this power; rather, a sustained effort to use it in the interest of the Spartan state. This is most obviously illustrated by the example of Fear.

The Spartan cult of Fear[10] is prima facie no less surprising than that of Laughter, since, as is well known, courage was regarded as the most cultivated Spartan virtue. Plutarch explains that 'the Spartans pay honour to Fear not as they do to the powers which they try to avert . . . but because they believe that their polity is chiefly maintained by fear'.[11] Although Plutarch refers to the fear of the disgraceful and of the laws,[12] one can hardly resist the temptation to apply his remark to the fear of the helots, whom the Spartans were always trying to neutralise (cf. Thuc. 4.80.2), *inter alia* by means of terror and occasional murders.

Like the uses of terror (and death), so the uses of laughter were appreciated by the Spartans and were applied in various ways aimed at consolidating the social order and promoting the norms of the so-called Lycurgan system.

Certain patterns of laughter were developed and encouraged at the common messes (*syssitia*), where the Spartans used to spend a considerable part of their time.[13] Laughter, however, was not introduced to these 'clubs' just as a casual pastime but was assigned educative and social functions of the utmost importance. The experience of laughter at the *syssitia* was even integrated within the educational system (the *agōgē*). For the Spartan ephebes 'institutionalised' laughter must have been highly significant in view of the strict seriousness otherwise imposed on their behaviour. Xenophon graphically describes (as an eye-witness and enthusiastic admirer) how they used to keep their hands under their cloaks, walk in silence, without looking around but keeping their eyes fixed on the ground, etc: 'you would expect a stone statue to utter a sound sooner than them'.[14] Even allowing for a certain measure of exaggeration in the description of the philo-Laconian Xenophon,[15] one can hardly doubt that those boys were afraid of indulging in free laughter.[16] Since laughter is partially a voluntary human reaction, it can often be suppressed, even when persons are amused (as it can also be forced when they are not), but the very attempt to suppress it may sometimes produce, particularly in the case of children, precisely the opposite effect, i.e. the explosion of a convulsive, 'mad' laughter which can hardly be controlled.[17] This mysterious faculty of laughter might have been one of the reasons for its deification.

In Sparta the control of the state over laughter was an integral part of the overall *étatisme*, as can most obviously be seen in certain aspects of the *agōgē* and the *syssitia*. Plutarch relates that when the Spartan boys were brought to the *syssitia* for educational purposes, they were witnessing not only the adults' political discussions, but also several sorts of amusement considered at Sparta 'worthy of freemen'; there they had to get accustomed to joking and jesting without buffoonery (*aneu bōmolochias*) and to endure jesting without displeasure. 'To endure jesting seems to have been a peculiarly Laconian quality', remarks Plutarch, adding however that if someone could bear the jesting no longer, he had only to ask and the jester ceased.[18] The restriction of jesting to the limit imposed by the sufferer's power of endurance was meant to protect social harmony in general and cohesiveness among the members of the same *syssition* in particular.[19]

The malice of laughter might sometimes have been combined

with a certain amount of affection, as often happens in amicable teasing. This is supported by many examples of what anthropologists describe as 'symmetrical or reciprocal joking relationships'. In these relations various persons are by custom allowed (sometimes even required) to tease or make fun one of the other without taking offence.[20] Such teasing, which presents a mixture of friendliness and antagonism, is symptomatic of the combination between elements of co-operation and competition in Spartan society. Moreover, the technique of sham conflicts may have been intended, *inter alia,* to obviate real ones and thereby promote social harmony. All in all, playful antagonism was one of the central elements of Spartan education.

The Spartan boys learned to jest and endure jesting not only by witnessing the adults' conversations at the *syssitia,* but also through jesting contests. Like the physical contests, these were inspected by the elders, whose purpose was to detect the most promising elements for potential leadership in the future.[21] Thus, dexterity in jesting must have been a serious criterion in the process of recruiting new members to the ranks of the Spartan elite. The jesting contests contributed to developing a certain type of wit which became proverbial in Greece.[22] Regardless of their strict historical accuracy, the Laconian apophthegms may be regarded as a significant source for the Spartan sense of humour. It is important to note that they are frequently dominated by an arrogant spirit of jocular aggressiveness well illustrated, even if in an extreme form, by the saying (ascribed to Cleomenes I) that the Spartans do not exterminate the Argives (despite their frequent victories over them) only because they need some trainers for the young generation.[23]

The agonistic character of Spartan education (which is highly impressive, even by Greek standards) can plausibly be associated with laughter: the perpetual physical contests, mimic battles and disputes within the framework of the *agōgē* provided the stimulus for the laughter of triumph, which often expresses the sensation of superiority experienced by the winners (and also by the spectators, who usually tend to identify themselves with the victor). This kind of laughter must not only have been allowed but even encouraged by the Spartan authorities within their efforts to cultivate love of victory (*philonikia*). It would be interesting to know whether the losers were allowed the 'luxury' of the defensive laughter.[24] The Spartans' devotion in encouraging love of victory tells against the idea that the expression of such laughter was tolerated. Worth mentioning here is the example of a Spartan (Paidaretos) reported to have gone away content and smiling after failing to be selected for the famous *corps d'élite* of 300 *hippeis*. The story goes that the ephors called him back and asked why he was laughing, at which he replied: 'Because I congratulate the State for having three hundred citizens better than myself.'[25] Despite its anecdotal character, this example may serve to reflect the intolerance of the Spartans towards a loser's laughter (note, by the way, that in the story his smile is equated by the ephors with laughter). The apophthegm itself in its turn suggests that the defence mechanism of a Spartan 'loser' could be directed to a standard type of reaction — expressing patriotic satisfaction over the excellence of fellow citizens. Behind the façade, however, animosity and tensions were operating with remarkable intensity.[26]

Laughter was also deeply appreciated within the framework of the Spartan education as a corrective weapon against those who were not sufficiently successful in coping with the challenges of the *agōgē* or were guilty of some misbehaviour. In these cases the maidens were encouraged to mock the 'failures' in public, a method reported to have been highly successful: 'The sting of their sarcastic jokes was no less sharp than that of serious admonitions, especially as the kings and gerontes, as well as the other citizens, were present at the spectacle.'[27] This technique was all the more efficient in view of the songs that the same maidens were instructed to sing in praise of those who had distinguished themselves. The corrective function of laughter was exercised in similar ways by another 'pressure group', the elderly men, who enjoyed a special position of authority in Sparta. This position enabled them to defend the Spartan code of behaviour by exposing to public ridicule deviations from its norms. The role of such laughter was strictly conservative.[28]

For additional aspects of the role played by laughter in Spartan society, particularly in the educative process, we have to return to the common meals. The satisfaction of hunger is considered to be a primary prerequisite of laughter,[29] whereas wine is generally recognised as one of its most efficient catalysts. It is therefore important to bear in mind that in Sparta the *syssitia* functioned also as *symposia*. Spartan drinking, however, had to be moderate, as was emphasised by the philo-Laconian oligarch Critias, who pointed out the relationship between moderate drinking and moderate laughter ('metrios gelōs').[30] At the *syssitia* the Spartan boys were shown the dangers of excessive drinking by a peculiar

5

anti-alcoholic lesson, in which laughter must have been a highly significant component.

The Spartans, we are told, used to compel the helots to drink a large quantity of unmixed wine and then exposed the intoxicated victims at the *syssitia* to teach young Spartiates the meaning of drunkenness.[31] The degradation of the human being under the influence of alcohol, coupled with a sensation of superiority in the spectators, is bound to arouse contemptuous laughter in the latter. Worth mentioning in this respect is the view advanced by Hobbes (*Leviathan*, Part I, Ch. 6) on the nature of laughter, a view which, although often and rightly criticised as too rigid and dogmatic, is highly significant as far as Spartan laughter is concerned. According to Hobbes, laughter is the 'sudden glory' arising from a sudden perception of our own superiority by comparison with the infirmity of others. This view of laughter appears to be perfectly adequate for describing the sensation of the Spartans at the sight of the drunken helots, with the possible exception of the spontaneity factor. However, in the case of the Spartan youths who for the first time in their lives assisted at this performance, the relevance of the spontaneity factor cannot be denied. For them, laughter *was* identifiable with a sudden glory emanating from the sudden recognition of their own eminence by contrast with the infirmity of the helots. Nevertheless, those who have criticised the rigidity of Hobbes' view have argued, among other things, that spontaneity or surprise is not always essential to laughter:[32] many comedians have their 'signature gags', which are expected by their public. One may assume that the Spartan audience expected those helots who were made to play the fool at the *syssitia* to follow certain comic patterns. Some of these patterns are inherent in the very symptoms of drunkenness: ridiculous and immoderate hilarity, for instance, one of the most frequent symptoms of drunkenness, is known to be itself an incentive for laughter. Thus, the difference between moderate drinking and excessive drinking could be demonstrated *inter alia* by the contrast between the sober laughter of the spectators[33] and the unrestrained laughter of the drunken helots. Furthermore, the comic performance of the helots included certain elements which were not based on the natural symptoms of drunkenness but were part of a traditional repertoire carefully arranged by the Spartan 'stage directors'. In the *Life of Lycurgus*, immediately after relating the didactic method of exhibiting inebriated helots at the *syssitia*, Plutarch adds that the Spartans made them sing and dance vulgar and grotesque ('katagelastous') songs and dances.[34] These songs and dances are most plausibly interpreted as part of the comic ritual performed at the *syssitia* (and possibly elsewhere as well) by drunken helots.

Anthropological studies provide significant analogies, *mutatis mutandis* of course. The purpose of the ritual clowns in the American-Indian culture, for instance, is to teach people what they should not do, by means of performing certain obscene and self-indulging acts in front of their audience.[35]

In Sparta the ritual of laughter was frequently connected with the ritual of social oppression. The laughter aroused by the helots' performance at the *syssitia* was aimed not only at drunkenness but also at the helots. The solidarity of the Spartans and their devotion to the so-called Lycurgan code of behaviour were encouraged by their joint sensation of superiority, which in turn was animated by a double contempt: for phenomena regarded as base by their code of behaviour (such as drunkenness) as well as for those who served to exemplify these phenomena — the helots. Shared laughter of derision by one social group at the expense of another social group creates a bond among the participants in laughter and consolidates the feeling of their social inclusion (on the basis of their joint aggressiveness).[36] Since the *syssitia* were an integral part of the military organisation, this sort of laughter was valuable additionally for the promotion of *esprit de corps*, which was also encouraged by other means (e.g. the unanimity required at the vote for the admission of new members, and the obligation of strict confidentiality regarding the discussions at each *syssition*).[37]

There is a tradition according to which the Spartans did not attend either comedy or tragedy so that they might not hear anyone speak either seriously or jestingly against the laws.[38] However, the absence of a developed form of drama should not lead us to the conclusion that the Spartans had no drama at all: the performance of the drunken helots provides an example of a dramatic ritual of laughter, a sort of comedy which, despite its rudimentary character, had an unmistakable message to convey to the audience.

One of the most important forms of comic *mimēsis* in Sparta was the dance. As we have seen, certain vulgar and grotesque dances were performed by the helots at the *syssitia*. The *kordax* was most probably one of them: it was notorious as an extremely vulgar and obscene dance, frequently associated with drunkenness. The *lombroteron* and the *mothōn* were other vulgar and indecent dances; our evidence on them is very meagre.[39] In the case of the *mothōn* the name suggests a connection with the social group of the *mothōnes* (or *mothakes*), and it is reasonable to infer that the dance was occasionally performed by some members of this group (probably by the *nothoi tōn Spartiatōn*, i.e. bastard sons of Spartiates born of helot mothers).[40]

We are not much better informed as far as the dance called *baryllika* is concerned: this was an orgiastic dance of comic and obscene character, performed (possibly in honour of Artemis) by men disguised in feminine masks (*brydalichai*).[41] Other dances of comic *mimēsis* included representations of satyrs, of old men leaning on sticks or of boys stealing fruit.[42]

The stealing motif is mentioned also by Sosibius, who, as already observed, had a special interest in the attitude of the Spartans towards laughter. This interest is further illustrated by one of his remarks concerning the character of comic amusement in Sparta: 'Among the Lacedaemonians there was an ancient fashion of comic pastime, not taken too seriously, because even in such matters Sparta follows simplicity.'[43] The meaning of Sosibius' remark that the Spartans did not take their comic pastime too seriously is conveyed by the context, which emphasises the archaic character of their comic *mimēsis* and its simplicity (as compared with poleis where the genre developed into a literary art). This is also clarified by Sosibius' examples of Spartan comic performance: the imitation of persons stealing fruit or of a foreign doctor 'talking in the manner portrayed by Alexis' (i.e. probably trying unsuccessfully to imitate the Dorian accent). Sosibius reports that those who pursued this kind of performance 'among the Laconians' were called *deikēlistai*, a term which is explained as 'maskers or mummers' (*skeuopoioi kai mimētai*).[44] There is an anecdote relating that Agesilaus, when asked by a famous tragic actor, Callippides, if the king did not recognise him, answered contemptuously: 'Aren't you Callippides, the *deikēliktas*?'[45] Being labelled a *deikēliktas* does not appear to have been flattering at Sparta,[46], and for Callippides this was certainly a grave insult. The reduction of a tragic actor of his calibre to the status of an actor of mime is typical of the Spartans' attitude to dramatic art.

Many of the above dances and mimes were most probably performed at the various Spartan festivals and in the Spartan theatre, the main function of which was to provide a place for the celebration of the festivals.[47] The question arises as to what active part, if any, the Spartiates had in these comic performances. Some scholars assume that their part was indistinguishable from that of the helots.[48] This assumption encounters serious difficulties. Plutarch's statement that the helots were compelled to sing and dance vulgar and grotesque songs and dances is accompanied by the remark that they were forbidden to perform songs and dances worthy of freemen.[49] The obvious reason for this was the same as that behind using helots in the anti-alcoholic lesson: the intention of associating the helots psychologically with ugliness, buffoonery and servitude, and of dissociating them from decorum, sobriety and freedom. This device, which was meant to consolidate the superiority of the Spartans, was based on the distinction between two mutually exclusive codes of behaviour.[50] The implication of this dichotomy was not only that the helots were forbidden to behave like Spartans, but also that the Spartans were not supposed to behave like helots. Consequently, the very logic which on the one hand prohibited excessive drinking as far as the Spartans were concerned and on the other hand imposed it on the helots, would have led to the same attitude with respect to vulgar and grotesque dances and other mimetic performances of similar character: those would be confined to the helots and probably also other underprivileged social categories (such as the *mothōnes*). This conclusion is further corroborated by the derogatory associations which the label '*deikēliktas*' appears to have carried at Sparta.

To be sure, the existence of a 'Lacedaemonian' comic actor (a *kōmōidos*, not merely a *deikēliktas*) by the name of Nikon, son of Eumathidas, is attested by epigraphic evidence for the mid-third century BC (258–257 or 254–253).[51] However, it is important to note that the inscription bearing Nikon's name refers to performances *outside* Sparta, actually to his participation at the festival of Sōtēria at Delphi. Moreover, the term '*Lakedaimonios*' could apply to both *Spartiatai* and *perioikoi*. If of Spartiate origin, Nikon may well have been one of those 'inferiors' (*hypomeiones*), who owing to impoverishment were deprived of their civic rights (cf. Xen. *Hell.* 3.3.6; 11; Arist. *Pol.* 1271a 35–7). This would explain what drove him to leave his city in search of a livelihood and to adopt the profession of a comic actor. By that time poverty had compelled many disfranchised Spartans to undertake various sorts of occupations which were regarded in their city as unworthy of freemen and citizens (Plut. *Agis*, 5.5)

The Spartan concept of comic performances appears to have influenced Plato's view of comedy in his last work, the *Laws*. When referring to the value of comedy, the Athenian, who in this work usually advances Plato's own opinions, remarks that a wise man cannot understand the serious without a knowledge of the ridiculous; one has to know the comic in order to beware of ridiculous actions. However, in Plato's view, most probably inspired by the Spartan model, this sort of imitation should only be assigned to slaves or foreign hired employees and never be performed by citizens (Plat. *Laws* 816E).

In Sparta the contrast between the two codes of behaviour, that of the citizens and that of the helots, seems also to have been expressed through one of the basic vehicles of comedy — the parody. Myron's statement that the helots received a certain number of beatings every year, regardless of any wrongdoing (in order to remind them that they were slaves), can most plausibly be interpreted as referring to a parody of the ritual beatings the Spartans inflicted on their boys.[52] This was part of a strange ceremony at which it was highly honourable for the boys to dare to steal as many cheeses as possible from the altar of Artemis Orthia at the price of enduring pain when scourged in the process.[53] Here it is worth stressing that one of the Spartan comic motives mentioned by both Sosibius and Pollux was the imitation of stealing food.[54] (By the way, the literal meaning of the word *bōmolochos* 'buffoon' is 'one who waits by the altar', presumably to beg or steal some of the offerings.)[55] On the reasonable assumption that the imitation of stealing, like many other comic performances, was assigned to the helots, it is most tempting to associate Myron's statement on the beating of the helots with their mimetic stealing. If this is correct, the message of such comedy could also be interpreted as a warning to the helots that they should not try to imitate the Spartans: the actors who were symbolically assigned the role of imitators had to be beaten in order to remind the helots of their servile status.[56]

All in all, in primitive or archaic societies (as well as among children) beating is a frequent detonator of derisive laughter at the expense of the victim. Witness, for instance, the laughter of the Achaeans at the expense of Thersites, who is bludgeoned by Odysseus.[57] Beating has to be accounted a potential incentive to laughter also in the pseudo-primitive society of classical Sparta (in which many primitive elements survived in an artificial form, being adapted to political functions). However, not all sorts of beating are liable to stir laughter and, even when they do, it is not always the same sort of laughter. The beating of the Spartan boys at the altar of Artemis Orthia could hardly incite laughter of contempt. Their beating appears to have been associated with a completely different kind of laughter. Plutarch reports (this time as an eye-witness of a late version of this ritual) that during the flagellation (which in many cases had fatal results) the boys endured their whippings cheerful (*hilaroi*) and proud.[58] Their cheerfulness may be interpreted as an artificial expression of obligatory ritual laughter, a possible survival of the tribal society closely connected with the original significance of the flagellation: a symbolic ritual death and a fertility rite. This interpretation is supported by the frequent association between ritual laughter, birth, death and fertility in primitive societies and in folklore.[59] On the other hand, in the case of the helots, contemptuous laughter could be expected from the Spartan audience because, like Thersites, the helots had become associated with ugliness, baseness and derision. The helots' cries of pain (as contrasted with the proud endurance of the boys) could only increase the stimulus of laughter among the Spartan audience by appealing to their sense of superiority. Moreover, the reasonable assumption regarding the beating of the helots as a parody has a substantial bearing on the problem of laughter: within a parody the comic effect is always produced by the contrast between the gravity of the original and the frivolity (or incongruity) of the imitation.

The attitude of the Spartans towards comedy can be further explored with the assistance of archaeology. The British excavations at the sanctuary of Artemis Orthia have discovered a great number of terracotta masks, which are generally interpreted as votive imitations (usually small in scale) of the wooden original masks. These were most probably used in the ritual dances and other mimetic performances (e.g. by the *deikēlistai*). The masks are of different standard types, among which the most frequent are the 'Old Women' (wrinkled faces) and the 'Caricature' types.[60] The first category can plausibly be associated with Hesychius' description of the *brydalichai* — the 'ugly feminine masks' (*aischra prosōpeia gynaikeia*) worn by male dancers (probably helots) performing an obscene dance in female disguise.[61] Similarly, the appearance of the masks classified as 'Caricatures', 'Satyrs' and 'Gorgons' justifies the general interpretation of them as reproductions of the masks which the helots (and perhaps additional categories of the underprivileged) were made to wear when engaged in other obscene performances mentioned above. Among the 'Caricatures' category, it is possible to distinguish roughly between 'sub-human' figures (whose physiognomy still presents some human resemblance) and the entirely grotesque types.[62] The grotesque features are often mingled with terrifying and morbid traits, a mixture inevitably reminiscent of the strange trinity Fear, Death and Laughter — divinities who, as already noted, were honoured in Sparta with special sanctuaries. The predilection for the grotesque appears to have been strongest in the group of masks which can roughly be dated to the sixth century, but it survived well beyond the archaic period.[63] Some of these masks are of a particularly repulsive character and stand in sharp contrast to the exemplars usually classified as the 'Youths' (unbearded male-type), 'Warriors' (bearded male-type) and 'Portraits', which in their turn may partly be interpreted as reproductions of the masks worn by the Spartans (particularly by the Spartan youths), at the dances they regarded as noble. The contrast between these types of masks appears to be an emblematic expression of the mental attitude and psychological associations of the Spartans regarding themselves and the helots. From this viewpoint it is particularly significant to note the moderate and self-confident smile on some of the 'Youth', 'Warrior' and 'Portrait' specimens, in contrast with the lascivious smile and repugnant grimaces appearing on many of the theriomorphic 'Caricatures' (or on the 'Satyr' and 'Gorgon' types of masks).[64] This contrast is all the more enlightening in view of the probability that the masks belonging to the period between the seventh and early fifth centuries (which actually constitute a vast majority) could have been manufactured not only by *perioikoi* but also by Spartiates.[65]

Anthropological research provides significant examples of bestiality traits imposed on a lower class within the framework of an asymmetric joking relationship aimed at preserving the social hierarchy. One of the most significant cases is that of the 'capakoban' ritual impersonators in the Easter rites of the Mayo Indians of Sonora. The capakoban, who are the lowest-ranking members of the community, are assigned obscene performances at which they wear masks resembling hairy animal-like heads and their movements recall those of dogs.[66] In the case of Sparta, the bestiality of the grotesque masks can most reasonably be associated with the attempts of the Spartans to dehumanise the helots (e.g. by their presentation as asses, their obligation to wear a special 'uniform' — the dog-skin cap and rough animal pelts).[67] The dehumanisation of the helots in its turn facilitated their murder by the *kryptoi*.

Originally a primitive rite of passage, the *krypteia* was preserved and institutionalised in the pseudo-primitive Spartan society, but it was assigned as its main function that of coping with the helot danger by policing and terrorising the helot population.[68] The murder of helots by the *kryptoi* has aptly been described in terms of initiative helot-hunting.[69] The Spartans are known to have been fond of hunting, a hobby which they appear to have inherited from their early tribal organisation.[70] Anthropologists have convincingly shown that, when an animal is killed in hunting, savage people express their sensation of triumph and relief by means of sardonic laughter.[71] Such reaction is all the more predictable when, in addition to its ordinary functions, hunting is meant to be an initiating experience. The dehumanisation of the helots and the helot-hunting character of the *krypteia* make it reasonable to think of sardonic laughter as a very likely reaction also of the initiated '*kryptoi*-hunters' at the sight of their helot victims. Furthermore, the episode concerning the murder of 2,000 helots, as related by Thucydides (4.80.3–4), certainly reveals among other things a most sinister aspect of the Spartans' sense of humour. The helots who were most feared by the Spartans, i.e. those who had been trapped through the false promise of freedom, were made to play the fool before their assassination: they solemnly had garlands put on their heads and did the rounds of the sanctuaries as if they had been freed. Their itinerary presumably included the sanctuaries of Fear, Laughter and Death — divinities who, ironically, personified essential elements of this episode.

In addition to the buffoons recruited from the non-Spartiate sections of the population, the Spartans had also some buffoons of Spartiate origin. The bachelors, for instance, were not only punished by legal sanctions but also subjected to certain methods of ridicule: in winter they were ordered by the magistrates to march naked round the *agora* while singing songs about themselves to the effect that they were justly punished for disobeying the law.[72] When it is divorced from the serious functions it sometimes fulfils and is inflicted as a punishment, nudity becomes degrading and, as such, an incentive for laughter at the expense of the victim. In the case of the bachelors, the stimulus of laughter was amplified by the incongruity between nudity and the cold of

13

winter as well as by the dissonance of the singing in that peculiar situation. Furthermore, their nude performance can be most plausibly interpreted as a parody of the solemn processions of naked dancers at the Gymnopaidiai festival (celebrated each summer in the agora) from which the bachelors were significantly excluded[73] (note the similarity of place and inversion of seasons). The spectators at the bachelors' performance were most probably encouraged (if not obliged) to laugh in order to increase the embarrassment and discomfort of the victims, and display satisfaction at (or at least apathy to) their suffering. Such derisive laughter is a conservative weapon directed against the social expression of non-conformity which those bachelors represented. This technique of mockery is akin to the corrective laughter utilised within the framework of the *agōgē* (through the agency of the maidens and the elderly men): it is the corrective punishment inflicted by a closed society upon the unsocial or non-conformist individual.

A closed or parochial society is liable to react with vehemently aggressive-defensive laughter of derision against any pattern of behaviour that deviates or simply differs from its strict norms and values. This may explain the Spartans' notorious contempt for foreigners, which is expressed in many Laconian apophthegms (frequently accompanied by symptoms of narcissism).[74] Within the Spartan society there could be no graver deviation from the standards of conduct prescribed by the so-called Lycurgan code of behaviour than to show cowardice in battle. No wonder that the most prominent category of buffoons whose origin was Spartiate consisted of the 'tremblers' (*tresantes*). Cowardice in battle was punished at Sparta by a series of legal penalties, the specification of which lies beyond the scope of this study.[75] What matters for us here is that in addition to the legal sanctions, the punishment of the 'tremblers' entailed certain opprobrious norms, the virtual effect of which was to transform the victims into miserable clowns: 'any passer-by may strike them if he wishes. Moreover, they are supposed to go about in a dirty and abject state, wearing cloaks with coloured patches, half of their beard shaven and half left to grow.'[76] According to Xenophon, the 'trembler' is also obliged 'to give way to others in the streets and rise even for younger men when he occupies a seat . . . he may not stroll about looking cheerful, nor may he imitate those who are without reproach, or else he must submit to be beaten by his betters'.[77]

It is significant that the *tresantes* are deprived of joy and laughter: this is an important aspect of their social exclusion which, by way of contrast, points again to the integrative function of laughter. On the other hand, their degradation involves certain patterns of derision which are reminiscent of those used in the case of the helots: the obligation to wear a sort of degrading 'uniform', the infliction of beatings, particularly when they broke the ban on imitating the *homoioi*, or merely as a reminder of their inferior status. These and similar patterns of derisive exclusion were components of an asymmetrical mocking relationship which brought into high relief the social superiority of the *homoioi*. Certain derision patterns have a symbolic significance. Shaving half of the beard, for instance, has to be associated with the proclamation the ephors used to issue on entering office, that the citizens should 'shave off their moustaches and observe the laws'.[78] The *tresantes* were to remind the other citizens through the ridiculous appearance of their half-beards that the laws of Sparta should be strictly obeyed. The message behind the above techniques of derision was clearly expressed by Xenophon: the citizens should prefer a beautiful death to an ignominious life.[79]

The humiliating laughter of Spartan public opinion was sometimes directed also towards citizens who, owing to certain circumstances, tended to be associated with the *tresantes* although legally they did not seem to have belonged to this group. The cruelty of the derisive attitude towards such men is reflected by Herodotus' stories about the two survivors from Leonidas' force at Thermopylae. Aristodemus, who was prevented by ophthalmia from taking part in the battle, got the nickname 'the trembler' and was treated in such a way that he chose to get himself killed in battle at his first opportunity.[80] Aristodemus' survival could not be tolerated at Sparta particularly in view of the death of his comrade who, invalided by the same disease, had preferred to ask his helot to guide him to Thermopylae in order to get himself killed there. However, in the case of Pantitas — if the story is accurate[81] — the Spartans had no extenuating circumstances whatsoever to account for the cruelty of their derisory treatment, since the only fault of the survivor (whom they are reported to have subsequently driven to suicide) had been obedience to orders: he was not killed in battle because he had been sent with dispatches to Thessaly.

Malicious mockery was also a sharp weapon in the struggle between various politicians and factions in Sparta. An extreme example is provided by the end of Antalcidas: mockery by political enemies (most probably the leading men of Agesilaus' faction) is reported to have been one of the main motives behind the decision of the famous Spartan politician to starve himself to death after the failure of an important diplomatic mission.[82] Sciraphidas (a contemporary of Antalcidas) also appears to have been the victim of a campaign of derision organised by political opponents (most probably men of Lysander's faction): he is reported to have been fined by the ephors because he had let himself be wronged by many (!).[83] Unlike the jesting exercises (within the framework of the *agōgē* or at the *syssitia*),[84] the campaigns of derision seem to have been utterly pitiless and, in spite of having been trained to endure the malice of laughter, the Spartans appear to have been no less vulnerable than the other Greeks[85] to mockery. The above cases of suicide resulting from derision can be supplemented by another example in which mockery is reported to have produced an extreme reaction. According to Herodotus (6.67) it was the torture of being mocked (not that of being dethroned) which determined Demaratus to defect. This example is particularly significant, since in all probability Herodotus accurately reproduced the story as it had been recounted by his Spartan informants. Hence, regardless of the psychological vector which really prompted Demaratus' reaction, the relevance of his case for generalising is vindicated by the current belief of the Spartans that he was motivated by vulnerability to mockery.

Derisive laughter could be used in Spartan politics also as an alternative to discussion, particularly in the assembly. An example of such use is suggested by Xenophon's account of the 'debate' preceding the adoption of the fatal decision to dispatch Cleombrotus' army on the mission which ended in the disaster of Leuctra. Prothous, a Spartan whose name is known only from this occasion, tried to convince his fellow citizens to adopt a different (and more prudent) course of action. Xenophon relates that the Spartans thought he was talking nonsense.[86] Since no discussion is reported to have taken place the most plausible interpretation of this statement concerning the reaction of the assembly is that Prothous' words triggered a wave of contemptuous laughter (presumably encouraged by the leading politicians, who gave the tone). Owing to its highly contagious nature, laughter could be effectively manipulated in political assemblies as a channel of propaganda, and in Sparta even more so than elsewhere in view of the Spartans' gregarious character and their aversion to long speeches.[87]

To sum up, laughter was used at Sparta as an important instrument for the consolidation of the social hierarchy, the promotion of harmony among the *homoioi* and the cultivation of the norms and values comprising their social code. It was manipulated in the service of the state within the *agōgē*, at the *syssitia*, at the various contests, in the Spartan theatre, in the *agora* or wherever else the authorities thought fit. The state exercised an impressive degree of control over the laughter of its citizens, i.e. over the questions where, when, why and how they should or should not laugh, as well as over the selection of the buffoons and their treatment. Derisive laughter, however, was used by various politicians and factions also as a means of promoting private or sectarian goals, and in these cases the function of such laughter was diametrically opposed to that of fostering concord among the *homoioi*. Thus laughter is associated in Sparta with the basic features of the polity: the *étatisme*; the conservative and strictly conformist outlook; the prevalent intolerance; the mixture of antagonistic and co-operative elements; the rigid social hierarchy; the survival of primitive, archaic elements adapted to political functions; the deliberately backward and crude character of civilisation; the extremely aggressive-defensive disposition of the *homoioi*; their mentality of superiority over outsiders and contempt for the underprivileged, particularly for the helots; and the degradation and dehumanisation of the latter. The view of Charles Baudelaire[88] regarding laughter as primarily diabolical and only secondarily human can find considerable support in certain patterns of Spartan humour.

The statue of Laughter was after all not out of place in the midst of austere Sparta, and its attribution to Lycurgus (of course, as an outstanding symbol of the Spartan *kosmos*, not an historical personality) seems perfectly sensible.

Notes

1. Arist. *de partibus animalium*, 673a 8; cf. Clem. Alex. *Pedagogue* 2.46.2.
2. H. Bergson, *Le rire* (Paris, repr. 1972), pp. 5–6.
3. For the presentation of laughter as a luxury reflex, see A. Koestler, *The art of creation* (London, 1964), p. 31.
4. Plut. *Lyc.* 25.4 (= Jacoby, *FGrHist* 595 F 19). For the cult of Laughter, see Steuding, in Roscher, *Lex.* III (1890), s.v. 'Gelos', coll.

Laughter in Spartan Society

1610–11; cf. Waser, *RE* VIII. 1 (1910), s.v. 'Gelos', coll. 1018–19.

5. On Sosibius, see E.N. Tigerstedt, *The legend of Sparta in classical antiquity* II (Stockholm, 1974), pp. 88, 365–6 and nn. 369–74, with bibliography. E. Kessler, *Plutarchs leben des Lykourgos* (Berlin, 1910), p. 79 and K. Ziegler, *RE* XXI. 1 (1951), s.v. 'Plutarchos', coll. 270, 281 doubted a direct consultation of Sosibius by Plutarch, but there seems to be no solid reason for their scepticism. The fragment concerning the statue of Laughter is probably quoted from Sosibius' work Περὶ τῶν ἐν Λακεδαίμονι θυσίων. Cf. M. Manfredini and L. Piccirilli, *Plutarco, Le vite di Licurgo e di Numa* (Milan, 1980), p. 274 (commentary by Piccirilli).

6. Arist. *Eth. Nic.* 1128 b 3; cf. e.g. M.A. Grant, *The ancient theories of the laughable* (Madison, 1924), pp. 25–6; D.H. Munro, *Argument of laughter* (Melbourne, 1951), pp. 83ff.; Koestler (above, n. 3), pp. 52, 61; N.N. Holland, *Laughing, a psychology of humor* (Ithaca, 1982), pp. 43–4; J. Morreal, *Taking laughter seriously* (Albany, 1983), pp. 20–37. On the coining of the neologism 'gelotology' as a technical term for the study of laughter, see G.B. Milner, 'Homo Ridens, Toward a Semiotic Theory of Humour and Laughter', *Semiotica* 5 (1972), p. 3, n. 1.

7. Plutarch is a central source for our subject as for many other Spartan topics. The reliability of his evidence depends mainly on that of his sources, which too often are hardly discernible. When they remain unknown, his testimony is to be used with due regard to criteria of plausibility, inner coherence and compatibility with other available evidence. On Plutarch's methods of writing and reliability, see e.g. P.A. Stadter, *Plutarch's historical methods* (Cambridge, Mass., 1965); Tigerstedt (above, n. 5), pp. 230ff.; 509ff., with further literature. Cf. recently D.M. MacDowell, *Spartan law* (Edinburgh, 1986), pp. 17–22.

8. On Sosibius' importance as a source for the study of laughter in Spartan society, see also below and nn. 43, 44. Th.W. Africa, 'Phylarchus and the Gods: The Religious Views of a Hellenistic Historian', *Phoenix* 14 (1960), p. 223, believes that Phylarchus was behind the digressions on Fear and the other *pathēmata*. This view, however, has been convincingly refuted by G. Marasco, 'Aristotele come fonte di Plutarco nelle biografie di Agide e Cleomene', *Athenaeum* 56 (1978), p. 173, who rightly points to Sosibius as the most probable source for the digression.

9. This is true also with respect to the cult of Sleep (Hypnos), on which see Paus. 3.18.1, who mentions it together with that of Death; cf. also Alcman, fr. 26.7,62 (Calame).

10. For the cult of Fear, see P.H. Epps, 'Fear in Spartan Character', *CP* 28 (1933), pp. 23–4; E. Bernert, *RE* XX.1 (1941), s.v. 'Phobos', coll. 311–12.

11. *Cleom.* 9.2

12. Ibid. 9.4–6.

13. On the Spartan *syssitia*, see e.g. H. Michell, *Sparta* (Cambridge, 1952), pp. 281–97; E. David, 'The Spartan *Syssitia* and Plato's *Laws'*, *AJP* 99 (1978), pp. 486–95; S. Hodkinson, 'Social Order and the Conflict of Values in Classical Sparta', *Chiron* 13 (1983), pp. 251–4. See also the paper of N. Fisher in this volume, pp. 26ff.

14. *Lac. Pol.* 3.4–5. The statement is concerned with the second stage of the *agōgē*, i.e. with the *paidiskoi*, and Xenophon refers to the

participation of youths at the *syssitia* in the same context. Cf. Hodkinson (above, n. 13), pp. 250, 252.

15. Cf. F. Ollier, *Xenophon, la république des Lacédémoniens* (Lyon, 1934), p. 33.

16. The interdiction of laughter in primitive ritual is often accompanied by the interdiction of speech, sleep, food and looking around, elements which are to a certain extent reminiscent of the Spartan experience. For these interdictions, see the analysis of V. Ja. Propp, *Edipo alla luce del folclore* (Torino, 1975), pp. 51–4 = *Theory and history of folklore* (Manchester, 1984), pp. 128–31 (hereafter referred to as *Edipo* and *Folklore* respectively).

17. Cf. A. Penjon, 'Le rire et la liberté', *Revue philosophique* 36 (1893), pp. 137–8.

18. *Lyc.* 12.6–7, cf. Plut. *Mor.* 631F. The obligation to desist from joking under such circumstances must have applied to jesting contests as well; see below and n. 21. In certain cases self-ridicule could have been used at Sparta (as elsewhere) as an efficient means of self-defence; see e.g. Plut. *Ages.* 2.3.

19. For the importance of these goals at Sparta, cf. Critias, fr. 6 (West), with Fisher (above, n. 13) pp. 26ff.; see also below.

20. See e.g. A.R. Radcliffe-Brown, 'On Joking Relationships', *Africa* 13 (1940), pp. 195–210; id., 'A Further Note on Joking Relationships', *Africa* 19 (1949), pp. 133–40 and esp. R.E. Moreau, 'Joking Relationships in Tanganyika', *Africa* 14 (1944), pp. 386–400.

21. Plut. *Lyc.* 17.1; 25.3. On the Spartan contests and love of victory, see also ibid. 16.8–9; cf. Xen. *Lac. Pol.* 4.2; Plat. *Rep.* 547D; 548C; see also Michell (above, n. 13), pp. 174–5; 190–3; A. Brelich, *Paides e Parthenoi* I (Rome, 1969), pp. 121–3, 155, 182, 192–3.

22. Cf. Plat. *Protag.* 342 D-E. The preceding passage contains certain remarks on the Spartans' love of wisdom which are partially sarcastic, but the sarcasm does not seem to have extended to the statement on the Spartans' excellence in prompt, brief and surprising ripostes, which is advanced in the specified passage as proof of the previous remarks and therefore expected to be commonly accepted by the readers.

23. Plut. *Mor.* 224B (17); for another 'Spartan joke', typical of the same spirit, see ibid. 232C (3) — irritated by one of the helots, a Spartan exclaims: 'If I were not angry I would kill you.' Cf. ibid. 210E (28), 229C (9) and *passim*. See also below, n. 74, for the apophthegms reflecting the Spartans' mentality of superiority coupled with contempt for strangers. For the collections of Spartan apophthegms, their possible sources and basic traits, see Tigerstedt (above, n. 5), II, pp. 16–30 and 298–309, with bibliography.

24. On 'defensive laughter' in general, see Munro (above, n. 6), pp. 22–8.

25. Plut. *Mor.* 231B (3); cf. *Mor.* 191F; *Lyc.* 25.6. On Paidaretos = Pedaritos (e.g. Thuc. 8.28), see P. Cartledge, *Agesilaos and the crisis of Sparta* (London, 1987), pp. 92, 145, 205, 288. For another story reflecting a similar mentality, cf. *Mor.* 234 A(34). For the 'three hundred' (*hippeis*), see U. Cozzoli, *Proprietà fondiaria ed esercito nello stato spartano*

dell' età classica (Rome, 1973), pp. 84–97, with evidence; cf. MacDowell (above, n. 7), pp. 67–8.

26. See Xen. *Lac. Pol.* 4.4–6; cf. Brelich (above, n. 21), p. 122.

27. Plut. *Lyc.* 14.6

28. Ibid. 25.3. On the conservative and corrective facets of laughter, see Bergson (above, n. 2), p. 150: 'Le rire est, avant tout, une correction. Fait pour humilier, il doit donner à la personne qui en est l'objet une impression pénible.' Cf. C.R. Gruner, *Understanding laughter* (Chicago, 1978), pp. 29–31.

29. See e.g. Penjon (above, n. 17), p. 138.

30. Critias, fr. 6. 14–16 (West); cf. Xen. *Lac. Pol.* 5.4–7 and see Fisher (above, n. 13) pp. 26ff. For *symposia* as a medium of laughter in Spartan society, see also above, p. 1.

31. Plut. *Lyc.* 28.8; *Demetr.* 1.5; *Mor.* 239A (30); 455E; Clem. Alex. *Pedagogue* 3.41.5. Diog. Laert. 1.103. Cf. Michell (above, n. 13), pp. 81–2; 189, whose view that this evidence is inaccurate seems to be part of his general attempt to embellish the Spartans' treatment of the helots.

32. Cf. Munro (above, n. 6), p. 142.

33. See above, n. 30.

34. *Lyc.* 28.9. For the dances, see below and nn. 39, 41, 42.

35. L. Hieb, *The Hopi clown ritual* (Ann Arbor, Michigan, Univ. Microfilms, 1979), cited by L. Feinberg, *The secret of humour* (Amsterdam, 1978), pp. 23–4. See also below, n. 66.

36. See E. Dupréel, 'Le problème sociologique du rire', *Revue philosophique* 106 (1928), pp. 228–60, who makes the important socio-logical distinction between laughter of inclusion and laughter of exclusion. S. Freud, 'Humour', *Intern. journal of psycho-analysis* 9 (1928), p. 2, stresses 'the triumph of narcissism' in humour. See also G. Devereux, 'La psychanalyse et l'histoire; Une application à l'histoire de Sparte', *Annales ESC* 20 (1965), pp. 18–44 and especially 31–40; cf. K. Lorenz, *On aggression* (London, 1966), p. 152.

37. Plut. *Lyc.* 12.8–11. See also above, nn. 18, 19.

38. Plut. *Mor.* 239B (33).

39. For the *kordax* (and drunkenness), see Dem. *Olynth.* 2.18; Theoph. *Char.* 6.1; Athen. 14.631D; Schol. to Aristoph. *Clouds* 540; cf. H. Schnabel, *Kordax; Archäologische Studien zur Geschichte eines antiken Tanzes und zum Ursprung der griechischen Komödie* (Munich, 1919); L. Sechan, *Dar. Sag.* IV.2 (1909), s.v. 'Saltatio', p. 1043; Warnecke, *RE* XI.2 (1922), s.v. 'Kordax', col. 1384. (For the performance of vulgar Laconian dances under the influence of excessive drinking, cf. also Hdt. 6.129.) For the λομβρότερον, see Pollux, 4.104. For the μόθων, see id. 4.101; cf. Aristoph. *Knights*, 697; Schol. to Aristoph. *Plut.* 279: 'μόθων, εἶδος αἰσχρᾶς καὶ ζουλοπρεποῦς ὀρχήσεως'. See also Athen. 14.618C; Photius, s.v. 'μόθων'. Cf. V. Ehrenberg, *RE* XVI.1 (1933), s.v. 'mothones', coll. 385–86; Michell (above, n. 13), p. 189.

40. These are mentioned by Xen. *Hell.* 5.3.9. For the association between this dance and slavery, see previous note. On the *mothakes* in general, see D. Lotze, 'Mothakes', *Historia* 11 (1962), .pp. 427–35; MacDowell (above, n. 7), pp. 46–51.

41. Hesych. s.v. 'βρυδαλίχα' (cf. id. s.v. 'βρυλλιχισταί') and Pollux,

4.104, who, however, seems to have confused the female choruses to Artemis with these comic and obscene dances. Cf. G. Dickins, 'Terracotta Masks', in R.M. Dawkins, (ed.), *The sanctuary of Artemis Orthia at Sparta, JHS* suppl. 5 (1929), p. 173; H. Jeanmaire, *Couroi et courètes* (Paris, 1939), pp. 520–2; L.B. Lawler, *The dance in ancient Greece* (London, 1964), p. 112, also interprets these dances as a form of transvestism. For the masks, see below and nn. 60–4.

42. Pollux 4.104–5.

43. Sosibius *ap.* Athen. 14.621D = Jacoby, *FGrHist* 595 F7; cf. Jacoby's commentary, IIIb p. 649 and L. Breitholtz, *Die dorische Farce* (Uppsala, 1960), pp. 115–21.

44. Sosibius *ap.* Athen. 14.621E-F = Jacoby, *FGrHist* 595 F7; cf. Suda, s.v. 'Sosibius' = Jacoby, *FGrHist* 595 T1. Cf. Hesych. s.v. 'δεικηλισταί'.

45. Plut. *Ages.* 21.8; *Mor.* 212F.

46. It is worth noting in this connection that according to Sosibius, (above, n. 44) the *deikēlistai* were called at Sicyon phallus-bearers.

47. For the Spartan theatre, see Hdt. 6.67; Aristoxenus *ap.* Athen. 14.631C = F 108 Wehrli; Polycrates *ap.* Athen. 4.139E = Jacoby, *FGrHist* 588 F1; Plut. *Ages.* 29.3; Paus. 3.14.1. See also H. Bulle, *Das Theater zu Sparta* (Munich, 1937), pp. 27ff.; L. Piccirilli, 'Il santuario, la funzione guerriera della dea, la regalità. Il caso di Atena Chalkioikos', in M. Sordi (ed.), *I santuari e la guerra nel mondo classico* (Milan, 1984), p. 14; I.K. Loucas, 'Λακεδαιμόνιοι Διονυσιακοὶ Τεχνιτες', *Horos* 2 (1984), pp. 149–60 (with French résumé).

48. See e.g. Dickins (above, n. 41), pp. 172ff.; J.P. Vernant and F. Frontisi-Ducroux, 'Figures du masque en Grèce ancienne', in J.P. Vernant and P. Vidal-Naquet (eds), *Mythe et tragédie en Grèce ancienne* II (Paris, 1986), pp. 37–40. Cf. also Michell (above, n. 13), pp. 188–9; P. Roussel, *Sparte* (Paris, 1960), p. 78.

49. *Lyc.* 28.9; cf. also in n. 39 above, especially Schol. to Aristoph. *Plut.* 279. On the other hand the most conspicuous example of a dance regarded at Sparta as worthy of freemen is the *pyrrhichē*, a dance of warlike character; see Athen. 14.630D-E; 631C.

50. See above, n. 36. Cf. also J. Ducat, 'Le mépris des Hilotes', *Annales ESC* 30 (1974), pp. 1455–8, who underlined the role of buffoons assigned to the helots: 'les Hilotes jouaient le rôle de "fous", de bouffons involontaires'.

51. See H. Collitz et al., *Sammlung der griechischen Dialekt-Inschriften* (Göttingen, 1884–1915), 2565, l. 59; A.S. Bradford, *A Prosopography of Lacedaemonians from the death of Alexander the Great, 323 BC, to the sack of Sparta by Alaric, AD 396* (Munich, 1977), p. 312, s.v. 'Nikon' (i); Loucas (above, n. 47), pp. 149ff.; 159–60, with further literature.

52. Myron *ap.* Athen. 14.657C-D = Jacoby, *FGrHist* 106 F2. Cf. Ducat (above, n. 50); p. 1458, who describes this as a 'copie caricaturale' of the beatings inflicted on the Spartan boys. The beating of the boys who had failed in the exercise of stealing (Xen. *Lac. Pol.* 2.8; Plut. *Lyc.* 17. 5–6) is less likely to have been the subject of this parody since it was not a ritual, but an *ad hoc* corrective measure, whereas the beating of the helots was an annual ceremony. For the flagellation ritual, see below and next note.

53. Xen. *Lac. Pol.* 2.9, with Ollier (above, n. 15), pp. 28–30 and Plut. *Lyc.* 18.1–2, with (Manfredini-)Piccirilli (above, n. 5), pp. 265–6 (*ad loc.*). According to Pausanias (3.16.10), flagellation was introduced by Lycurgus as a substitute for human sacrifices. The origin of this ritual is most probably associated with death and fertility, but later it was used at Sparta in order to serve the educative-military purpose of teaching endurance. The primitive-savage element of real death was reinforced in the late Hellenistic and Roman periods. See Plut. *Lyc.* 18.2; *Mor.* 239D; Lucian, *Anacharsis* 38. The flagellation of helots to death ordered by Nabis (Livy 34.27.9) may also have been associated with the same ritual. Cf. W. Den Boer, *Laconian studies* (Amsterdam, 1954), pp. 261-74. See also below and n. 58. For the use of flagellation in early fourth-century Sparta as an exemplary punishment of political criminals (in the case of Cinadon's conspiracy), see Xen. *Hell.* 3.3.11.

54. See above, nn. 42 and 44.

55. See Hesych. s.v. 'βωμολοχία'. Cf. R. Janko, *Aristotle on comedy* (London, 1984), p. 31, n. 2.

56. Cf. Devereux (above, n. 36) who points to the Spartans' extreme suspicion of helots' attempts to imitate the Spartan code of behaviour. If the symbolic meaning of stealing food was the appropriation of the vitality of the strong, as Den Boer maintains (above, n. 53), p. 262, the symbolic beating of the helots for imitating such an action becomes all the more intelligible (although the imitation was imposed on them). Cf. also Vernant and Frontisi-Ducroux (above, n. 48), p. 37: 'dans bien des sociétés, l'ordre, pour être raffermi, a besoin d'être périodiquement contesté, bouleversé pendant ces quelques jours de Carnaval où régne l'inversion: femmes vêtues en hommes, hommes costumés en femmes ou en animaux, esclaves prenant la place des maîtres'. One should, however, be cautious not to exaggerate the readiness of the Spartans to contest their own *kosmos*, even at festivals.

57. *Iliad* 2.265–70. Cf. R. Boston, *An anatomy of laughter* (London, 1974), pp. 29–31 and Koestler (above, n. 3), pp. 53–4. For the symbolic beating of clowns, see J. Levine, 'Regression in Primitive Clowning', *Psychoanalytic quarterly* 30 (1961), pp. 78–9, who follows Freud in stressing the role of humour in the release of libidinal, aggressive and infantile impulses (pp. 71–3).

58. Plut. *Mor.* 239D (40); cf. *Lyc.* 18.2.

59. See above, n. 53. For this aspect of ritual laughter, see S. Reinach, *Cultes, mythes et religions* IV (Paris, 1912), pp. 122–5, and Propp (above, n. 16), *Edipo*, pp. 59–60; 77–8 (= *Folklore*, pp. 134–5; 145–6). See also below, n. 71.

60. Dickins (above, n. 41), pp. 163–86; Vernant and Frontisi-Ducroux (above, n. 48). pp. 36–43. Cf. also J.T. Hooker, *The Ancient Spartans* (London, 1980), p. 94, who stresses the originality of these masks. For a different interpretation (and classification) of the masks, see J.B. Carter, 'The Masks of Ortheia', AJA 91 (1987), pp. 355–83.

61. See Hesych. (above, n. 41); cf. Dickins (above, n. 41), pp. 166–7 and pls. XLVII 1–3; XLVIII 1 and 3; XLIX 1–2.

62. Dickins (above, n. 41), pp. 176; 183–5. For the 'sub-human' type,

see e.g. Dickins pl. LVII 1. For specimens of the entirely grotesque, see pls. LVII 2; LVIII 3. See also below, n. 64.

63. Most of the masks actually belong to the sixth century, but some of them can be traced back to the early seventh, and the lowest chronological limit is the mid-third century; see Dickins (above, n. 41), pp. 164–6; cf. L.F. Fitzhardinge, *The Spartans* (London, 1980), p. 55.

64. See e.g. Dickins (above, n. 41), pp. 167–8 and pls. LI 3; LIII 1; LIV 2 and 4; LV 1–2. The self-confident smile on these masks, accompanied in most cases by a slight nuance of contempt, seems to betray the sensation of superiority characteristic of the *homoioi.* Cf. the lascivious smile and bestial expression, e.g. of the masks in pls. XLVIII 3; LVI 1–3; LVII 1–2; LXI 1; LXII 1. For the political, socio-cultural and religious purposes of masks, see I.A. Ebong, 'Mask and Masking', *Anthropos* 79 (1984), pp. 1–12.

65. See P. Cartledge, 'Did Spartan Citizens ever Practice a Manual Tekhne?', *LCM* 1 (1976), pp. 115–19, with evidence and further literature. Cartledge challenges the conventional view confining artisan activities at Sparta to *perioikoi,* arguing that at least until the early fifth century, Spartiates were not debarred from such activities. For the dating of the masks, see above, n. 63.

66. See D. Handelman, 'The Ritual Clown: Attributes and Affinities', *Anthropos* 76 (1981), p. 321.

67. Tyrt. fr. 6 (West); Myron (above, n. 52). Cf. Ducat (above, n. 50), p. 1458. Cf. E.A. Lane, 'Lakonian Vase Painting', *ABSA* 34 (1933/4), pls. 39b and 40a, for scenes of *kōmos* depicting the costume of animal pelts and anal intercourse.

68. For the *krypteia,* see H. Jeanmaire, 'La cryptie lacédémonienne', *REG* 26 (1913), pp. 121–50; P. Oliva, *Sparta and her social problems* (Amsterdam and Prague, 1971), pp. 45–7, with evidence and further literature; cf. also M.I. Finley, *The use and abuse of history* (London, 1975), pp. 165 and 239, n. 9; Cartledge (above, n. 25), pp. 30–2.

69. This has been stressed by P. Vidal-Naquet, *Le chasseur noir* (Paris, 1981), pp. 161–3; cf. Ducat (above, n. 30), pp. 1456–7, 1460.

70. For the importance of hunting at Sparta, see Xen. *Lac. Pol.* 4.7; 5.3; 6.3–4, with Ollier (above, n. 15), *ad loc.*; Isocr. *Panath.* 211; Arist. *Pol.* 1263 a 36–7; Plut. *Lyc.* 12.4; 24.5.

71. See e.g. E. Marshall Thomas, *The harmless people* (New York, 1959), pp. 99ff., who describes as an eye-witness the laughter of the Bushmen of the Kalahari desert of South-West Africa at the sight of the agony of a springbok hit by a bullet. Cf. also V.M. Ionov, quoted by Propp (above, n. 16), *Edipo,* pp. 60–1 = *Folklore,* pp. 135–6: 'Yakuts . . . when they see in the distance an elk felled by a crossbow, . . . jump up and down, leap, shout and roar with laughter.' I am not persuaded by Propp's attempt (ibid.) to identify the motive of this reaction with that inducing certain primitive peoples (e.g. the Sards, the Thracians and the Troglodites) to laugh when killing their own relatives (or witnessing their death and burial); see e.g. Timaeus *ap.* Suda, s.v. 'Σαρδάνιος γέλως'; Strab. 16.4.17 (776). The reaction of these primitive peoples may well have emanated from a belief crediting laughter with a magic power of nullifying death and recreating life; see Reinach (above, n. 59), pp.

123–5, with further evidence. This belief, however, can hardly be ascribed to the hunters.

72. Plut. *Lyc.* 15.1–2. For the other measures against bachelors in Sparta, see P. Cartledge, *Sparta and Lakonia, a regional history 1300–362 BC* (London, 1979), p. 310, with evidence.

73. Plut. *Lyc.* 15.2; cf. Paus. 3.11.9, who explicitly mentions the *agora* as the place where the festival was celebrated. To be sure, part of the festivities took place in the Spartan theatre as well; see above, n. 47. For the time of year at which this festival was celebrated, see B.D. Meritt, 'The Spartan Gymnopaidia', *CP* 26 (1931), pp. 70–84, with evidence.

74. See e.g. Plut. *Mor.* 209C (13); 212E (55–56); F (57); 213C (64); 214A (72); 215E (9); 220F (8); 221E (3); 224B (17); 229C (8); D (9) and *passim*. On provincialism and laughter at outsiders, see Dupréel (above, n. 36), p. 236. Paradoxically, the Spartans often appear to have been influenced by foreigners in their decisions over policy matters; see Hodkinson (above, n. 13), pp. 276–8.

75. See e.g. V. Ehrenberg, *RE* VI.2 A (1937), s.v. 'τρέσαντες', coll. 2292–7; cf. N. Lornaux, 'La Belle Mort Spartiate', *Ktema* 2 (1977), pp. 108–9; 111–13.

76. Plut. *Ages.* 30.3–4.

77. Xen. *Lac. Pol.* 9.4–6; cf. Ollier (above, n. 15), *ad loc.*

78. Plut. *Cleom.* 9.3 (= Arist. fr. 539 Rose); cf. MacDowell (above, n. 7), p. 155.

79. *Lac. Pol.* 9.1; 9.6; cf. Lornaux (above, n. 75), p. 112: 'ils (viz., les *tresantes*) jouent le rôle d'une vivante et dérisoire exhortation au courage'.

80. Hdt. 7.229–31. In view of Herodotus' description of the sanctions which Aristodemus' *atimia* involved, he does not appear to have belonged to the legal category of *tresantes,* as is often wrongly supposed: see e.g. W.W. How and J. Wells, *A commentary on Herodotus* II (Oxford, 1928), p. 231; Ph. E. Legrand, Hérodote, *Histoires* (Paris, Budé, 1951), p. 120, n. 1. In this case '*tresas*' seems to have been only a nickname.

81. Hdt. 7.232. The introduction of this story by 'legetai' may indicate the historian's uncertainty concerning its factual accuracy.

82. Plut. *Artax.* 22.6–7. For the high vulnerability of the Spartans to mockery see also below.

83. Plut. *Mor.* 239C (36). For his identification with the conservative ephor of 405–404 BC, who opposed Lysander's friends over the issue of foreign capital, see P. Poralla, *Prosopographie der Lakedaimonier* (Diss. Breslau, 1913), revised by A.S. Bradford (Chicago, 1985), s.v. 'Skiraphidas', pp. 113–14. Cf. also the case of Naucleidas, one of the ephors of 404–403, who had supported the policy of King Pausanias, Lysander's political enemy (Xen. *Hell.* 2.4.36), and was later to pay for this by being exposed to public ridicule on account of having become obese through luxurious indulgence (see Agatharchides *ap.* Athen. 12. 550 DE; Ael. *Var. Hist.* 14.7; cf. Poralla, ibid. s.v. 'Naukleidas', p. 95).

84. See above, nn. 18 and 21.

85. Susceptibility to mockery is an important motif in Greek literature: many epic and tragic heroes are tortured by the thought that they are (or might be) subjects of ridicule; see B.M.W. Knox, *The heroic temper* (Berkeley and Los Angeles, 1964), p. 30; D. Lateiner, 'No Laughing

Matter; a Literary Tactic in Herodotus', *TAPA* 107 (1977), pp. 173–82, at 173–4.

86. Xen. *Hell.* 6.4.3.

87. See e.g. Thuc. 1.86.1; 2.40.2–3; Plut. *Lyc.* 18.5; 19–20; *Mor.* 208C (3); 215E (7); F (9); 216A (15); 217D (5); 223F (12); 232D (1); E (2); 233B (19). For an additional illustration of the Spartans' gregarious behaviour, this time under the contagious influence of weeping, note their reaction to the news of Archidamus' victory over the Arcadians and Argives (with no casualties at all on the Spartan side) in the so-called 'Tearless Battle' (368 BC), which ironically turned out to be a tearful one; for, on receiving the news, Agesilaus, the gerontes and the ephors are reported to have shed tears of joy and to have infected all the public with their weeping. See Xen. *Hell.* 7.1.32; Diod. 15.72.3; Plut. *Ages.* 33.6–8.

88. *Curiosités esthétiques* (Paris, 1923), p. 379.

2

Drink, *Hybris* and the Promotion of Harmony in Sparta*

N.R.E. Fisher

This paper has its origin in other work in progress. In preparing a book on *hybris*, I had observed that ancient authors regularly comment on the absence of hybristic behaviour at Sparta, and that specific accusations against individual Spartans were relatively sparse; and when I was writing an essay recently on *symposia* and associations, it was clear that Spartan *syssitia* seemed to need special treatment when compared to archaic or classical *symposia* elsewhere, as did Spartan society as a whole.[1] Further, these phenomena seemed related, and might repay further thought as contributories to Spartan 'success', the overall theme of this volume.

Two qualifications should be made at the start. First, hardly surprisingly, in the absence of detailed evidence for 'ordinary life' and social relations inside Sparta, it is easier to ask questions and risk speculations than demonstrate secure answers. Second, the suggestions here that mechanisms to promote 'harmony' enjoyed some success even in the early fourth century BC must be seen against the background of steadily increasing tensions and contradictions at all levels of a Spartan society approaching its crisis.

We may start with a clear contrast. On the one hand, the

* Versions of this paper were presented at a seminar of the London Classical Society in May, 1986 and at the Colloquium of Classical Departments of the University of Wales at Gregynog in May, 1987; I am very grateful to both audiences for their helpful and critical comments. Thanks are owed especially to Anton Powell, Paul Cartledge and Stephen Hodkinson for further information, advice and encouragement, and to the first two for subsequent comment on my typescript. None should be incriminated in these speculations.

degree of control over drunkenness and *hybris* of Spartiates achieved by the state and its constituent organs does not feature very extensively in modern treatments of Spartan *eunomia* or its failure; on the other, it does receive a very prominent place in accounts, from the fifth century down to Plutarch, of what was special about Sparta, and is held to be one major reason for her success — at times, as we shall see, to the surprise or incomprehension of modern commentators.

This emphasis in ancient analyses on Sparta's control of the consequences of drinking may now be set out. An initial objection, however, may be anticipated, that this prominence owes much to the fact that for many such passages of ancient comment on Spartan convivial customs and institutions we are indebted to Athenaeus' *Deipnosophistai*. First, one should say that the existence of Athenaeus' work, and the whole sympotic genre, is itself a tribute to the centrality of convivial associations, customs and ideas in ancient societies, and to their value in determining the nature of different ancient societies.[2] Second, and obviously, Athenaeus selected, but did not invent, the lengthy accounts that he used of Spartan *syssitia* and their peculiarities, or those of other states. Nor was the conviction that drunkenness and *hybris* constituted major causes of *stasis* throughout Greece peculiar to him. Finally, and conclusively, those works on Sparta, or those which use Sparta as an example to follow or to avoid, which have survived in full lay equal emphasis on these matters.

These general accounts share for the most part an acceptance of 'bland' Spartan versions of their splendid system, and often a desire to recommend Spartan values, or a revised version of them, in contrast to Athenian: as so often with Sparta, it is convenient to start with the 'mirage' or the 'ideal type' before proceeding to consideration of the degree of contradictions and tensions in the system, and of the extent to which the operations of these rules and laws began to break down through the classical period.

The first passage to be considered comes from an extended philosophical discussion of drinking parties which has especially aroused scholarly puzzlement and inaccuracy. Of the opening two books of Plato's *Laws* Guthrie says that they contain an 'extraordinary eulogy, in several parts, and at tedious length, of properly conducted drinking parties, not stopping short of intoxication, as a beneficent educational institution', and that the whole is an 'odd, unsatisfying and inordinately long' introduction to education;[3] many other scholars are similarly condemnatory, while Saunders thinks that it is tolerable if you assume that Plato has tongue in cheek throughout the discussion.[4]

One need not deny Plato's capacity for humour or even for developing points at undue length, especially in this most baroque of his works, but such judgements reveal a failure to realise the importance of common meals and their conduct, and drinking generally, in fourth-century political thought.[5] It is also true that Plato anticipates that this discussion on drink may seem too much 'on a small matter', but he proceeds to justify it; the objection would be based on the obvious associations of drinking with play, festival and fun, and in responding Plato does not develop the obvious facts about the social dangers of drunkenness which have been implicit in the preceding discussion, but employs instead the more surprising argument that proper, sedately organised, but still drunken parties should be seen as an essential element in *paideia,* in the whole complex of education and socialisation through music, and dance, in the habituation of the proper use of pleasures and in the control of one's emotions (642a, and earlier). Hence it makes a good opening topic for the work.[6]

Commentators seem also to be led by boredom with the topic into lack of attention to its argument, specifically about what it says about the Spartan *syssitia*. Morrow, for example, imagines that the characters assert that Sparta, or the Dorians, practised 'stern prohibition' of wine:[7] and Guthrie summarises Megillus' argument as being that 'Drink simply weakens a man's resistance to temptation, and its prohibition in Sparta has been a source of strength'.[8] In fact, as Morrow knew,[9] wine was as regular at Spartan *syssitia* as it was essential in their rituals and sacrifices, and it is deep drinking (*methe*), not any drinking, that is the issue. Megillus the Spartan spokesman claims that the Spartan laws on pleasures are the best: that they

> eliminate what induces people to fall into the greatest pleasures and acts of *hybris* and all types of madness, and these you won't see anywhere in the countryside or in the towns under Spartan control, that is to say *symposia* and all the things that go with *symposia* and drive men forcibly to all sorts of pleasures; not one of us would not impose the severest penalties on anyone we saw engaged in a drunken *komos*, not even if he had the Dionysia as his excuse would we let him off, as I once saw people drunk on wagons in

your country, and at Tarentum among our colonists I saw
the whole city drunk at the Dionysia; but nothing like that
happens among us. (637a)

Here, and in the following discussion, it is clearly *symposia* and
deep drinking that are at issue (cf. 639d–e: it is *symposia, synousiai*
or *koinoniai* of *sympotai* that are neither at home nor legal [*epichorion*
or *nomimon*] in Sparta); and the Athenian poses the issue explicitly
at 639d–e: 'I'm not talking about drinking wine or not *tout court,*
but about *methe'* — should it be encouraged, as it was in many
states — 'whereas you (sc. Spartans) keep away from it (sc. *methe,*
not *oinos*) altogether.' This is the phrase that must have misled
Guthrie and Morrow into talk of 'prohibition'; but clearly they
were mistaken.

Plato's presentation of Spartan practice then is that it banned,
and effectively prohibited, exhibitions of public drunkenness by
citizens even at Dionysiac festivals, and at privately organised
clubs, associations, political groups and private parties which all
focused on shared drinking at their meetings;[10] and reasons for
such bans included the belief that drinking and forced jollification
led to excessive (presumably sexual) pleasures and acts of *hybris,*
i.e. quarrels and fights between members of the party, random
vandalism, violent or sexual assaults on the innocent in the
streets during the *komos,* or even politically motivated acts of
sympotic conspirators.

It was these types of behaviour that meant that *hybris* was a
common danger of the *symposion* which got out of control, and was
a major element in Solon's poetic analyses of the problems of
Athens, perhaps producing from him a law to restrain it, and
which, as practised by the likes of Alcaeus and his mates in
Mytilene, produced double penalties for drunken assaults from
Pittacus.[11] Plato's view is that the dangers are real, but the
remedy extreme; if the social occasions and the formations of
groups are tightly controlled, permitted drunkenness can train,
educate and reveal character. It is notable, before we leave Plato,
that the Athenian's immediate response to Megillus' claims of
successful abolition of drink-related problems is indeed the
natural claim against prohibition, that it is very difficult to
enforce given the weakness of human nature; but the example to
illustrate the judgement (such laws are fine if there is plenty of
endurance, but stupid if people are weak) is the notorious
slackness of the Spartan women, not the drunkenness of their

men. This might perhaps suggest that breaches of the Spartan rules about male organisations and drunkenness were not so blatant that they had to be recognised in this polite conversation (the remark about endurance seems a compliment to the Spartan system). The usual sneer about the looseness of Spartan women is dragged in instead, with the implication perhaps that among other vices they tended to get together and get drunk.[12]

Other late fifth and fourth century authors, mostly from the more or less committedly Laconising sections of Athenian society, offer comparable pictures, and support the close connection between, on the one hand, strict control over drunkenness and hybristic behaviour, and, on the other hand, Sparta's success in avoiding social tensions, disruptions and *stasis*.

The chief fragments of Critias' treatments in prose and verse of the superior Spartan *politeia* deal with drinking habits. Mac-Dowell has recently described these fragments as being mostly on 'domestic' topics, and not of legal interest;[13] it is true that specific laws are not mentioned, but it is none the less surprising that a scholar who has written so perceptively on Athenian law and on *hybris* should give the impression that drinking customs are essentially 'domestic', and indeed should use the term 'domestic' of Spartan male group activities.

The longest elegiac extract explicitly contrasts Spartan with other, no doubt specifically Athenian, drinking customs (while operating in the elegiac tradition of praise of moderate *symposia*). It claims that Spartans do not practise toasts and challenges, or pass the cups around to ensure that all get properly drunk; such habits lead to shameful stories, enfeebled bodies, loss of memory and reason, unruly slaves, and *oikos*-destroying extravagance. But Spartan *koroi* merely drink enough for cheerful and hopeful spirits, for *philophrosyne* and for moderate laughter (i.e. avoiding the sort of jokes that insult others, and hence lead to quarrels — in a word, avoiding *hybris*).[14] Such drinking is then praised as being in all ways beneficial (and not only for Spartans): physically, mentally, for one's property, for sex, for sleep, in summary for Health, Piety and *Sophrosyne*. The results, said to obtain particularly for the Spartans, are moderation in food and drink, no loss of capacity to work or think, and (as in Plato) no days given up to mass drinking at festivals.[15] One might well suspect a certain hypocrisy, as well as political purpose, in these lines, coming from a man of his circles in Athens who also praises the Sicilian invention of the cottabus and the sympotic poetry of

30

Anacreon;[16] though the extent of his commitment to a genuine Laconisation of Athens has been emphasised, perhaps over-emphasised, in recent years.[17] At all events the general picture proclaims Spartans' sobriety, self-control and care for their physical well-being, and equally their concern to preserve their properties, to avoid conflicts between citizens and to assert their authority over the slaves; one can compare Critias' remark that at Sparta the free men were the most free, and the slaves the most enslaved.[18] The particular need for Spartans to achieve such goals is self-evident.

The Xenophontic *Constitution of the Spartans* gives a very similar picture,[19] while adding some details; I share the view that, whenever it was written, Xenophon had read Critias' accounts recently, as well as having made use of his acquaintance with eminent Spartans.[20] In Chapter 5 we are again told that there is no 'compulsory drinking'; each drinks *ad lib.* to satisfy his thirst. Further valuable points are then made; opportunities for property-destruction through over-eating and drinking were absent, since the *syssitia* were all of mixed ages (and, he almost says, dominated by the elders), and so 'it is the custom for the conversation at the *philitia* to be about whatever one had done finely for the polis, so that there is the least possible *hybris,* the least *paroinia,* the least shameful deeds and talk', and the participants are all able to walk home without lights, and without stumbling.

More detailed information can be found in the potpourri of quotations about the Spartan *syssitia* in Book IV of Athenaeus (including a lengthy passage from the work of Dicaiarchos, so authoritative, we are told, that it came to be recited annually in Sparta);[21] at this stage two pervasive themes can be mentioned. First, we should note the concentration on the general frugality, and the lack of refinement of the fare — black broth, little meat, drinking from one's own cup and so on — the *topos* that starts with Regent Pausanias' contrast drawn at Plataea;[22] this *topos* occurs in Attic comedy as well as in political theorists or moralists, and also, for example, in Plutarch's picture of Alcibiades' chameleon-like adaptation to Spartan shaggy hair, cold baths and black broth.[23] Second, equally prominent is the emphasis on the attempts made by richer, or more able-bodied, Spartiates to gain prestige and offer patronage by contributing extra food at the *epaikla,* the session after the main rations have been eaten, especially the produce of the hunt, butchered and cooked at home: the idea is that any surplus wealth or extra good things should be shared with one's closest and permanent companions, and one main effect is to reward, with honour and powers of patronage, the donors, who are those who have achieved success in this intensely competitive, narrow world.[24]

So the 'authorised version' or 'mirage' is consistent. The *syssitia* are the only permitted occasion for dining and drinking in Sparta: *symposia* of *thiasoi,* or *orgeones* and the like, so common in Athens, seem unattested, and it is unlikely that groups such as the *gene* or the *phratries* dined and drank together at all regularly;[25] *symposia* of voluntary, politically-minded groups of *philoi,* or of wealthy young louts, are totally excluded in classical Sparta, whatever may have been the case in the time of Alcman.[26] Festivals are celebrated without public drunkenness, and with the involvement of the whole community, in many cases carefully organised in its social hierarchies.[27] The formal *syssitia,* themselves a little 'political system' (as Persaios puts it),[28] maintained strict control over the disorders of drink and the offences of verbal or physical *hybris.* All this is held to be a significant part of the explanation of Spartan success in avoiding *stasis* and achieving dominance; as a late anecdote featuring Leotychidas I puts it, the Spartans drink little so that they deliberate over others, not have others deliberate over them.[29]

Thus far the 'mirage': sources which offer a more detailed picture will permit some further speculation on the social and political effects of these institutions in Sparta, which may help to bring out the significance of this consistently dull portrait of Spartiate social life.

The fullest single account of the organisation of the *syssitia* is found in Plutarch's *Life of Lycurgus.*[30] The general ethos described there suits precisely the picture already sketched. For the details, daily attendance remained strictly compulsory 'for a long time';[31] the only acceptable excuse for not dining there, even for those over 30 who didn't sleep there, was to be delayed sacrificing or hunting, in which case portions of the food had to be sent to one's messmates. The story of Agis II's fine, after he refused to go one night when he had just returned from a campaign in Attica and wanted to eat with his wife (or wished to check up on Alcibiades?), was told to reinforce this strict requirement. It is true that, according to Herodotus,[32] the kings traditionally had the choice of going or not, and of attending private dinners elsewhere; it seems best to suppose, however, that the rules for kings were tightened in the fifth century, if not earlier;[33] just possibly, Agis was trying to recover lost freedom.[34] Similarly Plutarch mentions the modest drinking and walking home without lights, and the black broth; and he emphasises in particular the elements of socialisation in the conversations. He mentions political discussions and ideal models of 'free behaviour' for the boys; the ability of the members to make fun of each other without indulging in vulgar abuse (*bomolochia*) or giving serious offence; and the shared secrecy and mutual confidence that nothing said inside will be repeated outside, and that any joke that seems to be causing offence can be checked before it can lead to serious shaming or violence.

On the practical details, Plutarch gives an average of 15 for the membership, and describes the system of 'blackballing' of admission. It is true that Agis IV's proposed reconstitution of the *syssitia* was for 15 in all, with 200–400 members in each; but there is no reason to suppose he was attempting to reconstruct all the lapsed details and functions, and Plutarch is likely here to be following reliable, late fourth-century sources such as Aristotle.[35] So we may assume *syssitia* to have been small, intimate groups of perhaps 20+ at most before the fourth century;[36] and selection procedures attempted to ensure compatibility and continued harmony among the members of these clubs. In practice there must have been more and less exclusive *syssitia,* and the most obvious mechanism for selection would have been that of lovers seeking — competitively — to place their boys in their own, or in suitable, messes (there cannot always have been vacancies);[37] part of the point of the occasional presence at dinners of boys undergoing the *agoge* — as well as of adult spectators at their exercises in the *gymnasia* — will have been to scrutinise them for their suitability. No doubt this led to a good deal of jockeying and lobbying; a determined and respected lover could probably find a place in his *syssition* if his boy were well-connected, prosperous, and physically competent and attractive, but there must also have been cases where such a placement was not possible, and hence other people, and other *syssitia,* must have been involved; overall, 20-year-olds who had got through the *agoge* and had the capacity to keep up the payments must have been placed some-where. There were doubtless many situations of tension and conflict here; but mechanisms of resolution must have been applied, even if we lack evidence of the details.[38]

Despite the close-knit and secret atmosphere claimed for the messes, there seems room for further thoughts about occasional or not so occasional guests at *syssitia* dinners. Recent work on the preserved figures for mess-contributions may not be acceptable in detail, but it does profitably draw attention to the size of the contributions required, and hence the possibility that *syssitia* might often have wished to 'entertain' more widely bears further exploration.[39] Boys, as we have seen, were often invited and sized up, and the boys apparently sat while adults reclined, as elsewhere, if Persaios' language of hierarchical positions is accurate.[40] Further, the *syssitia* contributions may well have been used to feed the boys in their own 'junior' messes.[41] None the less the boys may not have consumed — or stolen — enough to account for the surplus. The helots may also have been substantial consumers: not only were they the cooks, carvers and waiters,[42] but some were also forced to attend as 'entertainment'. Reports that the Spartans got helots drunk and brought them to the *syssitia*, where they forced them to perform ignoble and ridiculous dances,[43] suggest that the helots may have occasionally performed functions at the *syssitia* that resembled in some ways duties performed by the buffoons and parasites, or the singers and dancers, at *symposia* in other cities.[44] This system may have served many purposes. It involved the helots in these allegedly convivial occasions, gave them more food and drink than some, at least, were usually allowed, and was hence in part a distinguishing privilege; yet it humiliated and degraded them at the same time, and reminded them of their permanently inferior position; and it reinforced for the full members of the *syssition* the importance of avoiding drunken excesses.[45]

Foreigners will have been entertained at *syssitia* at times; boys from other states attending the *agoge* may have received invitations,[46] and Spartiates could evidently entertain their foreign friends in their mess, and possibly elsewhere at festival time. A fragment of Ion of Chios seems to reflect such an occasion (see below); an anecdote tells us of a visit to a *syssition* of 'Hecataeus the Sophist', probably the Milesian; another describes how some Chians, entertained in the *ephoreion*, became disgustingly drunk, vomiting and defecating everywhere, but were tolerated, since their behaviour was compared to that of drunken helots, and they too were taken as examples of the superiority of the Spartan way of life; and a rich Spartan like Lichas could gain a panhellenic reputation for entertaining foreigners at the Gymnopaedia.[47]

The Ion of Chios fragment is intriguing, and might be more informative if more of it had been quoted, and if the text were more secure.[48] Like many another sympotic poem, it describes the mixing of the wine (using silver pitchers) and the washing of the hands, apparently involving some gold vessel; a Spartan setting is suggested, perhaps, by the salute to the king in the first line, and more certainly, in the third couplet, by the appropriately Spartan libations to Zeus, Heracles, Alcmene, Procles and the Perseidai.[49] The poem then encourages the communal drinking, playfulness, song, and general dancing and good cheer (*philophrosyne*); finally 'he for whom a well-formed female bed-partner is waiting/shall drink more nobly (*kydroteron*) than the others'. This playfully presented occasion when the king entertained, one presumes, members of the 'international aristocracy' at the royal mess, while not riotous, seems perhaps rather more luxuriously appointed and more given to communal deep drinking and fun than one might have suspected. Whether one should suppose that Ion has made the occasion more 'normal' in terms of the conventions of other Greek states and of the genre, whether the King's *syssition* let itself go when entertaining distinguished foreigners, or whether such events became even more austere through the course of the fifth century, is hard to determine.[50] I am not clear, either, how seriously we should take the last couplet. In a Spartan context, it should suggest men over 30, those allowed to go home to their wives, being told, in a *para prosdokian* joke, to drink more heavily than the rest; but the impression thus created of breaches in the restrictions on drunkenness should probably be treated with caution.

The idea that the *syssitia* were occasions when non-Spartiates could be present, some modest and controlled redistribution of wealth could occur, patronage could be exercised, and hierarchies reinforced, may perhaps be taken a little further. The decline in numbers of full members of the state from the mid-fifth century on was evidently accompanied by a marked increase in the categories of inferior statuses, and in the numbers in each of them: Spartiates demoted (through economic failure, incompetence in the *agoge*, or subsequent disgrace), bastards, or the different types of promoted helots. Some of these will have shared in the *agoge* (*mothakes* are called *syntrophoi* by Phylarchos);[51] many of them will have continued training in the *gymnasia* and served in the army, among men still grouped, probably, with their *syssitoi* in the *enomotiai* units.[52] The importance of the continual reinforcement of the solidarity of the small group in training, fighting and dining together has often been commented on;[53] one may cite, for example, the competitions on campaigns in Tyrtaeus-recitations, with meat as the prize;[54] Xenophon's view of the proper topics of conversation in the mess;[55] and also his remark that 'the eldest in each *gymnasion* should ensure that no one tastes his meal without having taken exercise',[56] which seems to suggest at least that fellow-*syssitoi* trained in the same *gymnasion,* though probably not that there was actually one *gymnasion* per *syssition,* and indicates one method by which the elders strictly supervised the younger members.

Hence the possibility may at least be raised that *syssitoi* who regularly trained and fought with particular *mothakes, hypomeiones* or even *perioikoi* may have at times selected some of them to be 'honoured' by an evening at the mess, apart from those who were permanently admitted to membership. Patronage, as has been said, was a very important element throughout Spartan society; in particular the provision of double rations to the kings was seen as an opportunity for them to honour whom they wished.[57] No doubt their guests were usually Spartiates,[58] but perhaps exceptions occurred. More generally, the offer and the withdrawal of such invitations, on a relatively personal basis, may have formed part of the complex of delicate relationships that Spartiates preserved with the inferiors, on whom they depended increasingly in the army, and of whose possible hatred they were well aware. For all the increasing tensions and hatreds, Cinadon did not succeed, and loyalty was still shown after Leuctra;[59] a process of divide and control, of partial sharing of the labours and the privileges (including military commands), with the hope of reinstatement for some, was used increasingly the more it was needed; and invitations to take an inferior place at the messes may have played their part as a change, presumably, from relatively unsocial evenings spent on (generally diminished) estates.[60] Certainly inferiors will not have been encouraged to form their own groups or clubs, like the *nothoi* of Cynosarges in Athens.[61] A 'mirage' of conviviality may have had its effect on such men, as well as the well-grounded fear of ridicule or elimination.

Some of these points may be summarised, in the form of a detailed comparison between the Spartan *syssitia,* as they operated from the mid-fifth to the mid-fourth century, and the types of *symposia* that flourished in Athens. This may help us to assess how well the Spartan institutions were designed for the promotion of harmony and fruitful competition; and whether they also produced tensions, and if so, how these were handled. Such a comparison between the two types of institution allows (at least) five points to be made.

First, in the *syssitia,* unlike the *symposia,* deep drinking and drunkenness were, we are consistently told, eschewed by the free participants; the emphasis was more on food than on drink, but even so luxurious foods and elaborate cuisine were largely absent. The provision of more interesting food, especially through the *epaikla* system, was seen rather as a mechanism for the exercise of patronage by the more successful, mitigating envy and sharing the wealth among close companions, and providing some approved honour in return for the donors. In theory, then, the harmony of the whole is preserved, in a timocratic manner, extravagance is severely limited, and the dangers of drunkenness and its ensuing insolent violence are controlled.

Second, Athenian *symposia* were of many different types, though the aristocratic drinking-sessions were doubtless the fashion-setters, and they were optional: Athenians had the choice of which associations, and how many, to join. Some were *ad hoc* groups of friends or acquaintances, others were settled, organised groups based on cult, politics, or other shared interests. But Spartan *syssitia* were part of the state and compulsory; they were all of the same type, devoted to identical activities and interests (if somewhat unequal in wealth, prestige or access to the inner circles of power); all tended to reinforce, especially through the strict rules governing dress, fare and topics of conversation, the rigid uniformity and monotony of the society.[62]

Third, Athenian associations that regularly met and drank together tended to be composed of men of similar ages, often — and perhaps most dangerously — of the relatively young (or the young at heart, like Conon).[63] As Xenophon pointed out, *syssitia* had members of all age-classes, and the men of age and experience set the tone; hierarchy in the *syssition* was extremely important, and within limits was competed for on the basis of a variety of criteria.[64] But the friendly, irresponsible, anarchy of snobbish or loutish young Athenians had no real counterpart in Sparta.

Fourth, Athenian *symposia* were the settings for free and open discussions, on a variety of ethical, theoretical, social, sexual or political topics (often in consciously playful imitation of more formal *polis* procedures); these might lead to conspiracies, political and legal planning, and at times blasphemies and acts of *hybris* against the city's gods and cults.[65] Spartan *syssitia* were

supposed to be secret, close-knit groups, and may well, as has
been suggested, have seen political discussions and gossip (as
well as gossip about boyfriends);[66] but it seems unlikely that they
could very often, if ever, have seen open speculation or seditious
plotting or plans for illegal acts, since the chances of a member
feeling obliged to inform the ephors or the elders would have
seemed too great. When Plato criticises the system of *gymnasia*
and *syssitia* on two counts, that they lead to *staseis,* and promote
pederasty, it seems to be Miletos, Boeotia and Thourioi that
provide the instances of *stasis,* and Sparta and Crete that are first
to take the blame for 'unnatural practices'.[67] The Laconiser
Critias, ironically for an habitué of the *symposia,* tried to suppress
Socrates' teaching and other forms of free thought in his new
Athens.[68]

Fifth, and perhaps most important, clashes between the ideas,
values and acts of many symposiasts in Athens and the interests
and laws of the *demos* were frequent, and the laws, including the
law of *hybris,* were often used against them, though perhaps not
often enough; but the Spartan *syssitia* were part of the state, and
their values were essentially the same. There were presumably
laws against hybristic abuses (cf. below); but the point is that no
systematic or structural conflict existed or could easily exist in
Sparta between the basic values and aims of the uniform *syssitia*
and the type of government and purposes of the Spartan state.

Summing up, it may be helpful, in the useful terms developed
fully by Basil Bernstein and Mary Douglas, to describe the
educational and social institutions of Sparta, in contrast to those
of Athens, as settings where the system, its rules, and the
discipline of its leaders alike imposed a 'restricted code', which
applied to the linguistic and rhetorical patterns, the range of
activities, the style of clothes and of commensality, and the very
capacity to think, of those who were, with greater or lesser success,
socialised into the society.[69] The *agoge* and the *syssitia* operated
with very severe limits on expressions of divergence, idiosyncrasy
or dissent, and there were no alternative institutions or small
groups to which a Spartiate might take himself without constant
fear of shame, rejection and public humiliation.[70]

Thus it is possible to endorse, and to develop, the types of
defence of Spartan convivial institutions as the promoters of
ordered and hierarchical harmony that we find in apologists such
as Xenophon. Further, some elements in (say) Xenophon's
analysis which other scholars treat as indications of grave

tensions and conflicts of values may rather be seen as indications of fruitful and beneficial competition for honour.[71] It seems to me that there is some truth in both ways of looking at these things; the difference might be expressed, in Greek fashion, by recalling Hesiod's discovery that there is a good as well as a bad form of *Eris*,[71a] i.e. that competition to succeed and excel in specific activities, within defined limits, without too much shame for those who do not succeed, is beneficial for the community. Xenophon himself recalls the distinction: 'here is the *theophilestate* and *politikotate eris*, that sets the goal for the good man to aim at', and it is a theme that undoubtedly appealed to Xenophon, who is keen in many of his works to see intense competitions established everywhere.[72] One could question whether all of these contests and indications of inequalities would seriously have upset the cohesion of the Spartan community.

First, one could say that the system of *epaikla* will have done something to reconcile the poorer members of a *syssition* to the undoubted inequalities, by insisting that the richer did not display their wealth in personal consumption and finery,[72a] but shared it with their closest comrades. Second, while limits were doubtless set to political discussion, yet the possibility for all to engage in small-scale discussions and grumbles, without going too far, will have done something to palliate the sense of exclusion from the inner counsels of elders, ephors, and perhaps from some of the other more exclusive *syssitia* such as the kings'. Interestingly, in the only political scandal that shows members of a *syssition* planning political action, the aim was to protect, perhaps foolishly, a member threatened with political disgrace: Sphodrias.[73]

Third, it is of course the case that the different qualities (such as birth, wealth, beauty, skill and courage in military and athletic spheres, and sound counsel) that could lead to varying degrees of eminence were not all found in the same people to the same degree; and that this must have induced tensions and frustrations among those who felt their talents insufficiently recognised.[74] But on the other hand this variety will in itself have enabled, for example, tough or clever men in lesser families to gain success and advancement, and in such ways have given some flexibility to an otherwise fairly rigid society.[75] Some minor success, perhaps, would have brought welcome praise at *syssition* level, more easily than at *polis* level, while success at national level would win particular praise, and be especially feted in the *syssition*, to which it would bring no little reflected glory.[76]

Especially suggestive here are the reported arrangements for the celebrations of election to the *gerousia*: the victor is offered honours, songs and food by relations and friends, and finally, at his *syssition,* he is in general treated as usual, except that he is offered a double set of rations there, the second of which he would give to the woman he honoured most highly. The high place of the *syssition* in the scale of a man's loyalties and the use of food as gifts of honour are particularly explicit here; it is evident, too, that though the victor is offered, temporarily, king-like honours (one may, *si parva licet,* compare the Roman triumph), he is also firmly reminded of his place, central to his identity, as an ordinary member of the *syssition.*[77]

Fourth, and most important, limits were set to the exercise of tensions and discontents among Spartiates by the ever-present consciousness of their privileged position and the need to preserve it: of the 'security against the helots' that dominated their institutions according to Thucydides (4.80), and the parallel need to keep divided and under control the other groups of inferiors. Consciousness of the much greater grievances of the lesser orders will have kept the full members of a *syssition* from expressing their own lesser resentments; the tensions of living in such a competitive society, great as these were for those who were not succeeding as well as they had hoped, would have been made more tolerable, or at least been repressed and controlled, by the constantly-felt need to avoid sinking to the levels of those they saw constantly around them.

These factors, and particularly the last, should be kept in mind as we return to the issues of drink, *hybris* and disorder in and out of the *syssitia,* and to two questions, postponed till now: whether in this area, as in others, the old laws were breaking down in the fourth century, and how individual instances of drunken disorder were actually handled in the society.

The statement 'there are no *symposia,* and no drunkenness in Sparta' is formally comparable to two other judgements, that 'there is no adultery in Sparta' and 'Lycurgus established as most shameful male relationships based on physical attraction and ensured that *aphrodisia* did not take place'.[78] Of these the one about pederasty is normally disbelieved, as Xenophon feared; the one about adultery seems to be believed to be mostly true, taken strictly;[79] what of the one about drink? No one will suppose no Spartiate ever got drunk at the *syssition;* but it needs evidence to persuade one that the rules for the conduct of *syssitia* had fallen largely or completely into disuse in Sparta in the early fourth century, or even soon after the battle of Leuctra.

Xenophon's gloomy chapter lamenting the abandonment of Lycurgus' laws seems relevant. It should be observed, first, that it might be merely an exaggerated outburst, written in an angry moment, and need not be taken to be saying that all the laws are blatantly ignored. In fact his examples mostly concern the arrogant, avaricious and power-seeking behaviour of those in the posts abroad or looking for them. None the less the themes of corruption by foreign contacts, and of delight in the possession of gold, might suggest that the *syssitia* were either perverted into debauchery, or by-passed while the real social action was elsewhere; equally, however, as has been suggested, it may well be that those complaints were produced mainly by the behaviour of Spartans abroad rather than at home, and that the state, through the ephors, did take control of such deviants on occasions.[80] Plato, as we have seen, did not seize the opportunity in the *Laws* to convict the Spartans of backsliding into drunkenness, though he hinted at other defects in the system, here and elsewhere.[81] Aristotle comes closer to it; quite unimpressed by the *syssitia*, he saw the damage done by the economic exclusions, and also said that the ephors lived in open luxury which had a bad effect on the rest who fled the excessively restricted life of the laws, and enjoyed 'bodily pleasures'. This seems much more serious a claim; it appears likely that in these sections of the *Politics* Aristotle is describing essentially the situation some years after Leuctra, and that by the time this book of the *Politics* was written the process which led to the complete breakdown of the *syssitia* by the mid-third century was under way.[82] Plato may still, by the 340s, have been reluctant to bring this out explicitly in the *Laws*, whereas Aristotle, perhaps a little later, was well prepared to see what was happening. The process of decline is hard to pin down, but a substantial breakdown of the *syssitia*-rules inside Sparta in the reign of Agesilaus seems hard to credit; tensions in these areas were no doubt growing, but, I suspect, less rapidly than in the areas of economy and inheritance.[83]

Finally, one should observe the remarkable readiness of Spartan authorities to use accusations of breaches of the rules of syssitic behaviour to damn their top-class deviants. The most famous case is that of Cleomenes I. The Spartan version of his fall, that he drank neat wine Scythian-style, seems to have defeated the other apparently attractive versions involving blasphemy and bribery of the Oracle.[84] There are also the accusations against Pausanias in Thucydides, apparently relying on Spartan stories, which include the wearing of Persian dress and the holding of Persian banquets — the reverse of Herodotus' portrait of Pausanias after Plataea; Herodotus probably disbelieved the official Spartan stories.[85] These and other cases[86] testify to the importance of the theme, and to the ruthlessness of Spartan *damnationes* of those they reject; conversely the praise of Agesilaus' sobriety and avoidance of *hybris*, his general obedience to the 'laws', and his concern to maintain cohesion through 'friendship', give the reverse, ideal, side.[87] The impression is given that the official Spartan myths and memories of their leaders paid more attention to breaches of the rules of sobriety, austerity and harmony between the equals than to maltreatment by Spartan officials of other Greeks.[88]

While the laws were still, for the most part, being obeyed, how were they enforced? Such little evidence as there is suggests that if the authorities had to take cognisance of a Spartiate fight, rape or piece of drunken vandalism, the ephors would in most cases dispense swift justice, acting as Aristotle says 'on their own judgements, not according to written rules and the laws';[89] and presumably they could impose fines, minor humiliations, or exclusion from citizenship and the *syssitia*, for serious offences.[90] But not only are no cases heard of (the authorities would be likely to keep them quiet): one may suspect that many cases that did occur might be dealt with as far as possible by the *syssition* itself, in self-defence, and in defence of Sparta's need of citizens, and in accordance with the motto of self-regulation and silence. (Whether transfers of *syssitia* could be arranged where irresoluble quarrels had arisen seems unattested, though it is likely enough that they could.) Many Spartan anecdotes emphasise the desirability of tolerance if one is wronged; but the saying of Chilon 'Settle if treated with *adikia*; achieve revenge if treated with *hybris*' suggests limits to this strategy, and that what was felt to be serious *hybris* had to be taken seriously.[91]

Finally, one may add some further reasons to accept the general picture that drunken offences, drunken violence, gross insults or sexual abuse (i.e. *hybris*) between Spartiatai or their wives were indeed unusual. In addition to the fact that the continuous presence, in one capacity or another, of helots may have had a strongly inhibiting effect on the expression of verbal insults or fighting, there are other points. The Spartiatai had been 'conditioned' to obey their elders, to obey the rules, and to respect each other, conscious of their precarious position, and brought up in the obsessively disciplined, authoritarian atmosphere of the 'restricted code'; all *syssitoi* constituted a ruling class, with a highly developed class-consciousness.

Further, opportunities for treating people with violence, insult and sexual abuse, whether after drinking or not, were in any case far from lacking. The 'tremblers' and the economic inferiors, or the confirmed bachelors, might receive their carefully graded insults and humiliations;[92] the progressive marginalisation of the failures, and their exclusion from full membership of the *syssitia*, made those remaining more conscious of their privileges and concerned to reinforce them. *Perioikoi* too, no doubt, were often treated violently or contemptuously by their rulers; indeed Isocrates described their treatment as abject *douleia,* involving all sorts of acts of *hybris,* with no defence against the right of the ephors to put them to death without trial, even though many of them contributed so much to the army.[93] The helots suffered most, of course, from the *krypteia,* from casual beating and presumably rapes and abuse (cf. the wishful musing of the Old Oligarch).[94] There was plenty of hybristic behaviour committed by Spartiates; but they would not so describe the acts, and they were not illegal. Equally, violent acts between future Spartiates in the *agoge* were brutal and frequent, but they were controlled, regularised, and even permeated the rituals; one need only mention the frequent whippings, and the many and varied team fights among the young, carefully encouraged and supervised by the elders.[95]

Thus the violence, the aggression and the *hybris* that were prevalent in Sparta were, like other features of the society, channelled to support the preservation of its curious structure and the needs of its 'law-abiding' elite, and were largely kept out of the *syssitia;* the control over the drinking habits of Spartans served the same purposes; and suggestions of the radical demise of such practices and controls seem, on the whole, to need to be treated with caution, at least down to the shattering defeat of 371.

Notes

1. Cf. my *Hybris* (Warminster, forthcoming), and my chapter on 'Greek Associations, Symposia and Clubs', in *Civilization of the ancient Mediterranean* (eds M. Grant and R. Kitzinger; New York, 1988). For a

survey of the recent profusion of *symposia*-studies, cf. P. Schmitt-Pantel, *Mélanges d'archéologie et d'histoire* (Ecole Française de Rome) 97 (1985) 135ff.

2. Cf. O. Murray, 'The Greek Symposion in History', in *Tria Corda: Scritti in onore di Arnaldo Momigliano* (Como, 1983), 258.

3. W.K.C. Guthrie, *History of Greek Philosophy* V (Cambridge, 1975), 325; cf. also authors cited by E. Belfiore, *CQ* 36 (1986) 421 n. 2.

4. *Ap.* Guthrie, V 382 n. 2.

5. Cf. Murray, 'Greek Symposion in History', 270f., G.R. Morrow, *Plato's Cretan city* (Princeton, 1960), 389ff. Common meals were of no little importance in the Academy and the Lyceum themselves: cf. Guthrie, *History of Greek philosophy* IV 20f., Morrow, 316f.

6. Cf. J. Gould, *The development of Plato's ethics* (Cambridge, 1955), 77ff., and recently Belfiore, *CQ* 36 (1986) 421 (n. 3).

7. Morrow, *Plato's Cretan city*, 48, 316.

8. *History* V, 325.

9. *Plato's Cretan city*, 390.

10. In the *Minos*, Plato (or whoever) claims that of all Greeks it is only the Cretans, and following them the Spartans, who abstained from *symposia* and drunkenness, and that this resulted in *eudaimonia* for Crete and Sparta alike (320). On Plato's presentation of *syssitia* in the *Laws* cf. also E. David, 'The Spartan *syssitia* and Plato's *Laws*', *AJP* 99 (1978) 486ff.

11. Cf. Murray, 'The Greek Symposion in History', 268ff., Humphreys, 'Evolution of Legal Process in Ancient Attica', in *Tria Corda*, 239, and, on the law of *hybris* in Athens, D.M. MacDowell, *G&R* 23 (1976) 14ff., and N.R.E. Fisher, *G&R* 23 (1976) 177ff.

12. On the allegations about the economic and social power of Spartan women, cf. P. Cartledge, 'Spartan Wives', *CQ* 31 (1981) 84ff., and now S. Hodkinson, *CQ* 36 (1986) 378ff., and this volume pp. 111–13.

13. *Spartan law* (Edinburgh, 1986), 15.

14. For the *hybris* of verbal insults see esp. Arist. *Rhet.* 1379a 30ff., 1389b 10ff., *Pol.* 1311a 38ff.

15. Critias fr. 6 West (=Athen. 432d–33b); also DK 88B32–37. Cf. F. Ollier, *Le mirage Spartiate* (Paris, 1933), 170ff., E. Rawson, *The Spartan tradition in European thought* (Oxford, 1969), 30ff.

16. Fr. 2 West (=Athen. 28b–c), DK88B1 (=Athen. 600d–e). Cf. S. Usher, 'This to the fair Critias', *Eranos* 77 (1979) 39ff., pointing out that this hypocrisy is elegantly exploited in Theramenes' dying game of hemlock *kottabos* (Xen. *Hell.* 2.3.56).

17. P. Krentz, *The thirty at Athens* (Ithaca, 1982), and D. Whitehead, 'Sparta and the Thirty Tyrants', *AS* 13/14 (1982) 105ff: against, cf. Cartledge, *Agesilaos* (London, 1987), 282.

18. DK88B37; he also attributed the motto *meden agan* to the Spartan Chilon, fr. 7 West. Cf. Ollier, *Le mirage*, I 172.

19. Xenophontic authorship of the pamphlet seems very probable to me, but decision on the date of composition, and on the relation of the apparently palinodic chapter 14 to the rest, is not easy. Cf. recently MacDowell, *Spartan law*, 8ff., Cartledge, *Agesilaos*, 56f., who is tempted

(more than I am) by the unitarian approach and late dating of W.E. Higgins, *Xenophon the Athenian* (Albany, 1977), 65ff.

20. Cf. Ollier, *Le mirage,* I 411, Whitehead (see n. 17), 116; against, MacDowell, *Spartan law,* 16.

21. Athen. 141a–c, Suda s.v. *Dicaiarchos,* cf. T.J. Figueira, 'Mess Contributions and Subsistence at Sparta', *TAPA* 114 (1984) 88f.

22. Hdt. 9.82.

23. E.g. Ar. *Birds* 1281f., Antiph. 44 (Kock), Plut. *Alk.* 23.

24. Xen. *Lak. Pol.* 5, Athen. 140c–141e; see esp. Molpis *FGH* 590 F2b = Athen. 141e: 'the cooks announce the names of those who have on each occasion brought something for the community (*eis meson*), in order that all may know the endeavour spent on the chase and the concern displayed on them'. Cartledge, *Agesilaos,* 178, compares the contribution of wheaten bread to the messes by the rich with the secretive storage of gold and valuables in private houses as symbols of 'the dissolution of the Lycurgan order'; but the comparison underplays the envy-reducing mechanism of reciprocal gifts, *philotimia* and *charis* designed to bind rich and poor mess-mates together; cf. A.J. Toynbee, *Some problems in Greek history* (Oxford, 1969), 312.

25. We hear of 27 Spartan *phratries* only in the passage of Demetrios of Scepsis (Athen. 141e–f) concerning the tents of representative groups at the Carneia; how, if at all, they are to be related to the military, the local, or the syssitic organisations, of whatever period, is wholly obscure. Cf. D. Roussel, *Tribu et cité* (Paris, 1976), 127ff. Many hero-cults are attested at Sparta, offered both to 'mythological' and to 'real' heroes (S. Wide, *Lakonische Kulte* (Leipzig, 1893), C.M. Stibbe, *Castrum Peregrini* 132/133 (1978) 6ff.); cult was no doubt offered by family and *gene* groups (cf. R. Parker, this volume pp. 144f.), by *phratries* and in state festivals; but there seems no evidence of private *thiasoi* identified by heroic cult.

26. Cf. frr. 17, 19, 95, 98 (Page); both elegant *symposia* and state *syssitia* may be involved in these poems, but certainty is impossible.

27. Cf. esp. Plut. *Lyk.* 21, Athen. 139d (the *Hyacinthia*), 674a (the *Promacheia*); cf. also Parker, this volume, pp. 142ff., and C. Calame, *Les chœurs de jeunes filles en Grèce archaïque* (Rome, 1977), I.3.2.

28. Persaios *FGH* 84F2 (=Athen. 140f); cf. Hodkinson, 'Social Order and the Conflict of Values in Classical Sparta', *Chiron* 13 (1983) 253. Each *syssition* seems to have a 'leader' (Persaios *FGH* 84F2), and a Spartiate official carver (*kreodaites*) and cook (*mageiros*); cf. n. 42 below.

29. Plut. *Lak. Apophth.* 224d.

30. Esp. ch. 12. On Plutarch's sources, and the problems of using the work, cf. Hodkinson, 'Social Order', 241 n. 8.

31. Presumably the terminal date for the observance of the rules Plutarch had in mind was the mid-third century, as in Phylarchos, *FGH* 81F44 = Athen. 141e–42f.

32. Hdt. 6.57.3.

33. Many of the 'traditional privileges' of the kings described in this chapter of Herodotus may already have been obsolete by the historian's day, most clearly the supposed power to declare war: cf. P. Carlier, *La royauté en Grèce avant alexandre* (Strasbourg, 1984), 250ff.

34. Cf. Carlier (n. 33), 267.

35. Plut. *Lyk.* 12.2; for Agis' reconstruction, *Agis* 8.

36. Cf. e.g. Toynbee, *Some problems,* 369ff., Hodkinson, 'Social Order', J.F. Lazenby, *The Spartan army* (Warminster, 1985), 13.

37. On the extent to which homosexual pair-bonding was institutionalised in the Spartan *agoge,* and virtually compulsory *de facto,* I would follow Cartledge, 'The Politics of Spartan Pederasty', *PCPS* 27 (1981) 17ff., Hodkinson, 'Social Order', 245ff.; MacDowell, *Spartan law,* 61ff. may be correct that there was not a law or strict allocation system assigning a lover to each youth, but this is not necessary for it to be the norm, or a crucial part of the educational structure.

38. Cf. esp. Cartledge, 'Pederasty', 36 n. 78, *Agesilaos,* 32f., Hodkinson, 'Social Order', 253. Such evidence as there is suggests that the messes were grouped together along the 'Hyacinthian Way' towards Amyclae (Athen. 173f, 39c, Paus. 7.1.8). How permanent or solid were the mess-buildings is unclear. Cf. H. Michell, *Sparta* (Cambridge, 1952), 287.

39. Esp. Figueira, 'Mess Contributions', 94ff. Earlier, U. Kahrstedt, *Hermes* 54 (1919) 279ff. In particular, in relation to the wine contribution, Figueira perhaps exaggerates the excessiveness of the amount if it was all consumed by the individual Spartiate (pp. 93–4), partly by comparing *per capita* rates of a whole population; one could add, for example, that farm workers in Languedoc consumed daily nearly two litres of wine in the fifteenth century (E. Le Roy Ladurie, *The Peasants of Languedoc* (Eng.Tr., Urbana, 1976), 63). None the less, the amount does not seem easily compatible with the emphasis on moderate drinking in the *syssitia,* and the boys, in the *syssitia* or in their 'junior' messes are not likely to have consumed much; it is reasonable to look for other regular means of disposing of the surplus.

40. Persaios FGH 584F2 (=Athen. 140e); describing the proceedings as 'a sort of *politeuma*', he distinguishes those reclining in first or second place, and those sitting on the *skimpodion;* cf. also Phylarchos *FGH* 81F44, Cic. *Pro Murena* 142a. On the importance of men reclining, and boys sitting, in various societies, cf. J. Bremmer, in Murray (ed.) *Sympotica* (Oxford, forthcoming).

41. Cf. Kahrstedt, *Hermes* 54 (1919) 284, Michell, *Sparta,* 288.

42. Individual helots no doubt attended their masters at the messes and served them. The menials concerned with the preparation of the food were presumably also helots, though the hereditary *technitai* called *mageiroi* (Hdt. 6.60), whose concern was the cults of the heroes Matton and Keraon, and who operated at (some, or all?) *syssitia* and on campaign, were presumably Spartiate. Cf. Wide, *Lakonische kulte,* 278, Michell, *Sparta,* 293, G. Berthiaume, *Les rôles de mageiros* (Leiden, 1976), App. II.

43. Plut. *Lyk.* 28 (cf. Ephraim David, pp. 6f. of this volume). In *Demetrios* 1, Plutarch expresses the point by saying that the Spartans got the helots drunk 'at the festivals' and brought them into the *syssitia;* but one should probably not suppose (as does e.g. J. Ducat, 'La Mépris des Hilotes', *Annales* 29 (1974) 1457) that the practice was restricted to festival occasions; indeed, at the major festivals, the *syssitia* did not operate. The practice may have started at festivals, and then been adopted in the messes, with what frequency it seems impossible to say.

44. Some, at least, of the *mothakes* were no doubt the result of liaisons between Spartiates and helot women (cf. Cartledge, 'Spartan Wives', 104); no evidence seems to support the suggestion that such women were admitted to the *syssitia* to perform roles comparable to those of flute-players and *hetairai,* unless the females appearing in a couple of sympotic scenes on Laconian vases (cf. E.A. Lane, 'Lakonian Vase Painting', *BSA* 34 (1934) 158f.) are to be interpreted in such a manner; though no doubt artistic borrowing from Corinth is present, and no implication for Spartan life is necessary.

45. Ducat, 'La Mépris des Hilotes', 1457f., emphasises the degrading and dehumanising aspects of the practice, and its value in inculcating contempt for helots among young Spartiates; Figueira, 'Mess Contributions', 97, suggests also a mechanism for recirculation of food as part of social integration. Ducat's doubts that the inculcation of the dangers of excessive drinking was also part of the purpose seem unnecessary.

46. Cf. G.L. Cawkwell, 'Decline of Sparta', *CQ* 33 (1983) 394f.; the most famous cases are Xenophon's sons and Phocion's son.

47. Plut. *Lyk.* 20.2, *Lak. Apophth.* 218b, 232f–3a; Xen. *Mem.* 1.2.61, Plut. *Kim.* 10.6. One is tempted to conclude that limited provision existed, especially for wealthy Spartans, to entertain friends and *xenoi* at private dinners at times of major festivals. Cf. also the material on Spartan *xeniai* and *proxeniai* in Whitehead, 'Sparta and the Thirty Tyrants', 117f.

48. Fr. 27 West; on the date and context cf. most recently West, *BICS* 32 (1985) 73ff.

49. West argues that the King in line 1 may be Dionysus or Wine, but that the deities imply a royal Spartan occasion; he suggests a visit of Ior with Cimon to Sparta *c.* 451/0 on peace negotiations, instead of the well-known visit in 462 previously postulated.

50. The difficulties of reconciling the tone of the poem with the supposed conduct of Spartan *syssitia* could be evaded by the suppositions that it was a more private dinner at festival-time, that a Spartan king was a guest when travelling abroad, or even that we have a group of ardent Laconisers; but none of these is as natural a reading as that which supposes the setting to be the royal *syssition.*

51. Phylarchos FGH 81F43 = Athen. 271e; cf. D. Lotze, 'Mothakes', *Hist.* 11 (1960) 427ff., and Cawkwell, 'Decline of Sparta', 394, Toynbee, *Some problems,* 343ff., for evidence on *mothakes.*

52. The details of this are complex and uncertain, but it still seems plausible that the *enomotiai* in the 'new army' were made up of members of (say) one or two *syssitia* and additional *perioikoi.* Cf. esp. Polyainos 2.3.11, 2.1.15, and e.g. Nilsson, *Klio* 12 (1912) 315ff., Toynbee, *Some problems,* 320ff., 369ff., Hodkinson, 'Social Order', 258f. Against, cf. Lazenby, *Spartan army* 12f. Xen. *Symp.* 8.35 suggests to me that a man might be stationed next to his lover in the Spartan army, or might not, and be next to a *xenos* (probably meaning a *perioikos,* cf. Hodkinson, 'Social Order', 253 n. 36): which would suit a system where *enomotiai* might be made up of men of different age-classes, from one or more *syssitia,* and also of *perioikoi.*

53. E.g. among ancient authors, Plato, *Laws* 633a, among moderns, Toynbee, *Some problems*, 320ff.

54. Philochorus *FGH* 324F216 = Athen. 630f., cf. Lycurgus 1.107, and cf. E.L. Bowie, in *Sympotica* (cf. n. 40). Helots were forbidden to sing such patriotic poetry, and some internalised the prohibition: Plut. *Lyk.* 28.10.

55. Xen. *Lak. Pol.* 5.6., above p. 31. Cf. the echoes in the boys' messes, Plut. *Lyk.* 18.2.

56. Xen. *Lak. Pol.* 5.8, accepting Schenkl's emendation *agymnastous ton sition geuesthai*; cf. MacDowell, *Spartan law*, 68f.

57. Hdt. 6.57, Xen. *Lak. Pol.* 15, *Ages.* 5. On the workings of patronage in Sparta, especially that of the kings, cf. now Cartledge, *Agesilaos*, Ch. 9, Hodkinson, 'Social Order', 263ff.

58. Assumed to be always Spartiates by Hodkinson, 'Social Order', 252 n. 34.

59. On Cinadon, cf. recently David, *Athenaeum* 57 (1979) 239ff., Cartledge, *Agesilaos*, 164ff. On reasons for the loyalty of inferiors, helots and *perioikoi* in the fourth century, cf. also Cawkwell, *Decline of Sparta*, 390ff.

60. This, as Stephen Hodkinson has pointed out to me, seems the most plausible answer to Finley's puzzle about where and how some, at least, of the 'inferiors' lived (*Economy and society in ancient Greece* (London, 1981), 34).

61. Cf. S.C. Humphreys, *JHS* 94 (1974) 88ff.

62. Cf. Thuc. 1.6.4, Arist. *Pol.* 1294b24ff., Toynbee, *Some problems*, 312, Hodkinson, 'Social Order', 252ff., 256. Limited exceptions only may have been provided at Sparta by dinners of the pseudo-kinship groups, and perhaps by private functions at festival-times.

63. Dem. 54, and many other cases.

64. Xen. *Lak. Pol.* 5, cf. also below.

65. Cf. S.C. Humphreys, *Family, women and death* (London, 1983), 16ff., Murray, in *Sympotica* (cf. n. 40).

66. Cf. the repeated 'motto' reported in Plut. *Lak. Pol.* 5: 'through that door no word goes forth', and Xen. *Hell.* 5.3.30., cf. D.M. Lewis, *Sparta and Persia* (Leiden, 1977), 34f., Cartledge, 'Pederasty', 29f., Hodkinson, 'Social Order', 253.

67. *Laws* 636a–c; Ollier, *Le mirage*, I 260 and Hodkinson, 'Social Order', 253 n. 38 seem not to observe this distinction.

68. Cf. Xen. *Mem.* 1.2.29ff., Whitehead, 'Sparta and the Thirty Tyrants', 125f.

69. E.g. B. Bernstein, *Class, codes and control* (London, 1971), M. Douglas, *Natural symbols* (Harmondsworth, 1973). Cf. also Parker, this volume p. 161f.

70. On the elements of the closed society indicated by laconic speech, limited literacy, and hostility to outside influences, cf. Cartledge, *JHS* 98 (1978) 25ff., Whitehead, 'Sparta and the Thirty Tyrants', 125.

71. I have in mind especially Hodkinson, 'Social Order', and many recent works by Cartledge, e.g. most recently *Agesilaos*, Ch. 12; the starting point was Finley's penetrating and very influential essay (*Economy and society*, Ch. 2).

71a. *Works and Days* 11ff.

72. *Lak. Pol.* 4.2–5; cf. also *Hell.* 3.4.16, *Kyr.* 1.6.27ff., etc. See also Redfield, 'The Women of Sparta', *CJ* 73 (1977/8) 157, who analyses Sparta's ideological commitment to substitute *philotimia* for *philochrematia,* and to institute a 'competition for conformity'.

72a. Chariot-racing, clearly encouraged at Sparta, brought honour to the *polis* and the *syssition* as well as to the individual, cf. n. 75 below.

73. Xen. *Hell.* 5.4.20ff., cf. most recently Cartledge, *Agesilaos*, 136ff., 156ff. More generally, Cartledge (*Agesilaos*, 131) argues that the mess-system will have fostered the oligarchic, anti-democratic and secretive nature of Spartan society, whereas Aristotle (in one place) treated it as a more 'democratic' element (*Pol.* 1294b 27ff.). My argument is rather that the 'illusion' of free, if severely limited, discussions open to all Spartiates in their messes will have helped to maintain a political consensus, through small-scale, pseudo-democratic procedures in a markedly hierarchical structure.

74. Cf. Hodkinson, 'Social Order', 252ff.

75. Paradeigmatic cases were those of Gylippos and Lysander, cf. e.g. Phylarchos *FGH* 81F43 = Athen. 271e. Many Spartan inscriptions attest the importance for Spartiates of victories gained at local and at more important games, most notably the remarkable record of Damonon, IG V.1.213.

76. Cf. the evidence for mess conversations already cited. On the glory brought by noble and 'heroic' death to Spartiates' relatives, *erastai* and no doubt their *syssitoi,* cf. C. Fuqua, 'Tyrtaeus and the Cult of Heroes', *GRBS* 22 (1981) 215ff, and Hodkinson, 'Social Order', 259; Spartans could only have a named gravestone if they died in battle, or in child-birth (Plut. *Lyk.* 27.3), and several examples exist (e.g. IG V.1.701ff., 1124ff.), while some reliefs with inscriptions attest the 'heroisation' of famous Spartans such as Chilon (Stibbe, see n. 25).

77. Plut. *Lyk.* 26. The modes of canvassing and election for the *gerousia* were open to the strongest manipulation from the top (cf. Aristotle's descriptions of them as *dunasteutike* and as childish, *Pol.* 1271a4ff., 1306a 18–20, and Cartledge, *Agesilaos,* 122); but, again, care is taken to inte-grate the successful man in his small-scale relationships.

78. Megillus, in *Laws* 637a, Plut. *Lyk.* 15.9–10, Xen. *Lak. Pol.* 2.12–4.

79. Cf. e.g. Cartledge, 'Pederasty', 19ff., and 'Spartan Wives', 104.

80. Cf. Cawkwell, 'Decline', 396. To what extent those who illegally imported gold and other wealth into Sparta spent it there (apart from buying land, horses and hounds), rather than gloated over it in their store-rooms, remains uncertain, though the sources insist unanimously that love of money was an increasingly divisive and destructive feature of Spartan life. Cf. also MacDowell, *Spartan law*, 118ff., David, *Sparta between empire and revolution* (New York, 1981), Hodkinson, below, pp. 95ff.

81. *Laws* 637b, above pp. 27ff. The *Republic* implies more serious criticism of Spartan society; the account of timocracy (*Rep.* 547–8) suggests that rich Spartans may both have hoarded and have spent money inside their own houses on their wives and 'on anything else they chose' (cf. also Xen. *Hell.* 6.5.27); but the maintenance of *syssitia* and gymnastic and military training, and respect for authorities, are still held

to be essential elements of the society. Cf. Cartledge, *Agesilaos*, 402ff., David, *AJP* 98 (1977) 486ff.

82. *Pol.* 1270b30ff. Cf. David, 'Aristotle and Sparta', *Ancient society* 13/14 (1982/3) 67ff., esp. 74ff., 91ff. Similarly, Aristotle's criticism of the *syssitia* as not really democratic (1271a 27ff.), in contrast to their presentation as an ideal at 1294b 27ff., and elsewhere, reflects the increase in inequalities of wealth and the failure of many of the poor to keep up their payments.

83. For these, cf. most recently Hodkinson, *CQ* 36 (1986) 378ff. and this volume, pp. 79ff.

84. Hdt. 6.84. Herodotus' further comment, that Spartans in his day say 'Scyth-ise it' when they wish to drink their wine less diluted, confirms that variations in depth of drinking were known, and discussed, in Spartan gatherings (? *syssitia*); it might be thought to confirm hints discussed above that rules against drunkenness may have been a little more relaxed in the fifth century, but caution is probably needed here too.

85. Thuc. 1.130; contrast Hdt. 9.82 and 8.1. Cf. e.g. P.J. Rhodes, *Historia* 19 (1970) 387ff.

86. E.g. the attempt by 30 traditional Spartiates to discredit Lysander at Ephesus (Xen. *Hell.* 3.4.8).

87. Xen. *Ages.* 5, 7.1–3, 8.1–2, 6–8, 10.2, 11.11–12. For the cunning, if ultimately short-sighted, political career underlying the idealistic picture of this most crafty of Spartan kings, cf. now Cartledge's extended study.

88. Cf. the treatments of Phoebidas and Sphodrias, and contrast the attacks of Isocrates, *Paneg.* 110ff., *Panath.* 176ff.

89. Xen. *Lak. Pol.* 8.4, Arist. *Pol.* 1270b 28–31, 1275b 9–13. Cf. now MacDowell, *Spartan law*, 129ff.

90. Cf. MacDowell, *Spartan law*, 42ff., 144ff. Two sources state particular penalties for abuse of boys: Aelian (V.H. 3.10.12) mentions a law of *hybris* for rape of boys, with a penalty of death or exile for both partners, and Plutarch *(Inst. Lak.* 237b–c) mentions a penalty of disenfranchisement for shameful intercourse by *erastai*. These reports have little plausibility (Cartledge, 'Pederasty', 31 n. 19); but the ephors and the other guardians of those in the *agoge* must have been able in principle to take action against the grossest sexual abuses, however these were defined in Sparta.

91. Stob. III.1.172, p. 118 Hense; cf. on these anecdotes P. Janni, *La Cultura di Sparta arcaica: I* (Rome, 1965), 43ff.

92. Cf. e.g. Hdt 7. 231f., Xen *Hell.* 3.1.9, *Lak. Pol.* 9, Plut. *Lyk.* 15.1–3, Lewis, *Sparta and Persia*, 30ff.

93. *Panath.* 178ff.

94. Plut. *Lyk.* 28 and the material collected by Cartledge, *Sparta and Laconia*, App.4; [Xen.] *Ath. Pol.* 1.16.

95. Xen. *Lak. Pol.* 2.2, 4.3–6, 6.2, Plato, *Laws* 633 b–c, Paus. 3.14. 8–10, Plut. *Lyk.* 16.5–9, 17.1–2; cf. the use of controlled jesting and abuse, Plut. *Lyk.* 12.4, 25.2–3. Cf. Hodkinson, 'Social Order', 245ff.

3

Was Kleomenes Mad?

Alan Griffiths

There are people who do quite confidently believe that Kleomenes I, King of Sparta between about 520 and 490 BC, became unhinged and by modern standards 'certifiable'. Some have attributed this to the drinking of neat wine, a habit learnt from Skythian visitors. Others have thought that he stoned himself into insanity with cannabis imported from the same source. Or that he was epileptic. Or that we can diagnose him, across the centuries, as a paranoid schizophrenic: it has recently been claimed that 'the story offers plenty of scope to the psychoanalyst' (Huxley 1983, 12), while Devereux and Forrest have been promising a joint interpretation along these lines for some time, though it has not yet to my knowledge appeared. Was he not, after all, the unwanted son of his father (Forrest 1980, 83)? And does his reported death by self-laceration not express in the clearest possible way a wish to attack the hating and hated father, turned — now that its real object is beyond his reach — destructively in upon himself?

The material that is pressed into service to support these speculations depends, I need hardly say, almost entirely on our text of Herodotos. I should add, in fairness, that others have been much less ready to accept Herodotos' account as a firm foundation for secondary and more advanced analysis, psycho- or otherwise. Here is a suitably cautious, if lurid, sentence from Macan: 'Through the mists of oblivion, rivalry, prejudice and afterthought the figure of Kleomenes looms as an enigma in Spartan history rather than as an intelligible and manageable agent' (Macan 1895, 89).

If we are to arrive at any sort of tenable position on this question, then, it is crucial that we should understand just what sort of a document Herodotos' 'book' actually is, from what sort of primary material it was composed, and thus how it is to be deciphered.

There has been some progress in this direction. Walter Burkert has demonstrated one way in which a superficially 'incredible', or 'mythical' story, when read with a sensitive awareness of fifth-century political pamphleteering (if one may so describe a process that was at this stage overwhelmingly an oral one), could be made to yield up meaning (Burkert 1965). In that case the issue was the doubt surrounding the legitimacy of Kleomenes' opposite number, Damaratos; and he showed brilliantly how the real question (was Damaratos the son of King Ariston, and thus legitimate, or of his mother's previous husband, and accordingly disqualified?) had been exaggerated in both directions under the pressure of Persian War faction-fighting. As the deposed and exiled Damaratos returned to Greece with the Persian army as satrap-in-waiting, his opponents grossly caricatured the less favourable version, and put it about that Damaratos' mother had been putting it about with the stable-boys; supporters claimed, equally wildly, but to the other extreme, that he had been fathered by a friendly neighbourhood hero. So we find ourselves presented with the compressed and fossilised remains of no less than four separate accounts, from which Burkert helped us to reconstruct the fully-articulated living originals.[1]

In general, however, I do not believe that we are yet in a position to apply Burkert's method more widely, for however regularly one reads and hears pious acknowledgments of the fact that Herodotos depended on oral sources, and that his own attitude to the material he gathered was in some sense pre-literary, I still do not find a proper awareness of this vitally important factor displayed in the way historians actually use his text as evidence.[2] This essay, starting out not from historical but from literary considerations, will try to lay some groundwork for discussion. I have tried to carry out some investigations into the conditions in which myths, folktales, popular narratives and rumours circulate, and it is the lessons that one can draw from this area of research that I think historians need to take into account before they attempt to squeeze yet more drops of infer-ential juice from the desiccated lemon that we call Herodotos. Let me quote from someone who does not just make ritual genuflections towards the altar, but in his work on the Delphic oracle has put into practice what he preaches (Fontenrose 1978, 128):

We hardly appreciate the great difference between his time and ours in the reporting of events, the preservation of records, the means of communication, the general state of knowledge. The Greeks had almost none of our facilities in communications and records; there was nothing of what we call media; there was little in the way of archives. We scarcely realise how much they depended on oral reports and how ready they were to believe what they were told.

Oral story-types, then, must occupy a place of central importance in any study of this kind: what their characteristics are, how they are transmitted, to what sort of personalities they tend to attach themselves. It is necessary to remember that they were used by Herodotos not just in contexts of what was for the author himself 'ancient history', but to illuminate events of recent times too. Xerxes, Peisistratos, Miltiades all have generic exemplary tales of this type attached to them; and so does Kleomenes, to whom we can — after a brief intermission — turn our attention.

Digression: how long did Herodotos think Kleomenes' reign lasted?

We may begin by trying to clear one small confusion out of the way. At 5.48 Herodotos records the death of Kleomenes' half-brother Dorieus in Sicily, adding

εἰ δὲ ἠνέσχετο βασιλευόμενος ὑπὸ Κλεομένεος καὶ κατέμενε ἐν Σπάρτῃ, ἐβασίλευσε ἂν Λακεδαίμονος· οὐ γάρ τινα πολλὸν χρόνον ἦρξε ὁ Κλεομένης, ἀλλ' ἀπέθανε ἄπαις, θυγατέρα μούνην λιπών, τῇ οὔνομα ἦν Γοργώ. ('If he had been able to stand having Kleomenes as king over him in Sparta, he would have ruled over Lakonia; for the kingship of Kleomenes didn't last very long, but he died without male issue, leaving only a daughter, whose name was Gorgo.')

It has long been recognised that this remark that 'the kingship of Kleomenes didn't last very long' is grossly and astonishingly inconsistent with the historian's own narrative, which chronicles the king's activities over a period of three decades. Macan described it as 'one of the most unintelligent and unintelligible mis-statements for which Herodotus is responsible'. No convincing solution to this problem has however been forthcoming.[3] Nor has it apparently been noticed that the sentence contains another inconsistency, of an internal, logical kind. For what is the meaning of the adversative ἀλλά, translated by Godley, Powell, de Sélincourt and most recently by Grene as 'and'?

All that is needed to restore both semantic coherence and Herodotus' reputation is the simple emendation of a single word: read εἰ for οὐ. 'For while it is true that Kleomenes had a pretty long reign, still he died without an heir . . .'[4] The idea is that because Kleomenes and Dorieus were almost the same age (5.41), and because Kleomenes died relatively young, Dorieus had (as it turned out with hindsight) only to sit tight and look both ways when crossing the road in order to succeed to the Agiad throne.

The sources of Herodotos' information about the King

First, some basic orientation concerning the transmission of information about Kleomenes' life and character. Argives, Athenians and other assorted Greeks had no reason to remember Kleomenes — who pursued an active and aggressive foreign policy — with affection; but they were not the only ones in that position. Spartan tradition itself (as reflected in Herodotos) regarded Kleomenes as a king who was only semi-legitimate. Anaxandridas not only married Kleomenes' mother reluctantly, for the sole purpose of getting an heir, but then proceeded to father three sons by the wife he had loved all along. The 'proper' line in the Agiad house continues through Leonidas, Pleistarchos and Pleistoanax, down to Herodotos' day; none of these would have had a good word to say for the interloper Kleomenes (cf. Jones 1967, 49). Gorgo, Kleomenes' daughter who was married at some stage to Leonidas, represents the King's only connection with the main line, and the only possibility of a favourable view establishing itself.

Kleomenes' position as an imposed and resented King becomes even more critical when we remember that this Agiad family was the one which normally played the dominant role in Spartan policy; certainly Herodotos thinks that it possessed inherently more τιμή, κατὰ πρεσβυγενείην (6.51).[5] On the other hand, this 'senior' house had a bad run of luck in the fifth century: Pausanias the regent disgraced, Pleistarchos short-lived, Pleistoanax in exile — Macan describes the whole line as being 'in eclipse' throughout the period. No doubt the start of the rot was ascribed by some to the disturbance caused by Kleomenes' kingship. There was certainly enough bad feeling around to make slanderous accusations of lunacy a likely charge from the opposing camp.[6]

Finally, in view of my initial hypothesis that we may expect to find some evidence not of history, not even of slanted history, but of free-floating stories of the malicious anti-tyrant type, we should note the fact that for long periods Anaxandridas and Ariston, and Kleomenes and Damaratos, ruled in parallel as head of the rival dynasties. It would not be surprising to find that stories about the opposing families had developed in parallel, as responding pairs; and the traditions about the disputed births of Kleomenes and Damaratos seem to lend a certain amount of prima facie credibility to that position.

An initial survey

It is immediately apparent that Kleomenes does not get a good press in the tradition that reached Herodotos. In particular, a whole series of allegations of outrageous or deranged behaviour is connected with the expedition that he led against Argos in the late 490s,[7] which culminated in the decisive victory of Sepeia but then somehow petered out. Let me briefly summarise some of the incidents of that campaign, in preparation for a more detailed examination later.

Kleomenes marched north and came to the River Erasinos, at or near the Argive border (see below, p. 65 and n. 36). The sacrifices were unfavourable, so instead of crossing over the King made a long detour, embarking his army on ships and landing it to the east of Argos. This is but one of many reports which associate Kleomenes with omens, oracles and portents: it is such a strong characteristic of the tradition — while not being always obviously pejorative — that I am inclined to accept it as genuinely Kleomenean. (It is not the intention of this paper to dissolve the King *entirely* into an amorphous minestrone of story-motifs.)

There follows the battle, won, according to Herodotos, by a

trick involving the issuing of false commands to the army in order to deceive the enemy. The survivors of the routed Argive troops are surrounded in a wood. Fifty of them are enticed out one by one by the promise that ransoms have been arranged, then butchered. When this no longer works, the whole grove is set alight, burning to death the remaining soldiers. The King casually asks the name of the wood: 'It belongs to the hero Argos', he is told. 'Then I shall not capture the city itself', he exclaims, 'for the oracle foretold that I should take Argos, but clearly I have anticipated the event, and having captured the hero Argos I shall not now secure what I really wanted, the enemy citadel of the same name.'

Kleomenes accordingly sends the bulk of his army home, and makes for Hera's temple. When the priest refuses him permission to sacrifice, he has him flogged. He then claims to see a flash of light on Hera's statue, which confirms that he has already achieved as much as is destined for him; so he leads his remaining troops back to Sparta, there to face the accusation that he failed to press home the final attack because of bribery.

The last act of the Kleomenes tragedy — Myres (1953, 77; cf. 174–6, 186–9) goes so far, too far, as to say that 'the "hero" of Books V and VI is not Dareios but Kleomenes, in the dramatic myth of *Kleomenes mainomenos*, a pendant to the Sophoclean *Ajax*' — is presented by Herodotos as involving some sort of defection to Arkadia, where Kleomenes raises an army sworn by the River Styx to follow his personal command wherever he may go. The Spartans anxiously recall and reinstate him, but he is too far gone: he starts smashing his staff into people's faces, is put by his relatives into the stocks (the nearest thing in Sparta, presumably, to a straitjacket), and finally, having somehow got hold of a knife, shreds himself from the toes up until he rips his guts out.

The basic question is simple. How much of this narrative can legitimately be treated as in any sense 'history' — distorted, prejudiced history, perhaps, but still with a kernel of truth which we may be able to winkle out once we have made some appropriate allowances — and how much should we rather classify as miscellaneous, all-purpose anti-tyrant folklore? We need to examine the details closely and set them properly in the context of traditions about other unloved leaders; especially, as will emerge, traditions about the Persian king Kambyses.

The battle of Sepeia and its aftermath (6.76ff.)

The first note of doubt is perhaps struck when we are told that
Kleomenes beat the Argives by wrong-footing them by the well-
known technique in which deliberately misleading instructions
are given to one's own side in order to lull the opposition into a
false sense of security. This trick is one of the regular stand-bys of
ancient textbooks of *strategemata,* and can be perhaps traced
elsewhere in Herodotos (1.63, cf. 4.111); and that it became at
least later a theme of popular folklore is shown by the fable at
Babrios 33, in which a farmer, finding that the grain-stealing
starlings always fly off as soon as he asks his lad for a sling,
arranges to use 'bread' as the code-word for 'sling', and thus
catches them unprepared (Aesop 298 Perry).

Next, the defeated Argives who took refuge in the wood. They
were first tricked into coming out one by one,[8] and once that
device had failed, incinerated *en masse.* Herodotos is fond of
holocaust stories of this type, usually set in an oriental context.[9]
We can detect a tell-tale sign, I think, of its generic nature, and of
its slightly imperfect application here, if we consider the little
detail of the 'brushwood piled up around the grove' with which
Kleomenes orders the helots to start the fire. True, some tinder
would be useful, but one would hardly bother to mention it if it
were not a regular feature of the situation in which it is absolutely
essential: the much more common scenario where it is an
essentially non-combustible *building* which the wicked king ignites
after having locked his enemies inside.[10] What we have here is a
case of 'formulaic momentum'.

Further: twice in Thukydides' account of the communal
violence in Kerkyra (3.81 and 4.47f; cf. also Xenophon *Hell.* 5.6,
9, an incident at Mantineia) we find similar stories of atrocities in
which the defeated side are trapped in barns or temples and some
are lured out to death, while the remainder meet a horrible death.
Now it is necessary to add, with some emphasis, that of course
such things happen in real life, and happen repeatedly. The point
I wish to make is that if we know already that we are dealing with
a grossly prejudicial tradition, as is the case here (and also in
reports of the *stasis* on Kerkyra), then we must give due weight to
the possibility that once the subject has been cast in the role of
archetypal war criminal, all the archetypal concomitant trimmings
may also be ascribed to him. We should remember the stories of
Belgian nuns raped by the advancing horde of Huns, with which

the British press made such effective propaganda in 1914; not to mention the many myths which gained ready acceptance during the Malvinas campaign, or the rumours during the British coal strike of 1984 that the miners' leader Arthur Scargill had 'a villa in Majorca', or 'a daughter at a Swiss finishing school'. And if such allegations can flourish unchecked in a world with easy access to printed and electronic media, how much less readily could they have been checked in the fifth century BC?[11]

What of Kleomenes' exclamation that he had been duped by fate into capturing 'the wrong Argos'? This too, as has of course long been recognised, is a widespread motif of the folktale; a very close parallel is found at 1.167, 4, where the Phokaians similarly mistake the hero Kyrnos and the island Kyrnos (Corsica).[12] Again, the *Certamen Homeri et Hesiodi* describes how an oracle predicts Hesiod's death in the wood at Nemea; Hesiod avoids the famous one but meets his end in an obscure homonym.[13] This application of the idea to a character's death is particularly interesting because Herodotos tells the same story of Kambyses, who expires at the 'wrong' Ekbatana (3.64); it is the first of many correspondences we shall note between the Persian and Spartan kings.[14]

Kleomenes at the Heraion

Several of the details given by Herodotos of the King's supposedly outrageous behaviour here can be paralleled elsewhere. First his arrogant defiance of the priest's protest that 'strangers may not sacrifice here' (6.81) echoes his earlier experience on the Acropolis at Athens, when he was told that 'no Dorian may enter' (5.72);[15] we may suspect some recycling. Second, his driving out of the priest and sacrificing in person finds a parallel in Herodotos' account of Pheidon of Argos at 6.127, who kicked out the Elean judges and organised the Olympics personally. Once more it is reasonable to conclude that typical tyrant-behaviour may account for the allegation. Finally, his flogging of the unco-operative priest is matched by the conquering Kambyses' whipping of the priests of Apis at 3.29.

Once in undisputed control of the temple, Kleomenes approached the goddess' cult-statue to seek divine guidance on his next move: staring at the image, he saw (so he is supposed to have claimed later, when under investigation) a flash of light appear from Hera's chest. This was not the sign he had hoped for. If Hera had approved his intention to go ahead and take Argos by storm, the light would have shone from her head; as it was, fire from the chest signified that he had now achieved all that was destined for him. The King acquiesced in this decision, and returned to Sparta.

This incident exhibits several features of interest. First, for once — or rather, twice: he has already obeyed the River Erasinos with good humour — it shows Kleomenes not as *deorum spretor* but as a pious mortal accepting the limits to action ordained by heaven; the usual contrast between Kleomenes and Dorieus is here sustained, but in inverse form, for it was Dorieus who (according to Herodotos) came to a bad end by violating his destiny, παρὰ τὰ μεμαντευμένα ποιέων (5.45).

Second, it presents us with the curious spectacle of Hera, the Argive goddess *par excellence*, being interrogated on whether she would like her favourite city to be destroyed (rather as she contemplates at *Iliad* 4.51ff.). This is not however as bizarre as it might seem: an important aim in any ancient siege was to steal (as in the case of the Trojan Palladion) or win over the gods of the defending city.[16] No doubt it was with the intention of making just such an attempt on the loyalty of the local goddess that Miltiades entered the temple of Demeter-outside-the-walls on Paros (6.134) — one of several significant links between the bad ends to which both leaders are said to have come.

What of the precise form of the oracle which Kleomenes sought? This too corresponds closely to other reports of Greek religious belief and mythological phenomena. In Greece, as in present-day Ireland, the faithful might observe a statue closely for signs of approving or disapproving movement: Athena's statue in Troy shifted on its base in horror at the rape of Kassandra, and Sinon claims in the *Aeneid* (2.172f.) that the eyes of the Palladion flashed fire in anger at its theft by Diomedes and Odysseus. In particular, people tried to predict from 'binary omens' of the form 'if x, a; if y, b'. Sometimes a god might be asked a direct question, as in the regular case of divination at Delphi, when the god was asked to choose, on behalf of the client, between two options, sometimes contained in sealed boxes. Or the development of a natural phenomenon might be scrutinised for its revelation of divine will, as when Dikaios the exiled Athenian interprets the meaning of the dust-cloud for Damaratos at 8.65, 3: if it moves towards the Peloponnese, it portends danger for Xerxes' army, if towards Salamis, his fleet.[17] Greek sailors, like Kleomenes here, would scan their ship's rigging anxiously for a binary fire-oracle: if a single flicker of St Elmo's fire should be seen aloft, Helen the ship-destroyer was present, and the omen boded ill; if two points of flame were visible, all was well, for the crew were safe under the protection of her brothers the Dioskouroi.

The binary distinction for which Kleomenes scans the statue is articulated on a vertical axis: will the sign appear on head or chest? As with the 'test your strength' machine at the fairground, the higher the better.[18] But here there is, I think, a special point to the image of 'fire on the head', for the context is that of city-sacking, and Greek epic tradition regularly uses language which symbolises the walls and citadel of a city as the 'head', or the 'holy' (or 'rich') 'veil' (κρήδεμνον) which is to be 'undone' by the attackers. There is thus a close and pointed homology between the topmost keep of the fortress of Argos, which Kleomenes aims to take with fire and sword, and the sign which Kleomenes hoped for, but did not find, on the head of the city's patron goddess.[19] Even if it is true that the archaic image of Hera at Argos was a pillar, we may still surmise that the statue could actually have been dressed with a veil, symbol of Hera's status as modest wife.[20]

At all events, though Hera fails to grant him his wish, she seems not to be particularly outraged by his question; not as good a protectress of her territory as was the Erasinos, for example.[21]

Kleomenes back at Sparta (6.82; 74f.)

The King returned to Sparta to face the inevitable charge that the reason for his failing to press home his assault on Argos was that he had taken a bribe; the same allegation as was made in 446, when Pleistoanax declined to administer the *coup de grâce* to Athens, and was relieved of his command and exiled (Thuk. 2.21,1). Then, after his curious *démarche* to Arkadia,[22] in which his attempt to make the local leaders swear an oath of loyalty by the Styx is probably a motif designed to pin on him the accusation of divine megalomania,[23] Kleomenes returned (or was brought back) to Sparta. Like Kambyses, who shoots the son of his faithful vizier Prexaspes (3.35) and kicks his pregnant wife to death (3.32), Kleomenes' madnes is supposed to have been demonstrated by acts of gratuitous sadism ('smashing his staff into the face of Spartiates', 6.75).

We may now focus on the manner of his death. Locked up in the stocks as insane, he is supposed to have sliced himself to bits from the feet up until he reached his vitals and expired. Once again we find that the career of Kambyses runs parallel: having stabbed the Apis bull in the thigh (though aiming for the belly: 3.29), he brings about his own death in an appropriately symmetrical way by accidentally piercing his own leg while mounting his horse (3.64).[24]

Nor is this all. There is another story about someone in the stocks at Sparta — that of the Elean Hegesistratos, which Herodotos tells at 9.37. Knowing that he faces certain death, Hegesistratos also gets hold of a knife (one begins to get the feeling that they come with the rations in Spartan prisons, like cyanide-laced *caffè* in the Regina Coeli), and also attacks his foot with it. This time, however, it is for a positive purpose: he cuts his foot off to enable him to escape from the stocks, then burrows out through the wall and hobbles off to Arkadia, where subsequently he has himself a wooden foot made to replace the old one abandoned in Sparta. This story certainly belongs to a group of mythical anecdotes involving locked-room mysteries,[25] and I think we should classify the Kleomenes story in that set too. Kleomenes escapes to Arkadia, then returns to hack himself to pieces from the feet up in a Spartan prison; Hegesistratos hacks his foot off in a Spartan prison, then escapes to Arkadia. Perhaps we can see an echo of Hegesistratos' prosthetic wooden foot — and a further link between the Kleomenes-Kambyses traditions — in Ktesias' story that Kambyses was *whittling a piece of wood* when he stabbed himself and thus brought about his own death.[26]

Kleomenes' supposed suicide, then, is what Lefkowitz (1981, 3; cf. 10 n. 37) calls an 'illustrative' or 'appropriate' death: because the King is alleged to have cut down sacred groves (6.75, 3),[27] and — as we shall shortly see — flayed a holy corpse, popular tradition provides him with a homologous end. Erysichthon, in myth (another tree-feller), and Miltiades, in 'history', also die self-inflicted deaths which correspond to the sacrilegious crimes they committed in life. The unsatisfactorily random and bitty quality of real life is restored to harmonious order by the use of standard and salutory ideal patterns; facts gradually but inexorably realign themselves to match inbuilt expectations, like iron filings subjected to a magnetic field.

Kleomenes at Anthene

We may continue this study of the Herodotean Kleomenes by turning to examine one of the few anecdotes about the King to be transmitted by a different route — in this case, Stephanos of Byzantion. Though the source may be so much later, and so apparently peripheral, its character ('a curious little story', Forrest 1980, 86) is all of a piece with the picture painted by Herodotos; and it will be necessary, if we are to succeed in interpreting what is a strange and difficult piece of evidence, to bear in mind the 'iconography' which we have already established for the King.

Here is the text (St. Byz. s.n. ʼΑνθάνα):

πόλις Λακωνική, μία τῶν ἑκατόν. κέκληται δέ, ὡς Φιλοστέφανος, παρὰ ῎Ανθην τὸν Ποσειδῶνος, ὃν Κλεομένης ὁ Λεωνίδου ἀδελφὸς ἀνελὼν καὶ ἐκδείρας ἔγραψεν ἐν τῷ δέρματι τοὺς χρησμοὺς ὧδε τηρεῖcθαι.

ὧδε add. R, om. cett.

'Anthene, town in Lakonia, one of the Hundred. Named, according to Philostephanos, after[28] Anthes the son of Poseidon, whom Kleomenes the brother of Leonidas killed and flayed, and wrote on his skin that (?) by his so doing the oracles were being kept (i.e. fulfilled?).'

To start with the smaller, more tractable problems: the MS R of Stephanos not only provides us with ὧδε, but omits the phrase 'after Anthes the son of Poseidon'; both seem clearly necessary for the sense of the passage, and I shall assume that Stephanos wrote them. Next: do we have *all* that Stephanos wrote? Meineke (*app. crit.* to his 1849 edition) thought not: *post* Ποσειδῶνος *fortasse lacuna indicanda erat: ineptum enim est Anthen, Neptuni filium, a Kleomene interfectum et excoriatum dici.* An eminently reasonable objection, one might suppose: how could a historical Spartan king of *c.* 500 BC kill and skin someone who must, as an eponymous founder, belong to legendary times? Meineke proceeded to suggest that Stephanos' first sentence ended after '*Poseidon*', and that he had continued '*From this town came Mr X, whom . . .*'. This proposal has succeeded in establishing itself as conventional wisdom ever since. Lobel: 'Clearly we have a mutilated story of the flaying by Kleomenes of some Anthenian';[29] Leahy: 'The original version must presumably, on chronological grounds,

have referred simply to an Anthenian' (Leahy 1958, 155 n. 45;
similarly, Huxley 1962, 140). Meineke's lacuna, then, constitutes
one of the two lines of interpretation of this passage for which
there exists a modern consensus. For the moment, I content
myself with the remark that Stephanos' entry runs perfectly well
as it stands (provided the 'chronological difficulty' can be
skirted), while the currently accepted reconstruction breaks the
note into two quite unrelated statements.

The other use to which this entry in Stephanos has recently
been put concerns its historical context, and its assignment either
to a known incident in Kleomenes' career or to traditional
allegations about his behaviour. Kleomenes, runs this now-
conventional approach, was as we know at daggers drawn with
his half-brother Dorieus; Dorieus took a party of Spartiates from
Anthene off with him on his ill-fated expedition to Sicily; thus
Kleomenes' killing-and-skinning operation on the hypothetical
'citizen of Anthene' falls into place as a (for him) typically savage
reprisal on the town for siding with his hated rival.[30]

All very neat. Unfortunately, this structure depends entirely on
a suggested emendation of Lobel's (n. 29), who tried to import
some Anthenians into a corrupt passage of Pausanias (3.16, 4):
ἰόντι δὲ ὡς ἐπὶ τὰς πύλας [of Sparta] ἀπὸ τοῦ Χιτῶνος, Χίλωνὸς
ἐστιν ἡρῷον τοῦ σοφοῦ νομιζομένου καὶ †'Αθηναίων ῥωτ†
τῶν ὁμοῦ Δωριεῖ τῷ 'Αναξανδρίδου σταλέντων ἐς Σικελίαν.
'Αθηνοδώρου Madvig, 'Ανθηνέων ἡρίον Lobel.

One can share Lobel's distaste for the otherwise unknown
'Athenodoros' proposed by Madvig (alive and well and to be
found in the Teubner Pausanias), without necessarily feeling any
inclination to accept his own solution. Dunbabin (1948, 352 n. 4),
after Wade-Gery, adopts the less speculative approach of simply
assuming that Dorieus took some Athenians with him. Admittedly, one hardly expects any such Athenians to be awarded the
honour of a tomb next to Chilon (!), but it is surely almost equally
improbable that Anthenian colonists should have been brought
back and buried in state — Kleomenes would hardly have
allowed it during his lifetime, and afterwards it would have been
too late to bother. At all events, one must insist that the text of
Pausanias is much too doubtful here for an emended version of it
to serve as the main prop for the assumption of a lacuna in a
different text, and for the substantive interpretation of that text.

Both the trees that have been barked up in recent years thus
turn out in my view to have been wrong ones. It is time to go back

and try to make sense of Stephanos'[31] text as it stands; and to do this we will have to provide answers to the following questions: (1) What was the significance of Anthene in Spartan history? (2) What was Kleomenes doing there? (3) How was it possible to skin a legendary character? (4) What part do the oracles play in the story?

The situation and significance of Anthene

Although the precise location of ancient Anthene has not been established, modern Meligou is one likely candidate, and its general whereabouts are not in doubt.[32] It was a close neighbour of the town of Thyrea (Paus. 2.38, 6), in the area known as the Thyreatis, the coastal strip NE of Mt Parnon also called the Dogstail Territory, Κυνουρία γῆ (Thuk. 5.41, 2). All this had traditionally been *Argive* land, and accordingly — an important point to bear in mind — its towns will have had Argive mythical oikists.[33] But with the growing territorial ambitions of Sparta in the sixth century, the area began to be disputed; and at the famous Battle of the Champions the Spartans won possession (Hdt. 1.82, according to whom the date is *c.* 546). Thereafter it became a constant bone of contention, like Oropos which the Athenians and Boiotians disputed for so long, or like Alsace, the Sudetenland or the Pola peninsula.[34] The Spartans settled the Aeginetan *Vertriebene* here in 431 (Thuk. 2.27, 2; 4.56, 2), a decision for which one would like to know the reason — perhaps to release as many Spartiates as possible for the coming conflict? Ten years later the Argives were still determined to recover the Thyreatis (Thuk. 5.41, 2); and after Chaironeia they were eventually successful.[35] To sum up: at the time with which we are concerned, as at others, Anthene and environs were the subject of fierce irredentist claims, and constituted a military and diplomatic hot potato. There must be a strong possibility that it is *this* feature that lies, somehow, behind the Kleomenean anecdote.

Kleomenes and Anthene

No explicit independent testimony links the King with the town; and, as we have seen, the Kleomenes-Dorieus-Anthene connection is too speculative to carry any weight at all. And yet there is a

well-attested historical event which puts Kleomenes right in this
area at a crucial moment: the battle of Sepeia, discussed above
(pp. 55f).

Kleomenes receives an oracle from Delphi promising that he
will capture Argos, the auld enemy. Setting out with a land army,
he crosses into Argive territory and reaches the River Erasinos,
only a few miles from the capital itself.[36] Here (as we have seen)
he encounters a set-back: the obligatory sacrifice to the river
elicits a negative response, and while he might, in a different
mood, have scourged and abused the recalcitrant water like so
many other emperors and tyrants, on this occasion he accepts the
divine decision with good grace and turns around.[37]

Baulked by the River Erasinos, if we are to believe Herodotos,
the King tries another tack and crosses the Gulf of Argos to reach
the area of Nauplia and Tiryns. He embarks his army for this
short voyage — after another sacrifice — 'at Thyrea', according
to Herodotos. This cannot be *literally* true, as we know from
Pausanias that Thyrea lay *c.* 2 km inland; there must have been a
nearby harbour which acted as its Peiraieus or Avonmouth. Some
maps actually put Anthene (or 'Athene') on the coast, suggesting
that it was this town which acted as Thyrea's port; but the
description of Pausanias (2.38, 6) provides no particular warrant
for this assumption.[38] At all events, this provides us with at least
one highly-charged emotional occasion on which Kleomenes may
have passed through the town in question; and it is possible that
this visit was preceded by an earlier call (marching north *en route*
for the Erasinos), and followed perhaps by a third (the return to
Sparta after the ignominious, or negligent, or criminal, failure to
seize the enemy city, Hdt. 6.81f.).

Two or three times Kleomenes may have passed this way:
confident on the first occasion, baffled and perhaps in vindictive
mood on the second and third. This provides us with the
historical context we need to make sense of our third problem, to
which we may now turn.

What did Kleomenes do to whom at Anthene?

To recap: Anthene was an Argive foundation; 50-odd years
previously the Argives had been expelled and Spartan colonists
installed; now the supposedly violent and unstable Kleomenes is
in the area, engaged on a campaign which first promises well,

then falters, then produces a famous victory at Sepeia, and is for some reason finally abandoned when the prize of Argos itself seems within reach.

Against this background, I suggest, the story told by Stephanos (Philostephanos) is perfectly credible — credible, that is, within the parameters of what is generally regarded as acceptable in ancient tradition. Perhaps on the second of the visits to Anthene I have hypothesised, perhaps on the third — in which case he will have come fresh from the holocaust in the sacred wood of Argos — Kleomenes needed to express in some dramatic fashion his frustration and his hatred of Argos.[39]

What better way than to pay a visit to the tomb of the ancestral hero of the town, the Argive Anthes son of Poseidon,[40] to dig up the remains, and to desecrate them publicly? For, although the participle ἀνελών in Stephanos has always been taken to mean 'killed' (and was probably so ïderstood by the author himself), in his source Philostephanos it may well have had the meaning 'disinter' which it bears at Thukydides 1.126, 12.[41]

And *that* passage is relevant not only for semantic reasons but for its content. Coincidentally, or maybe not, there we see Kleomenes on another of his foreign adventures, fishing in Athenian politics at the time of the expulsion of the Peisistratids and the feuding between Kleisthenes and Isagoras. Kleomenes and his allies, says Thukydides, not only drove out the current crop of Alkmaionids who were tainted by the Kylonian curse, but *dug up and threw out*, presumably with appropriate execrations, *the bones of former members of the clan.*

Now whether or not Kleomenes actually did outrage the ancestors of the Alkmaionids at Athens (a crime particularly horrible to Greek sensibility) is not the point at issue here. What is important is that if the 'historical' tradition ascribes such an action to him in one place, and at one time, it is very likely to duplicate the feature elsewhere. As at Athens, so too at Anthene he finds himself in what was (at least by origin) an 'enemy' town; and whereas no doubt the first action of the incoming Spartan colonists after the Battle of the Champions had been to placate and mollify the spirit of the presiding Argive hero, 50 years later the 'mad' king Kleomenes was bent on the symbolic and systematic extirpation of the enemy presence.

Two further items of analogous evidence may be added in support of this suggestion. First, the 'use and abuse' (to reapply Forrest's phrase) of heroic graves for propaganda purposes during the late archaic period in Greece is so well known as hardly to require documentation. The bones of Orestes, Teisamenos and Theseus were all conveniently 'found' (the first two by Spartans) and used *to establish claims to disputed territory*: just the situation with which we are now dealing. To grub up and expel an *enemy* founder's remains is of course a rather different matter, but it fits the pattern of behaviour well enough in general terms. A close parallel can be found in the savage treatment meted out about a century before by Kleisthenes of Sikyon to the cult of the hated Argive hero Adrastos (Hdt. 5.67); the significant difference being only that Herodotos represents Kleisthenes, out of respect for the Delphic oracle, as just stopping short of actual sacrilege at the tomb and the cult-site, while Philostephanos' Kleomenes has no such scruples.[42]

Second, we have already seen signs that close and mutual interpatterning seems to have taken place between the characters and actions ascribed by Herodotos to Kleomenes the Spartan and Kambyses the Persian; in this context we should note that Herodotos twice attributes to Kambyses in Egypt behaviour of the kind I am here suggesting was alleged against Kleomenes. He 'broke open ancient tombs in Memphis and inspected the corpses' (3.37, 1); and, in an access of rage against the Pharaoh Amasis, who had died before Kambyses could get his hands on him, he opened the mausoleum, dragged out the body, and had it *flogged, stripped of its hair, stabbed with cattle-prods* and finally *burnt* (3.16). Nor is this Kambyses' only connection with human skin: Herodotos reports elsewhere how he flayed a corrupt judge, cut his skin into strips, and used it to upholster the chair on which the judge's son, in turn, pronounced his verdicts; a powerful, if macabre, incentive to judicial rectitude (5.25).[43] This brings us conveniently to the allegation that Kleomenes 'flayed Anthes and wrote (?) oracles on his skin'.

Skythians, Epimenides, and human parchment

Paradoxically, it is for this final and most bizarre element of Kleomenes' treatment of Anthes that documentation lies thickest on the ground. Let us suppose, as a hostile ancient tradition would quite happily have supposed, that the disinterred bones of the legendary Anthes were found to have scraps of skin still adhering, mummified perhaps (another trace of Kambyses in

Egypt?). Why should Kleomenes have chosen, out of all the possible indignities that could be thought of, to write oracles, or to write about oracles,[44] on the tattered human vellum?

If we start by free-associating across the Herodotean thought-world which constitutes our proper frame of reference, we will recall first that the strongly antipathetic view of Kleomenes purveyed by Herodotos' Spartan sources accounted for his ultimate insanity by alleging that he had picked up Skythian bad habits from the delegation that visited Sparta — in particular, that it was from them that he had learned to drink his wine neat (6.84). But we may also remember that one of the most prominent characteristics of the Skythians, again according to Herodotos, is their unpleasant propensity to scalp their enemies and fashion fetish-like objects, anything from handkerchiefs to quiver-covers, from the skin (4.64). In this respect, then, the Anthes story will match very well the image of Kleomenes the Crazy Skythist.

But why turn the skin into an *oracle-book*, if that is what he did? This detail too can be fitted into a known context. Herodotos tells us (5.58) that for the Greeks of his age skins, διφθέραι, were an outmoded medium for the writing of texts; and we may deduce accordingly that any book being touted around in this form would be regarded as possessing, or would claim for itself, great antiquity. Not surprising, then, to find Euripides writing (fr. 627 N²) of 'ink-written skins, groaning with many an utterance of Loxias' — for any oracle-monger, like the infamous Onomakritos (7.6), would seek to enhance the credibility of the previous night's forgeries by inscribing them on a venerable scrap of leather.[45]

Kleomenes, we may surmise, probably had an oracle-book, and his enemies claimed that the skin on which it was written was that of the Argive hero whose grave he had desecrated at Anthene. We can strengthen this suggestion by taking up at this point an independent line of evidence whose relevance has already been recognised[46] — the ancient traditions about the involvement of Epimenides with Sparta.

Some 'facts' about Epimenides the Kretan: (1) During his lifetime, as well as purifying various cities including Athens and Sparta, he delivered inspired oracles foretelling future disasters in battle, for example the catastrophe that was to strike the Athenians at Mounychia (Plut. *Solon* 12); (2) In particular, he produced anti-Spartan prophecies — that is, perhaps, he made predictions of Spartan defeats which were intended to be self-fulfilling. Thus he foretold the Spartan defeat at Orchomenos (Theopompos 115 F 69, on which see Leahy 1958), and 'in a war between Sparta and [his homeland] Knossos, he gave prophecies unfavourable to Sparta, so that when they took him alive the Spartans killed him'.[47] (3) Most interestingly of all, according to the Souda, art. *Epimenides,* long after his death the prophet's skin turned up 'marked or tattooed, with writing' (γράμμασι κατασικτόν); and that these 'grammata' were in fact oracles is made likely by the existence of a proverb Ἐπιμενίδειον δέρμα, used to mean 'obscurities'. From this evidence Diels concluded, surely rightly, that there was in circulation at some time an oracle book known as 'Epimenides' skin', and that later tradition took this to mean not 'the vellum MS containing Epimenides' oracles', but a text reminiscent of Ray Bradbury's *The Illustrated Man* in which the future was laid out on genuine seerskin.[48]

Finally, what was it that Kleomenes wrote on the bookskin, or what was it that he showed written there? We do at least know from Herodotos (5.90, 2) that Kleomenes *did* produce old oracle-books and apply them to political ends:

> Moreover they [the Spartans] were spurred to action [in hurriedly reversing their anti-Peisistratid policy] by the discovery of certain prophecies of coming disasters at the hands of the Athenians — prophecies of which they knew nothing until Kleomenes brought them to Sparta. These prophecies had formerly been in the possession of the Peisistratidai, who left them in the temple on the Acropolis when they were expelled from Athens. It was here that Kleomenes found them and picked them up.[49]

This some 15 years before the Argive campaign. What he had done once he could do again. Did he pass off the Anthenian oracles as Epimenidean prophecies, as Leahy was inclined to think? But why then inscribe them (if that is what he did) on the skin of Anthes the Anthenian? Perhaps we should seek a more immediate and specific context. Herodotos tells us (6.76, 1) that it was the Pythia who encouraged Kleomenes to attack Argos in the expectation of capturing the city; but instead of, or as well as, this source, is it not possible that the superstitious King took some sort of oracle at the grave of Anthes just before his invasion of the Argolid, was encouraged to go ahead, and then wrought an appropriate revenge on the hero's remains when he subsequently found himself disappointed of his main objective?[50] We might tentatively envisage an enraged Kleomenes revisiting the grave of the Argive hero who, like the River Erasinos, had turned out to be protecting his own after all, and yelling 'I'll make sure your oracles come home to roost! I'll engrave them into your own skin!'[51] Some such condign punishment would in fact chime well with the death that the tradition records for Kleomenes himself: ripping himself up with a knife, just as he is said to have flayed the eponymous hero of the town of Anthene.

But tentative is all we can be. The tradition about Kleomenes' activities in Anthene, which were transmitted by the Kallimachean researcher Philostephanos down to Stephanos of Byzantion, can be defended as fitting very well into the general scheme of early fifth-century symbolic action and historiographical slander. There is probably a firm historical basis to the anecdote, connected with the Sepeia campaign. This kernel has been richly embroidered with contemporary material concerning oracles, and even if we cannot precisely pin down the significance of this, we may be confident of having identified the area in which significance is to be sought. Kleomenes may well have desecrated in some way the tomb of the Argive founder of Anthene; this tradition was then conflated with Kleomenes' well-known addiction to oracles, and other legends about Epimenides, to produce the confection that Philostephanos found and passed on.[52]

Traditions about Kleomenes and Kambyses

We may now pull together and summarise the several correspondences already noted between these two late sixth-century rulers. This can best be done in the following chart.

Some of the similarities have been noted before,[53] but not, I think, the sheer extent of the overlap. Two almost contemporary, deranged, dipsomaniac, priest-flogging, skin-stripping, sacrilegious, sadistic warrior-kings who are misled by place-name oracles and expire in circumstances symbolically retributive of their capricious cruelties? If one rejects the possibility that these two kings were genetic clones doomed from birth to mimic each other's behaviour, it is clear that there exists a case for claiming that either one king's story has been transferred to the other, or that both draw on a repertoire of classic 'wicked ruler' tales. The Kleomenes-Kambyses parallels are therefore an important piece

Was Kleomenes Mad?

Two 'Mad Kings' in Herodotos

Kambyses	Kleomenes
MAD: ὑπομαργότερος (3.29)	MAD: ὑπομαργότερος (6.75,1); cf. οὐ φρενήρης ἀκρομανής τε (5.42)
DRUNK: οἴνῳ προσκείμενος (3.34)	DRUNK: ἀκρητοπότης (6.84)
SACRILEGIOUS: flogs priests of Apis (3.29)	SACRILEGIOUS: flogs priest of Hera (6.81)
	burns down sacred wood of Argos (6.80)
stabs Apis bull (ibid.)	chops down sacred wood of Demeter (6.75)
	St. Byz. s.v. 'Ανθάνα:
drags out, flogs and burns corpse of King Amasis (3.16)	drags out and flays the corpse of Anthes and uses the skin to make oracle-books (?)
skin of judge used for upholstery (5.25)	
BRUTAL:	BRUTAL:
kicks, kills pregnant wife (3.32)	smashes staff into faces (6.75)
shoots Prexaspes' son (3.35)	
MISTAKEN about site of destined death: wrong Ekbatana (3.64)	MISTAKEN about site of destined conquest: wrong Argos (6.80)
DIES by 'accidental' self-inflicted dagger wound (3.64);	DIES by deliberately self-inflicted dagger wound (6.75)
(or (Behistun): suicide;	
or (Ktesias 688 F13 (14)): accidental death while whittling a piece of wood)	(Hegesistratos, another Spartan prisoner, later whittles himself an artifical wooden foot)

of evidence which must be taken into account when we try to assess the degree of defamation to which the memories of both kings have been subjected.[54]

What remains? Though I am much more sceptical about the evidential value of the text of Herodotos than most people, I am by no means a total agnostic. I recognise that valuable nuggets of real, historical fact may lurk among the folklore. The picture of Kleomenes as a man obsessed by prophecies, oracles and omens, even if it has become caricature, is unlikely to be wholly unfounded. In spite of the weight of adverse criticism, even in Herodotos some snippets have survived which allow us to glimpse a sharp, upright and forceful personality (3.148, he is a δικαιότατος ἀνδρῶν in refusing Maiandrios' bribes, and at 6.61, 1 (cf. 51) Damaratos is busy blackening his reputation in Sparta while he is in Aigina 'working in the best interests of Greece', trying to arrest the proponents of Medism). There are hints of a quick-witted, intelligent man with a good line in memorable repartee: see the story about the Aiginetan called Κριός at 6.50, 3, the 'I'm not Dorieus' crack (see n. 15) and·his laughing reaction to the sophist who tried to lecture him on bravery at Plutarch *Apophth. Lak.* 223e–f, §12. (The King's laughter reappears in more sinister form, reinforcing the image of the madman, earlier in the same chapter (223c), where Kleomenes is described as dying γελῶντα καὶ cεcηρότα, 'laughing and grinning'.)

All is not quite lost; but I do believe that the folklore constitutes a much larger part of the whole than is currently acknowledged; and that until we learn better to recognise the characteristics of the popular material, we shall not be in a position to distinguish nuggets from *nugae*. There is no clear watershed to be found between the Pharoah Pheros, who cured his blindness with the aid of a chaste woman's urine, and the historical King Kleomenes, nowhere that we can stand and say 'folktale this side, history that'. In our present state of knowledge, I should certainly regard any attempt to diagnose the particular clinical variety of the alleged psychosis of King Kleomenes as premature.

Notes

All references of the form '1.234, 5' are to the text of Herodotos.

1. Herodotos must have been aware of the cruel irony implicit in his story of Damaratos — of all people — advising Xerxes about the problem of the Persian succession (7.3), a problem which is simply a re-run of his own bitter experience at Sparta; but his report is, typically, completely dead-pan.
2. See the recent blunt comment of D.M. Lewis: 'Historians are not unaware that Herodotus' truthfulness has been challenged from time to time, but on the whole they take no notice. To speak frankly, they have to ignore such criticisms or be put out of business . . .' (Lewis 1985, 101).
3. Macan 1895, 83 ('The blunder seems to show how Herodotus will sacrifice consistency and probability for the sake of a point, especially a moral point'); How & Wells 1912, II 348 ('Possibly H. forgot the lapse of years'); Immerwahr 1966, 193 n. 13 ('the life of an impious leader is cut short as a punishment'); Hart 1982, 124f. ('carelessness').
4. For this use of apodotic ἀλλά see Powell's Lexicon s.v. §IV (seven examples — all, admittedly, in direct or reported speech rather than authorial), and LSJ I.2.
5. See White 1964, 141 n. 6: 'The Agiad was the senior royal house

and normally held the more important commands . . . If the Agiad king or his regent was for any reason considered unsuitable, the other royal house could supply the commander.'

6. After all, Pausanias was quick enough to round on Amompharetos at Plataia, and express his disagreement on strategy by calling him 'a madman, not right in the head' (9.55). Such accusations can start as momentary outbursts of anger but gain wider currency; alternatively, they may represent simply political hostility and incomprehension. The journalist Bernard Levin once wrote a piece in a newspaper belonging to the Murdoch chain (not the *Sun*) in which he attempted to brand Colonel Gaddafi ('obviously raving mad'), the Ayatollah Khomeini ('another raving madman') and Mao Tse-tung as 'literally insane' or, as he put it in a second article, 'a marble or two short'; see *The Times*, 15 May and 29 June 1984.

7. For the date, see Forrest 1980, 90, and Jeffery 1976, 125, who thinks of the expiry of a 50-year truce after the Battle of the Champions (so too Jones 1967, 53).

8. We may tentatively compare Helen trying to lure the Greek warriors out of the *wooden* horse; according to Apollod. *epit.* 5.14 there were 50 of them, as here.

9. Sesostris' brother (2.107), Pheros (2.111); compare the self-immolations of the Xanthians (1.176), Boges (7.107) and the Egyptian Nitokris (2.100). The Near-Eastern background to these stories is sufficiently illustrated by the parallel of Abimelech (Judges 9:46ff.); the Grimm Stories ##46 and 71 are examples of the theme's survival into modern times. When Herodotos applies the motif to *Greeks*, it is usually in a weakened form: Polykrates (3.45), Periander (5.92η), but cf. Arkesilas of Kyrene (4.164).

10. Burn 1962, 230f. explains the detail of the brushwood as a device to ensure the technical avoidance of blood-guilt; I do not agree with this interpretation, but find it interesting that Burn noticed the oddity.

11. We have to steer a difficult course between the Skylla of credulity and the Charybdis of unreasonable scepticism. On the one hand, it is easy to dismiss rumours of war like that reported by Iris Origo in *War in the Val d'Orcia*, 35f., that 'the Allies are dropping explosive lipsticks and dolls to maim women and children'. On the other hand, paranoid suspicion of all such allegations can become unduly paralysing: Gordon A. Craig, reviewing books on the Jewish Holocaust in *New York Review of Books* 14 iv 1986, p. 10, noted that 'As late as August 1944, when a group of respected American journalists entered the death camp at Maidanek and sent home detailed descriptions of the gas chambers, the crematoria, the piles of bones, and the storehouses for the personal belongings of the victims, *The Christian Century* reproached the American press for headlining this story and wrote that the "parallel between [it] and the 'corpse factory' atrocity tale" of World War I was "too striking to be overlooked".' Macan sums up fairly: 'Of course such things may happen, and may happen more than once; yet the repetition of similar stories tends to discredit.' (Macan on 5.17, 2, with some good examples; see also his App. IV §7.)

12. See Fontenrose 1978, Q93; and cf. 68f. with 69 n. 19 on the oracle

which encouraged Kleomenes, and his assessment of the tradition in general.

13. *OCT* Homer, ed. T.W. Allen, vol. V, p. 233f. See on this story J.A. Fairweather, 'Fiction in the biographies of ancient writers', *Ancient Society* 5 (1974) 231–75 at 271.

14. More general kinds of pre-emptive mis-fulfilment can be found at 6.107 (Hippias' tooth 'possesses his mother' and thus destroys Hippias' own chance of so doing); 1.120 (Kyros' boy-kingship — but here, by a nice twist, the Magi are deluded, for fate has *not* yet finished with making Kyros king); Plut. *Nikias* 13f. (Zeus Ammon promises that the Athenians will capture 'all the Syrakusans', but a ship they seize turns out to contain a complete citizen-list!); and Apollo's ambiguous prophecy to Agamemnon, on which see C.W. Macleod, *Homer: Iliad XXIV*, p. 2).

15. Macan saw that his reply ('I'm no *Dorieus*, I'm an *Achaian*') contained a joke on his half-brother's name.

16. Compare the Roman *evocatio deorum*, for which see Austin on *Aen.* 2.351 and Richardson in *JHS* 101 (1981) 186.

17. Compare 1 Sam. 6:7–9 (Which way will the cow-cart go?); 1 Sam. 14:8ff. (Which of two orders will the Philistines call out?); 2 Kings 2:10 (Will Elijah vanish or not?). Robert Darnton, *The great cat massacre and other episodes in French cultural history* (1984), 47, reports a French tale: 'When he sees Death standing at the foot of the bed, he knows the patient will die; when at the head of the bed, live.'

18. For Romans too, fire on the head is an encouraging sign: see Verg. *Aen.* 2.683 and Ovid *Fasti* 6.636 on the *apex*; perhaps too the halo of the Christian saint.

19. Cf. too perhaps Fontenrose 1978, Q80: Apollo tells the consultants, asking whether to rebuild their city or move, 'ἄκρον λάβε καὶ μέcον ἕξειc', 'Seize the top and you'll secure the middle.'

20. For the pillar-goddess, see E. Simon, *JdI* 82 (1967) 286f., 291. She wears' a *polos*, not a veil, on two fourth-century coins: see C.M. Kraay and M. Hirmer, *Greek coins* (1966), ##517, 518.

21. Two further speculations: (1) Was the choice of fire as an image determined or influenced by the fact that Hera's temple contained an ever-burning lamp (Burkert, *Greek religion*, 61)? (2) Did the 'flash of light from heaven' (3.28) which was supposed to descend upon the cow destined to bear the Apis bull (so closely connected with the fate of Kambyses) also help to shape the Kleomenean incident?

22. But not to Thessaly: at 6.74, 1 read Cελλαcίην, with D. Hereward, *CR* 1 (1951) 146.

23. It is a curious fact that, in spite of the assumption in both Homer and Hesiod that this is an oath which binds male and female deities alike, all actual examples in early epic concern *goddesses*: Hera at *Iliad* 14.271 and 15.37; Kalypso at *Odyssey* 5.185, Demeter at *H.H.Dem.* 259 and Leto at *H.H.Ap.* 85. At *H.H.Hermes* 519, Apollo invites Hermes either to κατανεύειν or to take the oath by the Styx; we are not told why he ignores the latter option and chooses to nod in assent, but we might speculate that Apollo was testing the godling to see whether he yet knew that (as is the case with many oaths in classical Greek) swearing by

the Styx was a practice confined to females.

24. At least, the wound is 'accidental' in Herodotos; the meaning of Dareios' Behistun inscription, which records Kambyses as having 'died his own death', is less clear (for references to recent discussion, see J.M. Balcer, *Herodotus and Bisitun* (*Historia* Einzelschrift 49), p. 52). Persian kings had trouble getting on and off their horses: see Dareios himself at 3.129. Compare too Ktesias' account of the death of Kyros, also wounded in the thigh (ὑπὸ τὸ ἰσχίον εἰς τὸν μηρόν') by an Indian javelin in battle, and brought back to die in camp (*FGrHist* 688 F9(7)), and Miltiades' leg-wound which festered like Kambyses' (6.134–6).

25. Hegesistratos' foot left behind in the cell is a relative of the unaccountably headless corpse which King Rhampsinitos of Egypt finds in his triple-locked treasury, and the detached arm which the thief uses so cleverly in the same story (2.121); compare too the hilarious saga of the disembodied heads (one found in a locked room) at Nikolaos of Damaskos, *FGrHist* 90 F44.

26. *FGrHist* 688 F13(14): ξέων ξυλάριον μαχαίρᾳ διατριβῆς χάριν, παίει τὸν μηρὸν εἰς τὸν μῦν, καὶ ἐνδεκαταῖος τελευτᾷ.

27. Cf. Frontinus *strat.* 2.2, 9: Kleomenes, fighting against Hippias in 510 BC and afraid of the enemy cavalry, littered the battlefield with tree trunks to impede their charge. This is not explicitly linked with the Demeter sacrilege, but a connection is surely likely.

28. LSJ s.v. παρά C.III.9? A late usage.

29. *CQ* (1927) 50.

30. Huxley 1962, 140 n. 552; Forrest 1980, 86; Cartledge 1979,145f.

31. Philostephanos', that is, of course. A Kallimachean paradoxographer from Kyrene, he was an enthusiast etymologist of toponyms; see F. Gisinger, *RE* xix. 104–18.

32. See W.K. Pritchett, *Studies in ancient Greek topography*, III 116–21 (= *UCalPubl in ClassAnt* 22 (1980)); Cartledge 1979, 189 and 145, with map on p. 186; R.A. Tomlinson (*Argos and the Argolid,* 1972) oddly refers to the town as Athene (sic) throughout his treatment of the Thyreatis (45–7); this mistake, an inevitable corruption in all MSS traditions, is also to be found on many maps (e.g. Murray's Atlas), but the founder's name in our passage is of course decisive evidence for the correct spelling.

33. Cf. Pausanias 3.2, 2: 'The Kynourians are supposed to be Argive by birth; they say that their founder was Kynouros the son of Perseus.' Herodotos claims to be able to identify an 'aboriginal Ionian' substrate under the Argive surface (8.73, 3).

34. On territorial disputes between Argos and Sparta, see further Pausanias 2.20, 1 and 7.11, 2, and Strabo 1.4, cap.7.

35. See Walbank on Polybios 4.36, 5; 9.33, 12; and 18.14, 7; also Pausanias 2.38,6.

36. The modern Kefalaki? (So Levi on Paus.2. 36, 6.) Burn (1962, 228) puts it *south* of Lerna, in direct contradiction of Pausanias. It is not clear whether (as is simply assumed by Jones (1967, 53)) the river constituted the actual border between the then-accepted Argive and Spartan territories; this is denied by Huxley 1983,10 n. 66. If the river is said to be 'protecting his own' (6.76; contrast the betrayal of Nineveh by

the Euphrates, at Diod. 2.26, 8; it ought, one would think, to be wholly in Argive territory; yet perhaps it could be regarded as 'Argive', even though marking the border, from the perspective of a Spartan invasion force. According to Euripides, *Elektra* 410 (cf. Paus. 2.38, 7), it is the R. Tanaos which uno *tellures diuidit amne duas*. On the other hand, we do expect to find some account of the dramatic and symbolically-loaded moment at which the general crosses water to enter enemy territory (Kroisos crossing the Halys, etc.); and for Spartan kings this departure from the homeland was marked by particularly crucial rituals: see Thuk. 5.54, 2; 55, 3, Xen. *Lak. Pol.* 13.2 and *Hell.* 5.1, 33; 5.4. 37; 6.4, 19; 6.5, 12; and especially the story at 4.7, 4, where Agesipolis — also engaged in an Argive invasion — dismisses the idea that an earthquake might be a bad omen for the Spartans on the grounds that 'if Poseidon had disapproved of our expedition he would have shown his displeasure while we were at the border'. See also Robert Parker, pp. 155ff. of this volume.

37. Compare Tydeus' refusal to cross the Ismenos in the face of unfavourable omens at Aesch. *Seven against Thebes* 378ff. On Kleomenes' erratic and unpredictable attitude towards religion, oscillating violently between piety and sacrilege, see Forrest 1980, 86: 'no one used or abused religion so much as he'; also Jeffery 1976, 126 and O. Murray, *Early Greece*, 252. We must remember of course that this is an image presented by the historiographical tradition, and that such images, once established, are powerfully self-reinforcing.

38. The fact that Anthes was a *son of Poseidon* may perhaps be suggestive, though.

39. Or perhaps his feeling of triumph (depending on whether the actual capture of Argos was his objective or not)? Compare the relish with which Gideon flogs the elders of Succoth after his victory over the Midianites (Judges 8:13–16).

40. Also, incidentally, said by Pausanias to be founder of Antheia, one of the original constituent towns of Troizen (2.30, 8; see Schneider on Kall, *Hymn* 4.41); and cf. 9.22, 5 on Anthedon in Boiotia.

41. ἀναλαμβάνω is more usual in this sense. ἀναιρέομαι means 'pick up off the battlefield *for* burial'.

42. Another case of this kind of desecration is attested for the grave of Nikias, first century BC tyrant of Kos: according to the epigrammatist Krinagoras (*A.P.* 9.81 = Gow-Page *GP* 1891ff.), 'his corpse returned to the sunlight: the citizens levered apart the closures of his tomb and hauled the wretched man out for punishment, a second death'. (See too the remark of 'J', the lemmatist of the Palatine MS.) A better-known example is that of Amphipolis, founded by the Athenian Hagnon: when the Spartans took control, the citizens buried Brasidas in the place of honour in the agora, and transferred their founder-cult to him (Thuk. 5.11; see T.J. Cornell, art. 'Gründer', *RAC* XII.1112, cf. 1140); on the unspecified 'buildings' associated with Hagnon, destroyed at the same time, see now I. Malkin, *Religion and colonization in ancient Greece* (Leiden 1987), 228–32.

43. The idea of recycling the corpse of a buried enemy for 'useful purposes' appears again in Ailian, *v.h.* 6.8: the Egyptian eunuch Bagoas took his revenge on Artaxerxes Ochos (who had been poisoned in 337)

by digging him up, feeding his flesh to cats, and 'fashioning his thigh-bones into sword-hilts'. That this is a variant of the Kambyses-Amasis story (as Ailian himself seems aware) is shown by the twin features of *the substitute burial* and *the killing of the Apis bull* which the author reports.

44. On the meaning of the phrase see n. 52 below.

45. See on skins and writing C.H. Roberts, *ProcBritAcad* 40 (1954) 182 and 172 n. 1.

46. See Leahy 1958.

47. Pausanias (2.21, 3) is the only person to record this war, though Huxley 1962, 67 is prepared to believe in it.

48. Diels *SBBerl* 1891.1.399, unconvincingly challenged by Dodds, *The Greeks and the irrational*, 142,163 n. 43; though the fact that tattooing is a punishment may be relevant, in view of the hostility between Epimenides and the Spartans, and their capture and execution of him.

49. So, rightly, de Sélincourt for ἀνέλαβε (see Powell's Lexicon). Godley (Loeb) and Grene talk of 'recovering' and 'regaining' (and Grene translates κομίσαντοc as 'brought back'); but there is no implicit suggestion that the oracles had previously been in Spartan hands. Note that Hippias is fully conversant with their contents (5.93, 2). On the careful guarding of oracle-books concerning the fate of cities see W.R. Halliday, *Greek divination*, 51–3.

50. Two points here: (1) for oracles other than the Pythia, cf. Pausanias 10.9 fin. on a prophecy by the Sibyl concerning the outcome of an Argive-Spartan battle over Thyrea; (2) for threats against unfavourable prophets, cf. Od. 2.178, Theoc. 6.23ff. — and the famous chickens in the Punic War.

51. Shakespeare provides an uncanny parallel: at *Titus Andronicus* V.1.135–40, Aaron the Moor proclaims:

> Oft have I digged up dead men from their graves
> And set them upright at their dear friends' doors,
> Even when their sorrows almost were forgot;
> And on their skins, as on the bark of trees,
> Have with my knife carved in Roman letters,
> "Let not your sorrow die, though I am dead."

I have been unable to identify a likely source.

52. To return, finally to St. Byz.: the text ('ἔγραψεν ἐν τῷ δέρματι τοὺς χρηcμοὺς ὧδε τηρεῖcθαι') can hardly be sound as it stands. One might suggest τελεῖcθαι or perhaps (cf. e.g. Polyainos 1.18, Matth. 1.22, John 13.18) πληροῦcθαι: 'he wrote on the skin that the oracles were, by his doing this, being brought to fulfilment'. The idea would perhaps be that, faced with an unfavourable prophecy of some kind, he was trying to bring it to a premature completion in a harmless form: as the Median experts thought that Kyros' boy-kingship pre-empted the possibility of his ruling a second time as an adult. Or is he remembering his misunderstanding of 'Argos' and angrily exacting punishment from yet another eponymous hero? It is hard to see exactly what is meant.

53. R. Bichler, 'Die Reichsträume bei Herodot', *Chiron* 15 (1985) 125–47 at 137, with n. 44, has an acute, if unspecific, comment on the parallels: 'dazu [viz. Herodotos' account of Kambyses] bietet die

Geschichte des Kleomenes manch erstaunliche Entsprechung in Aufbau und Detail . . . Diese innerherodoteischen Parallelen sind in ihrer Konsequenz für die Beurteilung von Herodots Arbeitsweise noch zuwenig gewürdigt.'

54. Which image was formed first, or did they develop reciprocally by mutual reinforcement — perhaps in Herodotos' mind? Certainly in the case of Kambyses, we can be confident that the picture of him as an impious violator of Egyptian religious custom is false; on the contrary, local Egyptian evidence (see Brown 1982, 397 n. 33) shows that he took the greatest care *not* to cause offence in precisely this sensitive area. No doubt Egyptian resentment will have been compounded by Herodotos" need, for ideological reasons, to conduct Kambyses along the path that takes all oriental potentates from arrogant πλεονεξία to an appropriate death; this is all the more necessary because Kambyses *succeeded* in his conquest of Egypt.

Bibliography

Brown, 1982: T.S. Brown, 'Herodotus' portrait of Cambyses', *Historia* 31.387–403

Burn, 1962: A.R. Burn, *Persia and the Greeks. The Defence of the West 546–478 BC*, London

Burkert, 1965: Walter Burkert, 'Damaratos, Astrabakos und Herakles: Königsmythos und Politik', *MusHelv* 22.166–77

Cartledge, 1979: Paul Cartledge, *Sparta and Lakonia. A regional history 1300–362 BC*, London, Boston and Henley

Dunbabin, 1948: T.J. Dunbabin, *The Western Greeks*, Oxford

Fontenrose, 1978: Joseph Fontenrose, *The Delphic Oracle. Its responses and operations, with a catalogue of responses*, Berkeley, Los Angeles, London

Forrest, 1980: W.G. Forrest, *A History of Sparta*, 2nd edn, Oxford

Hart, 1982: John Hart, *Herodotus and Greek history*, London

How & Wells, 1912: W.W. How and J. Wells, *A commentary on Herodotus*, Oxford

Huxley, 1962: G.L. Huxley, *Early Sparta*, London

Huxley, 1983: G.L. Huxley, 'Herodotus on myth and politics in early Sparta', *ProcRoyalIrishAcad* 83,C,1.1–16

Immerwahr, 1966: H.R. Immerwahr, *Form and thought in Herodotus*, Cleveland

Jeffery, 1976; L.H. Jeffery, *Archaic Greece: the city-states c. 700–500 BC*, London and Tonbridge

Jones, 1967: A.H.M. Jones, *Sparta*, Oxford

Leahy, 1958: D.M. Leahy, 'The Spartan defeat at Orchomenus', *Phoenix* 12.141–65

Lefkowitz, 1981: Mary R. Lefkowitz, *The lives of the Greek poets*, London

Lewis, 1985: D.M. Lewis, 'Persians in Herodotus', in *The Greek historians: literature and history. Papers presented to A.E. Raubitschek*, Stanford, 101–17

Macan, 1895: R.W. Macan, *Herodotus, the fourth, fifth and sixth books*, Vol. II

Myres, 1953: J.L. Myres, *Herodotus, father of history*, Oxford

White, 1964: M.E. White, 'Some Agiad dates: Pausanias and his sons', *JHS* 84.140–52

4

Inheritance, Marriage and Demography: Perspectives upon the Success and Decline of Classical Sparta*

Stephen Hodkinson

The reasons for Sparta's crisis and decline in the early fourth century have long been the subject of debate. Already in the same century widely differing opinions were expressed by Xenophon, Isokrates and Aristotle, as well as later by writers such as Polybius and Plutarch. Modern scholarship has been equally divided and the controversy has continued unabated in the 1980s with the divergent interpretations of David, Cawkwell and, most recently, Figueira and Cartledge.[1] The fact that the Spartan social system appears, in the face of various tensions which I have analysed elsewhere,[2] to have maintained an underlying stability for over a couple of centuries from perhaps the mid-seventh century onwards and then to have undergone a more rapid period of transformation and collapse from the later fifth and early fourth centuries, must form the essential backcloth for the interpretation of any particular aspect of the social system. The subjects of this essay — inheritance, marriage and demography —

* Earlier versions of this paper have been presented to the British School at Athens Centenary Conference on Sparta at the University of Newcastle-upon-Tyne in February 1986 and to the Greek Polis seminar at the University of Oxford in February 1987, as well as to the series of seminars which has given rise to this volume. I am grateful to participants on all three occasions for their stimulating discussion. I also owe a particular debt to a number of colleagues for their help in producing the models of landholding below: to Professor E.A. Wrigley and Dr. Richard Smith for advice and for permission to use their published tables of family composition distributions; to Dr. Theo Balderston for help with the mathematical calculations required to extend them to produce the figures given in Table 4.1; and, above all, to Sarah Davnall of the University of Manchester Regional Computer Centre for constructing and running the computer program which produced the results incorporated in Table 4.2 and Figure 4.1.

are in fact closely linked with the question of the viability of Spartan society in ways which I hope to demonstrate.

Spartiate landownership and inheritance

My discussion starts with one of the most fundamental aspects of Spartan society, that of property and wealth; and, in particular, the ownership and inheritance of the most important form of property, land. In most societies whose economies are dependent primarily upon sedentary agriculture the distribution of land and the rules governing its tenure and inheritance exercise a fundamental influence upon the nature of the social system, and there is every indication that the same was true of classical Sparta. My present concern lies exclusively with land held and inherited by the Spartiates, the full citizens, who directed the affairs of the Spartan state and owned most of the best land in Lakonia and Messenia. It is abundantly clear from evidence in Herodotus (6.61.3; 7.134.2), Thucydides (1.6.4), Xenophon (*Lak. Pol.* 5.3; 6.4; *Hell.* 6.4.10–11) and Aristotle (*Pol.* 1270a18) that throughout the classical period there were marked inequalities in Spartiate ownership of land. These passages, among other evidence, include specific references to activities which required larger than average estates. One example is the maintenance of horses for chariot racing and the cavalry.[3] Another is the provision by the rich to the common messes of extra donations of bread made from wheat, a higher-status and less reliable additional cereal crop compared to the barley which all citizens grew to provide the *alphita* (barley meal) for their *compulsory* mess contributions and for the subsistence of their families.[4] Beyond this point, however, we move into areas that are highly controversial. Since the 19th century there has been considerable dispute concerning the nature of land tenure and inheritance. Since I have recently made my own contribution to this debate, rather than repeat myself at length, I shall simply summarise here the main conclusions of my study.[5]

My main negative contention was that there is little of value to be extracted from the accounts of later writers upon whom scholars have often relied. Two main interpretations, founded especially upon the evidence of Plutarch,[6] have been prominent: one according to which each citizen was merely the life tenant of an indivisible lot which reverted to the state on his death;[7]

another according to which this indivisible lot passed down by primogeniture to the man's eldest son.[8] Both versions stem from a belief that in the archaic period there had been an equal redistribution of land and that the individual lots allocated in that redistribution had been maintained intact into the fifth century BC. On this view the individual landholder had no right to alienate his lot, either in whole or in part, whether by gift, by sale or by testamentary bequest. Proponents of these interpretations do often suggest that richer citizens also owned other land which was more private in character; but even on this view the more important category of land was still the type subject to strict regulation. In my study I concluded, firstly, that Plutarch's testimony is contradictory (as is suggested by the existence of two different interpretations of his evidence); secondly, that the systems of land tenure and inheritance outlined above are impracticable; and thirdly, that the esential elements in Plutarch's accounts, namely the supposed redistribution of land, the maintenance of indivisible lots into the fifth century and the systems of land tenure and inheritance themselves, can all be shown to be the products of fourth-century and later invention.

In place of the interpretations just described, I argued that, by reasserting the correct methodology of giving primary consideration to contemporary or near-contemporary evidence, it is possible to construct a more reliable interpretation, according to which land tenure was fundamentally private in character, with only a minimum of state regulation and with women enjoying considerably more property rights than has previously been realised. The evidence suggests that there were two types of land, one of which was called the 'ancient portion' (*archaia moira*).[9] A landowner was prohibited from selling the ancient portion and sale of other land was shameful; but otherwise there is no evidence for further restrictions concerning either type of land. A person could alienate his land by means of gift or bequest (Arist. *Pol.* 1270a19–21), a right which predates the early fourth century (Xen. *Ages.* 4.5; Plut. *Ages.* 4.1) when the almost certainly fictional law of Epitadeus was supposedly passed (Plut. *Agis* 5.2–3). A landowner without a male child could also control the disposition of his land, either directly, by adopting a son (Hdt. 6.57.5), or indirectly, through the choice of any husband for his heiress (Hdt. 6.57.4; Arist. *Pol.* 1270a26–9; only an unbetrothed heiress was obliged to marry her next of kin,[10] and even he might give her in marriage to whomsoever he wished). The basic method by which land was transmitted down the generations was partible inheritance, division among the owner's children (Arist. *Pol.* 1270b1–6; cf. Xen. *Lak. Pol.* 1.8–9). In the absence of children, the inheritance was shared among the nearest kin, starting on the male side (Xen. *Ages.* 4.5; Plut. *Ages.* 4.1).

Women were also landowners. When there were no sons, the daughter(s) inherited the estate (Hdt. 6.57.4); but even when there were sons, daughters still probably received a portion. It is possible that Aristotle's statement (*Pol.* 1270a23–4) that women owned approximately two-fifths of the land reflects no more than a fourth-century increase in the size of dowries or marriage settlements which daughters received from their parents. The more likely explanation, however, is that Spartiate women had long possessed the same inheritance rights as did their counterparts in fifth-century Gortyn on Crete: namely, the right to half the portion due to a son.[11] (This share was probably normally given to a girl at her marriage as a pre-death or 'anticipated' inheritance, as happened at Gortyn.) That Spartiate women possessed rights of inheritance even in the presence of sons, not just in their absence (I shall henceforth refer to these different systems as *universal female inheritance* and *residual female inheritance*, respectively) is also suggested by the existence of several royal intra-lineage marriages, including one as early as the mid-sixth century.[12] All these marriages were clearly aimed at the concentration of property and each involved a woman with a surviving brother or other close inheriting kinsman, implying that these women had the right to some property inheritance alongside the male heirs. Spartiate inheritance, therefore, operated on the basis of diverging devolution, according to which the property of both father and mother passed into the hands of children of both sexes.

The implications of universal female inheritance

Before turning to the implications of these practices of tenure and inheritance, it is relevant to comment briefly upon the genesis of the overall system of landownership of which they were a part. It seems likely that this system in its fundamentals went back to the seventh century when so many aspects of Spartan society seem to have been reshaped as part of the compromise between different interests which was involved in the creation of a united body of citizen *homoioi* (equals, peers or similars). In the sphere of landholding this compromise must have involved bringing the property of poorer citizens up to a basic minimum level at which they could have been expected to provide their compulsory mess contributions (failure to provide which meant loss of citizenship) and feed their families. This basic minimum may have been set quite high; but, apart from this, the compromise involved the retention of existing inequalities. The practices of private tenure and partible inheritance I would also view as a matter of the retention of previous usages comparable (though of course not necessarily identical) with those evident elsewhere both in the early archaic period (e.g. Hesiod, *Works and days* 37–9, 341, 379–80; cf. *Odyssey* 14.199ff.) and throughout Greek antiquity.[13] These practices were now applied, I suggest, to newly-distributed holdings as well as to pre-existing estates. A compromise of this sort is a much more plausible product of the crises of the seventh century than the unrealistic schemes in Plutarch; and it was made more acceptable for ordinary *homoioi* by the practice of institutionalised sharing (Xen. *Lak. Pol.* 6.3–5; Arist. *Pol.* 1263a35–7), by the distributive mechanisms which operated within the common messes,[14] by the restrictions upon ostentatious expenditure by the rich[15] and by the uniform clothing, equipment and, to a large extent, lifestyle shared by all citizens (Thuc. 1.6).[16]

The achievement of a workable compromise in this crucial field must have been important psychologically in sustaining the unity of the *homoioi*; but what about its long-term practical effects? Here I want to examine in some detail the implications of the inheritance system, focusing in particular upon the effects of the system of universal female inheritance for which I have argued, in order to suggest some ways in which it may have contributed both to Spartan society's long-term stability and to its ultimate decline. I want, in particular, to stress two related but conflicting implications.

The first is that a system of universal female inheritance tends *in itself* to produce less inequality among both individuals and families than a system of residual female inheritance only. Or, to express it more accurately, the inequalities generated by the former system are more graded and less sharp. The reason is that when all daughters as well as sons inherit at least some land, it is divided more evenly among more persons; and when those daughters marry, the combined husband-wife landholdings show less marked inequalities from one family to the next.

The correctness of these observations can be tested by a computer programme designed to make a systematic comparison of the theoretical implications of these two inheritance systems: residual female inheritance and universal female inheritance in which a daughter's portion is half that of a son. The programme postulates a model population of 10,000 married couples, in which each couple owns 1 unit of land in Generation 1.[17] On the assumption that the population remains stable and that any child born has a 0.5 chance of surviving beyond its parents' deaths, it is possible to calculate the resulting *family composition distribution* (that is, the numbers of *surviving* sons and daughters produced by each of the 10,000 couples).[18] This is given in Table 4.1, in which Columns I & II list various combinations of surviving sons and daughters to a maximum of four sons and four daughters. Column III indicates the number of families with the stated combination of surviving sons and daughters. (So, for example, on the bottom line there are 16 families with four sons and four daughters.) Columns IV & V give the total numbers of surviving sons and daughters produced by each of the combinations within the population as a whole. (So, to continue our example, the 16 families with four sons and four daughters produce a total number of 64 sons and 64 daughters.)

On the basis of this family composition distribution each family's 1 unit of land can then be divided among its surviving children, according to the different rules of the two inheritance systems. Land belonging to families with no surviving children is reallocated in whole units to the other families on a selective proportional basis. (There are 2126 units of land to be distributed among 7874 families with surviving children; consequently, 27% of these families receive one unit. So, for example, of the 16 families with four sons and four daughters, 16 × 0.27 = 4 (4.32) families receive one extra unit of land in addition to the unit they already possess.) This additional land is then divided among the families' children in the same way as their original landholding.

The outcome is that under both inheritance systems the sons and daughters who form Generation 2 of the model population own widely varying amounts of land. This is shown in Table 4.2 which illustrates the point already made concerning the levelling effects of universal female inheritance. Although its impact leads to a slight lowering of the size of the smallest male holding (0.2 unit as opposed to 0.3: compare Columns 1 & 4), this is more

Inheritance, Marriage and Demography

TABLE 4.1   Family composition distribution

I	II	III	IV	V
Combinations of		Number of	Numbers of	
Sons	Daughters	families	Sons	Daughters
0	0	2126	0	0
1	0	1191	1191	0
0	1	1191	0	1191
1	1	1028	1028	1028
2	1	578	1156	578
1	2	578	578	1156
2	0	514	1028	0
0	2	514	0	1028
2	2	366	732	732
3	1	244	732	244
1	3	244	244	732
3	0	193	579	0
0	3	193	0	579
3	2	165	495	330
2	3	165	330	495
4	1	112	448	112
1	4	112	112	448
4	0	82	328	0
0	4	82	0	328
4	2	78	312	156
2	4	78	156	312
3	3	76	228	228
4	3	37	148	111
3	4	37	111	148
4	4	16	64	64
		10000	10000	10000

than compensated for by the fact that the 6874 poorest women who are landless under the system of residual female inheritance possess amounts varying between 0.1 and 0.4 units under universal female inheritance (compare Columns 2 & 5). When both sexes are considered together (Columns 3 & 6), although the median size of all individual landholdings is 0.3 under both systems, the 75th percentile (the median of the 50% of larger landholdings) differs considerably, falling within the 1.0 unit band under residual inheritance but only the 0.7 band under universal inheritance. This clearly demonstrates the lesser degree of overall inequality resulting from the latter system.

TABLE 4.2   *Generation 2 individual landownership*

Amount of land (in units)	Numbers of landowners					
	Residual female inheritance			Universal female inheritance		
	(1) Men	(2) Women	(3) Both sexes	(4) Men	(5) Women	(6) Both sexes
2.0	852	322	1174	322	321	643
1.3	0	0	0	278	0	278
1.0	3220	1147	4367	1303	1147	2450
0.8	0	0	0	378	0	378
0.7	579	156	735	1134	434	1568
0.6	0	0	0	287	0	287
0.5	2834	839	3673	1436	1151	2587
0.4	0	0	0	1359	354	1713
0.3	2515	662	3177	2546	2948	5494
0.2	0	0	0	957	2039	2996
0.1	0	0	0	0	1606	1606
0	0	6874	6874	0	0	0
	10000	10000	20000	10000	10000	20000

How does this affect the landholding of families as opposed to individuals? In order to assess this, the individual men and women need to be paired off to form couples. (The model assumes that all individuals who survive the deaths of their parents will marry, but only once.) This marriage-making is also done on a selective proportional basis, such that the same proportion of men at any given level of landownership is married to each group of women with a different level of wealth. (The purpose of this is to maintain the focus upon the inherent logic of the inheritance systems by not introducing additional social factors such as any tendency towards marriages between persons of similar wealth.) The combined landholdings of each husband and wife pairing can now be calculated. Figure 4.1 indicates the outcome at the stage of Generation 3 couples. It concentrates upon the position of the 7,500 or so poorer families who own 1.2 units of land or less. Since each Spartiate had to provide a fixed contribution in kind to the common messes or else lose his citizenship, the position of poorer families under these model inheritance systems is the most critical in demonstrating their inherent implications. (Landholding among the 2,500 or so richer families in fact rises sharply under both systems from 1.2 units to 4.7 units under universal female inheritance and to 6.0 units under residual inheritance.)

FIGURE 4.1 *Family landholding in Generation 3 (ca. 7,500 poorer families)*

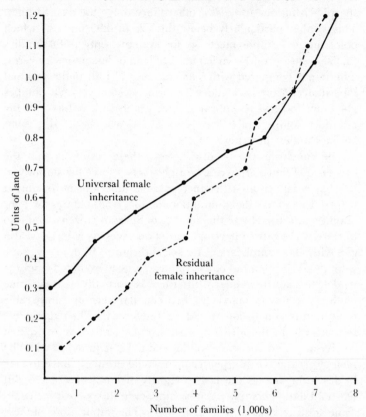

The graphs in Figure 4.1 show for the two inheritance systems the approximate number of Generation 3 families (indicated on the horizontal axis) who possess landholdings equal to or less than the numbers of units indicated on the vertical axis. (The graphs are approximate in that for convenience of exposition the sizes of holdings have been rounded to the nearest 0.05 unit and the numbers of families to the nearest multiple of 250.) The graphs demonstrate that under both systems the majority of families own holdings smaller (many *much* smaller) than their ancestors' original one unit of land. They also demonstrate, however, that the extent of poverty is considerably less under universal female inheritance (shown by the continuous line). The higher starting-point and the flatter graph of *universal* female inheritance indicate a less unequal distribution of wealth than the sharply-rising one of *residual* inheritance only (the dashed line). This applies particularly below the size of 0.95 units at which point the two graphs meet. So, for example, only 1,588 families (1,500 on the graph) own 0.5 units of land or less under universal inheritance compared with 3,836 families (3,750) under residual inheritance. Moreover, under the former system very few families (14 only; too few to appear on the graph) are reduced to the minutest holdings of 0.2 units or less as against 1,561 (1,500) families under the latter.

The conclusion to be drawn from these results is that the existence of female inheritance rights was a force for stability in that, in comparison with other possible inheritance systems, it helped to reduce the diminution of the landholdings of poor families, and thereby of the number of Spartan citizens, and also to restrict the rate of development of an excessively large wealth gap with all its implications for social disunity. If, moreover, one were to take account of one variable expressly excluded from the model, the fact that in real life there is normally at least some tendency towards marriages between partners of comparable wealth, this conclusion would be reinforced. When daughters inherit only in the absence of sons, only a minority of women receive any land and these would tend to be acquired as wives by men of greater wealth; poorer men would normally have to take brides from among the large majority of landless women. But when all daughters inherit something, even the poorest men gain some addition of land with their wives. The implications of these model inheritance systems are, therefore, not mere theory, but would apply with even greater force in real life. Acceptance of the hypothesis of female inheritance in the presence of sons would, consequently, help to explain the longevity of the Spartan socio-economic system, how and why it achieved two centuries or so of comparative stability before social disunity and the decline in citizen numbers became serious problems in the later fifth century.[19]

The other, contrasting implication of universal female inheritance, however, is that, although it tended to lessen long-term inequalities in landownership, it did so at the cost of considerable continuous *short-term* instability. When not only men inherit land, but women also, and those women receive at least a portion of their inheritance on marriage, land changes hands both down the generations and between the sexes at every adult death and at every marriage.[20] The ownership of specific holdings is drastically reorganised every generation and may be continually reallocated from one lineage to another because daughters are constantly inheriting land from both father and mother and ultimately bequeathing it to children whose father may be from an entirely different lineage. In addition the parental landholdings are subject to far greater division when daughters inherit in the presence of sons, a division which varies considerably in its effects from family to family, according to not only the total number of children but also the ratio of sons to daughters. For example, the grandchildren of couples with only sons stand to gain increased inheritances as those sons marry propertied wives without losing any of the parental property to sisters; whereas couples with more daughters than sons give away more land with those daughters than is brought in by the wives of their sons.

These phenomena of continual movement of land, its constant reallocation among different lineages, multiple division of the inheritance and extreme short-term variability in property levels, all of which arose directly from Sparta's particular system of diverging devolution, must have been important preoccupations for Spartiate families concerned for the well-being of their descendants. There was, moreover, a lack of direct mechanisms for remedying their most serious effects. In some societies the landholdings of families without children would lapse out of cultivation and become available for exploitation by families with too many children; but in Sparta the helots maintained the cultivation for whomsoever inherited on grounds of kinship, not of need. There is no evidence that the kings, in their role as adjudicators between claimants to the hand of unbetrothed heiresses, provided any help by allocating such women to sons from larger families.[21] Nor is there evidence for a reservoir of public land for such sons to exploit, such as existed in Ptolemaic and Roman Egypt which practised an even more extreme form of universal female inheritance.[22] Furthermore, whereas the Egyptians utilised purchase and sale of land as a means of adjusting property holdings affected by partible inheritance,[23] these activities were in Sparta restricted by a combination of legal prohibition and social disapproval. Only through adoption (Hdt. 6.57.5) could some evening-out of property be achieved, though probably largely within kin groups rather than between them. Consequently, it was in the sphere of marriage that Spartiates had to seek solutions to their problems.

Diverging devolution and Spartiate marriage practices

The anthropologist Jack Goody, in a statistical analysis of several
hundred societies, has noted a high degree of association between
inheritance systems of diverging devolution and specific kinds of
marriage practices which seem designed, from the viewpoint of
individual households, to minimise the various difficulties described above.[24] In many respects marriage customs at Sparta
accord well with the general pattern pointed out by Goody. He
notes, for instance, the frequent coexistence of diverging devolution with the practices of monogamy and polyandry, as opposed
to polygyny,[25] and this is precisely what we find in Sparta.
Herodotus (5.39–40) indicates that when King Anaxandridas II
in the mid-sixth century took a second wife *in addition to* his first
one, who was barren but whom he was unwilling to divorce, it
was a very un-Spartan practice which he performed only on the
express orders of the ephors and *gerontes*, who themselves adopted
this counsel only as a measure of last resort for fear that the Agiad
line would die out. When Anaxandridas' fellow king, Ariston,
voluntarily took a third wife, he adopted the more usual practice
of divorcing his second spouse (Hdt. 6.63.1). Polyandry is
attested by Polybius (12.6b.8), who says that it was a long-
standing custom and quite usual for three, four or even more
brothers to have one wife. Both monogamy and polyandry can be
interpreted as practices designed to limit the number of legitimate
children that a man sired and hence the division of the
inheritance. Other Spartiate customs tended in the same direction. It seems that a woman typically married at a later age than
in most Greek states, perhaps between ages 18 and 20, thus
reducing her years of potential fertility.[26] The practice of wife-
borrowing (Xen. *Lak. Pol.* 1.8–9; Plb. 12.6b.8; Plut. *Lyk.* 15.13;
Comp. Lyk.-Numa 3.3; *Moralia* 242B) also enabled one woman's
fertility to be divided between two men; Polybius specifically
remarks that it was when a man had begotten sufficient children
by his wife that he would give her to a friend.

Goody also notes a significant correlation between the existence
of diverging devolution and a high degree of control over female
marriage aimed at ensuring that one's womenfolk married
persons of similar or higher status (the practices of homogamy
and hypergamy). Once again we see these practices in Sparta. A
woman's marriage was decided by her male *kyrios* (legal
guardian).[27] Herodotus (6.57.4) implies that it was a father who

normally betrothed his heiress; and Aristotle (*Pol.* 1270a26–9) states that, if the father did not do so, that right fell to the *klēronomos* — in my view, her male next of kin. Although matrimonial rites may have included a symbolic marriage by capture (Plut. *Lyk.* 15.4–9), which was on one infamous occasion exploited by King Damaratos, who carried off the woman betrothed to Leotychidas (Hdt. 6.65), it seems that it was Leotychidas' method of acquiring a wife which was the orthodox one and that normally marriages were preceded by a betrothal approved by the bride's parents or next of kin.[28] The tendency towards homogamy and hypergamy which resulted from this control over female marriage can be seen through a variety of evidence. One illustration is the episode (see refs, n. 10) in which Lysander's daughters were deserted by their suitors when the poverty of their inheritance became known. Such a marriage would have meant a drop in status and wealth for the suitors and for their potential children, despite the fact that the girls' father had been one of the most prestigious and influential men in Sparta. Similarly, as early as the mid-sixth century, when King Ariston wanted to replace his wife, he selected a woman from a prosperous family who was the spouse of his closest friend (Hdt. 6.61–2). Ariston's choice of a woman already married was unorthodox, but otherwise the story of this well-born female being the ideal partner for a king's friend and for a king himself is quite typical.

The phenomenon of a girl from a leading, non-royal family marrying into a royal house is a classic case of female hypergamy which must have been reasonably frequent in Sparta. The sources mention several examples from the fifth century, such as the marriage of Eurydamē, daughter of Diaktoridas, to King Leotychidas II (Hdt. 6.71), that of Eupolia, daughter of Melesippidas, to King Archidamos II (Plut. *Ages.* 1.1) and that of Kleora, daughter of Aristomenidas, a leading Spartiate with connections in Boiotia, to the future king Agesilaos II (Paus. 3.9.3). But it is the mid-sixth-century episode mentioned above in which King Anaxandridas II was compelled to take an additional wife which provides the most vivid illustration of the passion with which such alliances with the royal houses were sought and jealously guarded by the girl's kin. Anaxandridas' first wife was his own niece (his sister's daughter); but his second wife came from a different lineage, being the daughter of Prinetadas and granddaughter of a certain Demarmenos. The second wife produced a male child; but then the first wife straightaway became pregnant, whereupon the kinsfolk of the second wife expressed with such vigour their suspicions concerning her fortuitous conception of a prospective rival for the throne after several years of barrenness that the ephors were obliged to attend the birth to guarantee that the pregnancy was genuine and a false baby was not smuggled in. The value this same kin group put upon achieving distinguished marriages for their womenfolk is further indicated by the fact that another granddaughter of Demarmenos, Perkalos, daughter of Chilon, was betrothed to Leotychidas, the leading member of the junior branch of the Eurypontid royal house (Hdt. 6.65). Perkalos was indeed such an attractive match that, as we have seen, Leotychidas' senior kinsman, King Damaratos, stepped in and seized her for himself before the marriage was consummated. Here we see a leading Spartiate lineage, perhaps related to the famous ephor Chilon, attempting to further the status of its descendants by marrying two of its womenfolk into the two royal houses.

Homogamy and hypergamy can also be seen in the practice of wife-borrowing. Xenophon's remarks about the kind of wife a man would request to borrow imply that she would be of similar status or better. Furthermore, Philo (*On Special Laws* 3.4.22) informs us that the Spartiates permitted marriage between uterine half-siblings (*homomētrioi*, children of the same mother but of different fathers). This would have allowed the woman's sons and daughters by her different partners to be exchanged in marriage. The whole complex is clearly one of homogamy, with the added bonus of concentrating the parents' properties for the benefit of their grandchildren.

Another form of homogamy was the practice of marriage between close kin. In addition to the three examples already noted (cf. n. 12), at least two additional cases can be cited — the marriage of King Kleomenes I's daughter, Gorgo, to her step-uncle Leonidas (Hdt. 7.205.1) and the late-third-century case of the marriage of King Archidamos V to the daughter of his cousin Hippomedon (Plb. 4.35.13). Close-kin marriage had the advantage that not only did it ensure that the amount of property brought by the bride was consonant with the status and wealth of the groom and his parents, but it also retained the property of a kinswoman within the kin. Close-kin marriage was especially important to the royal houses which were the richest and most prestigious lineages in Sparta. It was often their best option to avoid marriages below their station and the dispersal of their property and therefore their power.

Problems of interpretation

At this point we must confront the problem of the limitations of our evidence. Some of the marriage practices considered above, such as monogamy, hypergamy and close-kin marriage, are attested through episodes dating as early as the mid-sixth century. Others, however, such as wife-borrowing and polyandry, become apparent only in sources writing in the fourth century or later. It is important to consider whether the whole range of marriage practices should be viewed as long-standing concomit-ants of inheritance by diverging devolution or whether some came into prominence rather later than others. The issue of course is not just whether a specific practice began only at a certain date. Whatever its longevity, an equally important question is how common it was. For example, did Xenophon highlight wife-borrowing for its symbolic significance out of all proportion to its frequency? Or was its frequency in the early fourth century the reason why he drew attention to it? (Note his claim that Lykourgos 'permitted many such arrangements'.) And if so, for how long had it been frequent? Unfortunately, the sheer paucity of prosopographical information concerning Spartiate marriages imposes severe limits upon our capacity to answer such questions from the evidence of the sources alone. Similarly, although we see the royal houses practising close-kin marriage as far back as the mid-sixth century, lack of evidence prevents us from knowing whether it was already then a widespread practice or whether the royal houses with more property at stake were exceptional in this regard.

These questions are important because of the tendency of these marriage practices to counteract the inheritance system's moderating influence upon the development of inequality. If implemented by a significant number of individual households, the impact upon the delicate balance between levels of population and of landownership was potentially disastrous. Here we begin to touch upon the subject of Spartiate demography because limitation of family size, marriage of like to like and concentration of property are all factors which have justifiably been invoked by historians as both symptoms and causes of the citizen manpower shortage (*oliganthrōpia*) which destroyed Sparta, according to the famous account of Aristotle (*Pol.* 1270a33–4). The decline in Spartiate numbers was closely connected with the increasing poverty of many ordinary citizens and with their potential and actual inability to provide the monthly mess contributions necessary for the maintenance of their citizen status. The issue of the precise timing and rate of decline has been the subject of considerable disagreement among historians, linked as it is with problematic calculations of the size of the citizen body at certain dates based upon extrapolations from the size of Lakedaimonian armies. The debate over whether we should double Thucydides' figures for the forces at Mantineia in 418, for example, is notorious.[29] Critical scrutiny of army figures is clearly necessary; but, equally clearly, that alone is not going to resolve the continuing controversies, and I would suggest that consideration of the wider issues of inheritance and marriage patterns may open up a helpful perspective upon the subject.

Constraints of space prevent full exposition here of the variety of opinions concerning the development of Spartiate *oliganthrōpia*. Most interpretations, however, fall within one or other of two broad categories. First, there is the 'gradualist' approach which views the decline in citizen numbers as a long-term process extending over more than a century at least, with an ever firmer tightening of the screw as the inherent deficiencies of the system of land tenure and inheritance, exploited by the acquisitiveness of leading citizens, reduced more and more Spartiates to a level of poverty at which they failed either to maintain their mess contributions or to reproduce themselves through attempting to limit the number of their heirs. Perhaps the clearest recent exposition of this kind of view has been provided by Cartledge.[30] Even when scholars of this school view this process as accelerating under the impact of the Peloponnesian War and its aftermath, they still see it as originating long beforehand. In contrast to the gradualist position stand interpretations which view the decline as taking place more dramatically, the key event being for many scholars the earthquake of *c.* 465 in which losses are judged to have been sufficiently large to have caused a sudden permanent drop in Spartiate numbers. In recent times Toynbee, and now Lane Fox and Figueira, have adopted this kind of view.[31] Other historians would lay greater emphasis upon the acquisition of empire in 404 which is said to have led to the passing of the supposed law of Epitadeus which, it is claimed, wrecked Sparta's inheritance system;[32] there are even those who implausibly ascribe all Sparta's problems to this putative law.[33]

The significance of wealth as a determinant of status

As presented so far, my analysis of the implications of the system of inheritance could in principle be adduced to support either of these two broad approaches. The moderating effect of the inheritance system might seem to support the gradualist position whereby inequalities increased slowly from the seventh century onwards until they began to have a serious impact in the fifth century. On the other hand, several of the marriage customs aimed at limiting family size and achieving the concentration of family property could be viewed as later developments stimulated by the consequences of the earthquake and/or the acquisition of empire. This brings us back to the problem already mentioned, that a direct answer to questions concerning the age and frequency of these marriage customs is not possible from the evidence of the sources alone. We can, however, make some progress by considering the conditions under which these marriage practices would be most likely to flourish. Here Goody's work is once more illuminating because it suggests that it is the degree of social stratification based upon inequalities in property ownership which is the key underlying factor.[34] In societies heavily influenced by such economic stratification families are typically very concerned about the level of wealth of potential spouses for their children, since that will affect the status of the family and its descendants. One could further hypothesise that this in turn might lead to the practice of family limitation.

This perspective is helpful, first, because it suggests that at least some of the marriage practices in question should be viewed not as indissolubly-linked concomitants of inheritance by diverging devolution but rather as customs whose frequency, and even existence, might be altered by the social context; secondly, because the degree of social stratification based upon unequal ownership of wealth is a factor about which it is possible to make some assessment, however imperfect. This subject takes us right to the heart of the nature of Spartiate society. In an earlier study I attempted to assess the relative importance of a variety of factors in the determination of a man's status.[35] It seems clear that throughout Spartan history some lineages were continuously more important than others and that differential ownership of land was a major factor in their importance. The self-imposed restrictions upon the Spartiates ensured that land was the only form of property through which substantial wealth could be accumulated. Land-rich Spartiates could gain status through patronising their messmates with extra donations of produce, animals and game from their estates (Xen. *Lak. Pol.* 5.3; Athenaios, *Deipnosophistai* 4, 139B–141E) or by lending their horses and hunting dogs for the use of poorer men (Xen. *Lak. Pol.* 6.3; Arist. *Pol.* 1263a35–7). Landed wealth must also have enabled leading Spartiates to sustain the guest-friendships with leading men from other states which are attested throughout the classical period.[36] As Goody has noted, however, 'criteria of ranking are rarely single-stranded',[37] and this was especially true in Sparta where the significance of differential landownership was restrained within certain limits by the new social order of citizen *homoioi* which emerged out of the compromises of the seventh century. This social order entailed a common life-cycle within which there was a large degree of uniformity in lifestyle for all citizens (with the exception of the kings and their immediate heirs) supported by an ideology which stressed the priority of collective interests over private ones. Within this system status was acquired partly through seniority, partly through conformity to specified types of action and standards of behaviour required in different situations, ranging from absolute obedience to authority to vigorous competition with one's peers.

For a considerable period the competing claims of uniformity, seniority and merit are likely to have been significant counter-vailing influences against the monopoly of high status by the rich. The role of differential landownership as a source of status distinctions does seem, however, to have developed considerably from the mid-fifth century onwards. This is suggested, above all, by the evidence that the overwhelming majority of Spartiate victories in the four-horse chariot race at Olympia occurred in the period from *c.* 450 onwards: ten out of fifteen victories won by eight out of Sparta's eleven victors (see Table 4.3). This is a phenomenon to which one should give full weight because not only was chariot racing, with its high costs of breeding and maintaining horses, a most expensive sporting activity within the capacity of only the wealthiest of men,[38] but the Olympic four-horse chariot race was the most important equestrian event at the most significant panhellenic gathering. Expenditure and success on this scale carried withthem an unmistakable claim to social and political influence, using large-scale property as a power base, as Davies has demonstrated with reference to Athens.[39]

TABLE 4.3 *Spartiate victories in the Olympic four-horse chariot race*[40]

Date	Name	Moretti no.
548	Euagoras	110
544	Euagoras	113
540	Euagoras	117
504	Damaratos	157
484	Polypeithes	195
448	Arkesilaos	305
444	Arkesilaos	311
440	Polykles	315
432	Lykonos[41]	324
428	Anaxandros	327
424	Leon	332
420	Lichas	339
396	Kyniska	373
392	Kyniska	381
388	Xenarches[42]	386

The pattern of Spartiate victories outlined in Table 4.3 is worth elaborating in a little detail. The main expansion of interest in regular panhellenic chariot-racing competitions on the part of the elite of the Greek *poleis* seems to have taken place in the first third of the sixth century.[43] Between this time and the second Persian invasion of 480–479 three Spartiate Olympic victors are known, a record second to that of Athens (four victors). From this period there is also the evidence of a Panathenaic amphora dated *c.* 525–500 and dedicated in the temple of Athena Chalkioikos on the Spartan *akropolis*, a prize for a four-horse chariot victory in the Athenian games.[44] After the Persian wars, according to Pausanias (6.1.7), the Lakedaimonians became the most ambitious (*philo-timōtata*) of all the Greeks in the breeding of horses, an interest perhaps stimulated by the distribution of captured Persian horses among the army after the battle of Plataia (Hdt. 9.81). But there is no record of any definite Spartiate Olympic victories until 448 when Arkesilaos' first victory initiated the unparalleled string of seven victories out of eight Olympiads, achieved by no fewer than six different Spartiates, which Moretti places between 448 and 420. After 420 no Spartiate was able to compete until Elis had been disciplined at the end of the Peloponnesian war (Thuc. 5.49–50; Xen. *Hell.* 3.2.21–31). But then further victories followed in the first third of the fourth century, not only those listed in Table 4.3, but also one by Eurybiades in the four-horse chariot race for foals in 384 and by Euryleonis, a Spartiate woman, in the two-horse chariot race of 368 (Moretti nos. 396 & 418).

On its own this evidence suggests that participation in competitive horse breeding for chariot racing became more widespread and enthusiastic among leading citizens from the mid-fifth century. How reliably can the evidence for Olympic victories be used as an indicator of more general trends? It is true that some of the details of Moretti's catalogue are uncertain and that Olympic victors probably represent only a small subset of a larger field of competitors in both panhellenic and purely local festivals. There can be little doubt, however, concerning Moretti's overall schema which places the bulk of Spartiate victories after 450; and it is hard to believe that their sudden virtual monopoly of victories in this period does not reflect some significant deep-rooted development. Further evidence of such a development comes from the uniquely rich testimony of the dedication to Athena set up by Damonon which records 47 four-horse chariot-race and 21 horse-race victories won by himself and his son at eight different local festivals in Lakonia and Messenia over a period of at least 12 years.[45] The dedication has normally been dated to the 440s or 430s, but more recently a date in the early fourth century was suggested by the late Miss Jeffery on the grounds of the style of its relief as well as of the letter forms.[46]

If this is correct, Damonon's activities may fit into the context of the criticisms which King Agesilaos II made against those who bred horses for chariot racing (Xen. *Ages.* 9.6), arguing that such studs were a mark only of wealth, not of manly virtue (*andragathia*). Agesilaos' criticism is a clear indication that in the early fourth century many leading Spartiates were exploiting their wealth in this way to enhance their status. This indication is confirmed by the details of Damonon's dedication in which he boasts no fewer than three times that his victories were won with fillies bred from his own mares and his own stallion (11.15–17, 20–3 & 27–9). Damonon's self-advertisement was a particularly blunt version of a practice already developed by Sparta's

Olympic four-horse chariot race victors. The victory dedications of ten of these eleven persons are known to us; and again a change is evident in the period after 450. It was then that Spartiate dedications at Olympia commenced the custom of always including a statue representing the victor in place of the previous practice of dedicating only a model of the chariot.[47] The culmination of this increased emphasis upon the personal prestige of the owner came with the dedications of Kyniska (Paus. 5.12.5; 6.1.6) which included model bronze horses and a statue group with an inscription acclaiming the first female Olympic triumph (*IG* V 1.1564a; *Greek Anthology* 13.16). That she was honoured posthumously with a hero shrine in Sparta itself (Paus. 3.15.1) demonstrates the prestige that chariot-race victories could bring.

Kyniska's involvement in this self-glorification was doubly ironic: first, because her brother Agesilaos had supposedly urged her to emulate male participants precisely in order to discredit the sport; secondly, because he also scorned the making of personal statues as being appropriate to wealth rather than virtue (Xen. *Ages.* 11.7; Plut. *Ages.* 2.2). Behind Agesilaos' criticism of chariot-horse breeding and personal statues there clearly lurked a fear that his rivals might outstrip him in prestige. To this threat he himself responded not by spurning horse breeding but by rearing many horses for the army (Xen. *Ages.* 9.6). He thus took advantage of another avenue for gaining status by horse breeding which had opened up in 424 when Sparta began to use a cavalry of its own for the first time (Thuc. 4.55). By the early fourth century the cavalry, some 600 strong, was a regular part of the army and the horses were provided by the very rich (Xen. *Hell.* 6.4.11).

In view of this evidence for the late-fifth century development of competitive breeding of horses, whether for chariot racing or the cavalry, it comes as no surprise that almost nine per cent of adult Spartiates known to us by name in the period 432–362 have names incorporating the words *hippos* (horse) or *polos* (foal), compared with less than three per cent in the preceding period from *c.* 600 to 433;[48] or that horses were one of the main topics of conversation between Kings Agesilaos and Agesipolis II (Xen. *Hell.* 5.3.20); or that the early-fourth-century (Platonic) dialogue *Alkibiades* I, after highlighting the size of Spartiate estates, should single out their horses for special mention among all the other livestock grazing in Messenia (122D). Isokrates' criticism (6.55) indicates that citizens were still devoting their resources to 'feeding teams of ravenous horses', even when Sparta was in dire straits after the loss of much of Messenia in 370/69. Attitudes and behaviour in late-fifth- and early-fourth-century Sparta are a perfect exemplification of Aristotle's generalisation (*Pol.* 1289b33–5) that among wealthy Greeks the number of horses a man kept was a determinant of social differentiation.

In sum, the evidence for the increased concentration upon horse breeding as a source of prestige suggests that, although disparities in wealth had long been one important factor among several determinants of social differentiation, their significance had increased considerably by the mid-fifth century and continued to develop thereafter. This picture of Sparta's development is similar to the transition from the timocratic state to the oligarchic state described in Plato's *Republic* (547A–555B). Although an artificial construct, Plato's 'ideal type' of the timocratic state is clearly influenced by the Sparta of real life (cf. esp. 547B–D). It is essentially a compromise between virtue and wealth which changes towards oligarchy as new ways of expenditure are invented and wealth and wealthy men become esteemed more highly than virtue and men of merit. Eventually status becomes equated with the possession of wealth. Plato's model of the changes occurring within his ideal timocratic state, based upon his perception of contemporary political realities, provides a valuable corroboration of the developments suggested above.

Spartiate population trends: causes and effects

We are now in a position in the following two sections to investigate two related hypotheses which are suggested by the evidence just considered. The first hypothesis, already suggested by some earlier scholars,[49] is that the upsurge of ambition in horse breeding was connected with the twin processes of decline in citizen numbers and concentration of property. If our picture of the increasing importance of economic stratification from the mid-fifth century onwards is correct, there should be some evidence of parallel developments in these spheres. The second hypothesis, which will be treated mainly in the next section, concerns the significance of Spartiate marriage practices. Given the high degree of association which Goody has detected between economic stratification and several of the marriage practices discussed earlier, it is plausible to suggest that they increased in frequency (and some perhaps even originated) as the fifth century progressed.

These hypotheses fit in well with certain trends observable in Sparta's demographic history. As Figueira has recently pointed out,[50] Spartiate population trends up to the Persian wars appear to have been rather different from those evident from the later fifth century onwards when the citizen body was declining in numbers. Herodotus (1.66) connects the Spartans' aggression against Tegea in the early sixth century with their strength in numbers. The purpose of their campaign was to divide Tegean territory among themselves with the natives as helots. They may have put this into effect in the Thyreatis after winning it from Argos in *c.* 545. In the Battle of the Champions, which was part of this successful campaign, the Spartiates were prepared to face the loss of 300 warriors in a fight to the death against an equal number of Argives (Hdt. 1.82). In *c.* 520 Dorieus, disgruntled that the kingship had been given to his half-brother Kleomenes I, was permitted to take a body of Spartiates with him on his colonial expedition (Hdt. 5.42). This evidence for the period up to *c.* 520 suggests a need for additional land, which may be an indication that impoverishment of poorer families was perceived as at least a potential danger; but otherwise there is no hint that citizen numbers were anything but buoyant.

Forty years later at the time of the second Persian invasion in 4809 there is a hint of a different trend. The *homoioi* were said to number as many as 8,000 (Hdt. 7.234) and the Spartiates despatched 300 men to Thermopylai whom Leonidas was ultimately willing to sacrifice in battle. On this occasion, however, the selection of only men with sons may suggest some concern to preserve lineages from extinction; and, unlike the 300 at the Battle of the Champions, those at Thermopylai were sent not as a lone force but as part of an advance guard over 5,000 strong which was itself intended to be reinforced before it met the Persians (Hdt. 7.202–6). By the later fifth and early fourth centuries the trends evident in the sixth century had clearly reversed. In 425 when considerably fewer than 300 citizens were trapped on Sphakteria and about 120 of them subsequently captured, the Spartans were demoralised and went to great lengths to ensure their survival and return (Thuc. 4.14–41, 108, 117; 5.15). The figures for Lakedaimonian armies show that citizen numbers were in decline; and Aristotle, viewing the whole process with the benefit of hindsight, attests the phenomenon of widespread impoverishment and loss of citizen status (*Pol.* 1270a15–b6; 1271a26–37).

This outline of Sparta's demographic trends appears to indicate that both gradual and dramatic change was involved. The implications of the sixth-century population buoyancy are well summarised by Wrigley's observation that at normal pre-industrial mortality levels there must always be a substantial number of large families if demographic decline is to be avoided.[51] The evidence that for a considerable period during the sixth century this did not lead to such significant poverty as to cause a widespread loss of citizen status and decline in citizen numbers is compatible with the argument above that under a system of universal female inheritance landed inequalities would develop at a comparatively more moderate rate with a lesser degree of impoverishment of the poor. Even under this system, however, in the long run the requirement of compulsory mess contributions meant that Spartiate numbers either had to decline demographically or they would shrink for economic reasons as inequalities gradually deepened and poor families lost citizen rights. By 480 one or both of these processes seem at last to have been happening — Sparta's withdrawal from military adventures outside mainland Greece during the reign of Kleomenes I, *c.* 520–490, might be adduced as further evidence for such a development — and after the Persian wars the decline doubtless continued.

The concentration of property suggested by the upsurge in competitive horse breeding developed, therefore, as part of a gradual long-term process. We should not, however, ignore the role of short-term contingent events which exacerbated the impact of long-term trends.[52] The quarter-century from the second Persian invasion to the battle of Tanagra in 458 (or 457) was an extremely difficult period militarily during which Spartiate manpower is bound to have suffered. After the loss of almost 300 men at Thermopylai, 91 Spartiates were killed the following year at Plataia (Hdt. 9.70). At some time during the 470s and 460s, in addition to a campaign in Thessaly (Hdt. 6.72), the Spartans had to meet two serious challenges in the battles of Tegea and Dipaieis (Hdt. 9.35). At the latter battle they had to fight against great odds — in a single line, according to Isokrates (6.99) — against almost all the Arkadians; although victorious, they may have suffered significant losses. Then in the helot and Messenian revolt of 464–460 at least one contingent of 300 men was wiped out and there was a major battle at 'the Isthmos' or Ithome (Hdt. 9.35, 64). Finally, there were great losses at the battle of Tanagra in which 1,500 Lakedaimonian troops were involved (Thuc. 1.107–8).

In addition, there was the great earthquake that struck Sparta in *c.* 465 which several scholars have seen as a turning-point in Spartan demographic history. It is unfortunate that the sources for this event are all late (Diodorus 11.63.1–2; Plutarch, *Kimon* 16.5; Polyainos 1.41.3; Aelian, *Varia Historia* 6.7) and probably somewhat exaggerated. Diodorus claims that more than 20,000 Lakedaimonians perished; the other sources state that only five houses in the *polis* remained undemolished and Plutarch narrates a suspiciously dramatic story in which the young men (*neaniskoi*) fortuitously escaped the deaths suffered by the youths (*ephēboi*) through dashing out in pursuit of a hare just before the collapse of the stoa inside which they had been exercising. Nevertheless, there remains a core of precise and credible information, namely, the demolition of private houses killing many persons and the deaths of the *ephēboi* whose collective tomb Plutarch actually saw. Since the quake took place during daytime, the persons killed within their houses are likely to have been mainly females of all ages and boys under age seven, since older boys were engaged in the public upbringing and adult males also typically spent their days outside the home (e.g. Xen. *Hell.* 3.3.5; 5.4.28). The *ephēboi* I would interpret, with Figueira, as the 18 and 19 year-olds, rather than the 13–19 year-olds as Toynbee suggests.[53]

Systematic computer modelling of the possible demographic effects of this arbitrary mortality due to war and natural disaster lies beyond the scope of this paper. But with the aid of a plausible model life table, such as the Princeton Model South, mortality level 3, growth rate 0,[54] the likely consequences of the earthquake and of subsequent Spartiate deaths in the helot revolt can be approximately sketched. First, there will have been an immediate drop in citizen numbers. If one were conservatively to add a further 200 deaths in war to the 300 casualties attested in just one engagement, this would have represented 6.25% of the *homoioi* (adult males of age 20 and over), on the generous assumption that overall numbers had not declined from the 8,000 mentioned in 480. Furthermore, the complete elimination of the 18–19 year old *ephēboi* removed a group who within two years would have formed 5.8% of the *homoioi*. Even allowing for the fact that natural mortality would in those two years have depleted some of those killed in battle, that would still have meant by about 463 a loss of *c*. 11.5% of the *homoioi* solely attributable to earthquake and war.

Second, there will have been consequences for subsequent reproduction. One critical factor here will have been the level of mortality among the female population and males under seven. For the purpose of the present illustration this may be set at the figure of 5%. The disruption of this proportion of fecundable marriages would have prevented any return to previous population levels without a correspondingly large increase in the birthrate. In fact, the rate of reproduction is likely to have fallen still further, partly because of changing marriage patterns to be discussed later, but also because of the additional disruption of marriages due to the 500 male deaths in battle. On the assumption, *exempli gratia*, of a standard five-year age difference between husband and wife, with the age of male marriage at 25 and female marriage at 20, the crucial factor would have been the number of deaths among males aged 25–49, since they would have been the partners of women aged 20–44, who will have accounted for over 99% of Sparta's marital fertility.[55] If deaths in battle were spread evenly among men aged 20–49 and the 500 dead represented 6.25% of the *homoioi*, then the level of mortality among men aged 25–49 would have been 8.7%. After the deduction of the proportion of those killed (5%) who would have been widowers because of the earthquake, war casualties would still have reduced the overall level of marital fertility by over 8%, on top of the 5% removed by female deaths in the earthquake. Even allowing for some remarriage of war widows to earthquake widowers, the effect in terms of further decline in citizen numbers is likely to have been considerable. Owing to the significantly greater impact of war casualties upon the reproductive male age groups in comparison with the male population as a whole, fertility levels will have been appreciably lower than those of mortality. This situation would, moreover, have continued for many years because of the depleted numbers of males continuing to reach marriageable age, due to war casualties among the 20–24 year-olds and the elimination of the 18–19 year-olds. Finally, the smaller cohort of females born from *c*. 465 would have attained marriageable age from *c*. 445 onwards, at precisely the same time as the cohorts of 0–6 year-olds reduced by the earthquake, thus further fixing a considerably lower ceiling for future Spartiate numbers.

Besides their purely demographic effects, significant loss of life and subsequently reduced reproduction will have directly affected the distribution of landed property. Many Spartiates will have inherited additional land which would not otherwise have come their way. For example, many persons will have gained larger inheritances, either immediately or later, through, for example, the sudden death of siblings, nephews or nieces who would have been entitled to a share in the parental property or of parents who would otherwise have produced more children. Although citizens of all levels of wealth will have benefited from such random mortality, the overall result will have been increased economic differentiation. Richer persons with deceased relatives will have gained considerably more property in comparison not only with those whose relatives survived but also with poorer beneficiaries, simply because their deceased relatives will themselves generally have had a greater actual or potential inheritance. The likely demographic repercussions of this increase in inequality will be considered in the following section.

Definitive assessment of the relative importance of the long-term structural and short-term contingent factors discussed above is of course impossible because of the paucity of evidence. Even given the moderating effects of universal female inheritance, the gradually deepening inequalities inherent in the system were bound at some stage to reach a critical point beyond which the twin processes of property concentration and impoverishment of the poor became so dominant as to lead to widespread loss of citizenship and a significant decline in Spartiate numbers. Whether that critical point had already been reached before the earthquake cannot be known. Equally, since the number of Spartiate deaths in the earthquake and in warfare is uncertain, one cannot fully assess the impact of their likely demographic and material implications upon the development of Spartan society. What we can say, however, is that long-term and short-term developments pulled decisively in the same direction and that both help us to see why from the mid-fifth century Sparta takes on the aspect of a more sharply economically stratified society.

Changing marriage patterns: causes and effects

It was the increasing concentration of property resulting from these combined factors which, I suggest, enabled and stimulated leading Spartiates to develop their passion for horse breeding; and their very success and the status it brought probably exercised reciprocal effects by promoting an increased acquisitiveness at the expense of poorer citizens. It is in this context that I would posit the increasing significance of the marriage practices discussed earlier (homogamy, close-kin marriage, wife-borrowing, uterine half-sibling marriage and polyandry) which served to retain land within the kin group and to limit the number of heirs. These were all means by which wealthy families could seek to ensure that the property of their descendants was maintained in a society in which their status increasingly depended upon it. These methods could also help poor families to avoid slipping still further into impoverishment in an age in which marriage above one's station is likely to have been harder than ever to achieve.

Other factors may also have contributed to these developments. In some societies increased levels of in-marriage or systematic exchange of siblings between families have been known to occur as a response to a perceived need for solidarity in situations of 'environmental stress'.[56] The crises of the 470s onwards — Sparta's loss of her leadership over the eastern Greeks, serious disaffection in her Peloponnesian allies, an internal threat to her way of life from the regent Pausanias, the helot and Messenian revolt, a dangerous war with newly-democratic and imperialist Athens and, above all, the disfavour of the god Poseidon manifested in the shattering earthquake — may have developed a general sense of insecurity in a universally hostile environment and a psychological need to 'marry-in'. Moreover, close-kin marriage could in part have resulted from attempts to restore the size of the holdings of one's descendants at a time of subsistence crisis, as in areas of early modern Cumbria.[57] The long helot revolt of 464–460 may have caused difficulties for many citizens in getting sufficient produce from their estates, making close-kin marriages appear a prudent means of guarding against future crises by ensuring that existing holdings remained within the kin group and did not have to contribute to the upkeep of spouses (and their children) drawn from outside the kin.

This variety of potential influences suggests that there were strong reasons in mid-fifth-century Sparta for the growth of marriage customs aimed at concentrating property and limiting the number of heirs. These may also have been supplemented by more direct efforts at family limitation within marriage, although the evidence is not clear on this subject. When added to the long-term effects of the inheritance system and the dramatic short-term increase in mortality of the 470s and 460s, these developments are likely to have made a major contribution to Sparta's demographic problems. At this point my analysis differs from that of Figueira, who suggests that Spartiate numbers may have resumed a slow increase after the earthquake until the disaster at Pylos in 425. He doubts whether a fall in fertility could account for the extent of Sparta's citizen decline.[58] I would argue, however, that it is within the context of the *combination* of factors discussed above that the growth of marriage practices which concentrated property and limited the number of heirs became of critical importance in helping to bring about rapid decline. Wrigley has pointed out that at normal rates of mortality in preindustrial communities, a society

> would run into great difficulties if any significant proportion
> of the population was so moved by concern for solving its
> immediate problems of heirship that it kept family sizes
> down to a level that appeared rational in the local context of
> the immediate nuclear family.[59]

Among the Spartiates, a closed elite with virtually no recruitment from outside and an economic qualification for continued membership, the difficulties created by the combination of factors referred to above must have been considerably more serious even than those posited by Wrigley.

These difficulties, moreover, may have been further compounded by higher child mortality deriving from the deleterious genetic effects of increased levels of inbreeding. All human beings carry on average at least one gene (and, more probably, between three and five) with a lethal recessive mutation potentially active in the years up to early adulthood.[60] Since each person has two copies of every gene (except those on the X and Y chromosomes in men), one from each parent, the fact that one gene is non-functional is usually irrelevant if the other copy is functional. If, however, both copies of a vital gene are non-functional, illness or death will normally result. Because each person carries some 10,000 or more vital genes the chances of an unrelated husband and wife both carrying recessive mutations in the *same* gene and both passing that same gene on to their offspring are extremely low. Close kin, however, share a proportion of their genes owing to their common ancestry. When inbreeding takes place, the chances of both parents carrying and passing on recessive mutations in the same gene are very much greater than with marriages of unrelated couples. In marriages of first cousins, for example, the chance of both parents passing on recessive mutations in the same gene to any given child (the coefficient of inbreeding) is as high as 1 in 16 as opposed to approximately 1 in 100 million with unrelated couples.[61] Studies of the children of inbred marriages in modern communities have consistently found significantly increased levels of neonatal, infant and juvenile mortality in comparison with children of outbred marriages within the same communities, not to mention more frequent congenital malformations likely to impair the reproductive capacity of those affected. To continue the particular comparison started above, 'mortality appears to be approximately doubled by first cousin parentage'.[62]

These genetic effects do not in themselves lead to population decline in communities practising a high level of inbreeding, as is demonstrated by the demographic increase of certain closed North American religious sects such as the Old Order Amish.[63] Social, economic and cultural factors rather than genetic ones normally determine the general direction of population trends. Indeed, if population size *is* increasing, the long-term effect of increased mortality among the offspring of consanguineous marriages may be beneficial because recessive mutations will thereby tend to be selectively eliminated.[64] But within a population like that of classical Sparta, which was already declining in numbers for socio-economic reasons and probably increasingly attempting to limit fertility, the genetic and demographic effects of higher levels of inbreeding can only have been harmful. Furthermore, close-kin marriage in Sparta often involved higher coefficients of inbreeding than those of the first-cousin marriages studied in modern communities. In the marriage of King Anaxandridas II to his sister's daughter, which produced the future king Kleomenes I (a man whom some claimed to be mentally unstable: Hdt. 5.42; 6.75; but cf. the counter-arguments of Alan Griffiths in this volume (pp. 51ff.)), the coefficient of inbreeding was double that of first-cousin marriages: one in eight as against one in 16. The same coefficient applied in marriages of uterine half-siblings and in cases in which a sole heiress was married to her father's brother as her next of kin.[65] If, as I have suggested, close-kin marriages increased in frequency during the fifth century, the resultant increase in child mortality is likely to have been even more dramatic than those indicated by modern statistics. This in turn will have made heirship strategies considerably more difficult for those couples who had entered consanguineous marriages because of economic imperatives and for whom the avoidance of too many heirs was a vital objective. The risks of 'overinsurance', resulting in loss of status by the next generation, or of 'underinsurance', causing the line to die out, will have been sensibly increased by the genetic effects of a growth in close-kin marriage.[66]

Our analysis, therefore, has uncovered a significant combination of reasons why the apparently buoyant population trends of the sixth century were dramatically reversed from the fifth century onwards. From this perspective it becomes possible to comprehend the astonishing rate of decline in Spartiate numbers from 8,000 in 480 to a maximum of 1,500 in 371.

The failure of Sparta's leaders

It is clear not only that Sparta's leaders were aware of the problem of the declining number of citizens, but also that they tried to counteract it by stimulating the birthrate in a variety of ways. First, the institutional controls upon the timing of male marriage seem to have been altered. In the fourth century Spartan males normally married in their twenties; but until age 30 they were severely restricted in performing the normal roles of a husband. They could not reside with their wives, meetings were limited and furtive, and they were prohibited from entering the market to obtain their family's household necessities (Xen. *Lak. Pol.* 1.5; Plut. *Lyk.* 15.4; 25.1) These restrictions were, I suggest, survivals from an earlier period when men were not permitted to marry until 30 when they finally left the *agōgē* and became fully adult. At some point therefore the male age of marriage was lowered; and in addition an upper age limit (perhaps 30) before which a man had to get married was imposed (Xen. *Lak. Pol.* 1.6; Plut. *Lys.* 30.7; *Moralia* 228A; Pollux 3.48; 8.40). Compulsory marriage was now enforced by elaborate sanctions against offenders (Xen. *Lak. Pol.* 9.5; Klearchos, fr. 73 Wehrli; Plut. *Lyk.* 15.1–2; *Moralia* 227 E–F). Secondly, incentives were established to encourage greater numbers of sons. Fathers of three sons were given exemption from military service and fathers of four exemption from all public duties (Arist. *Pol.* 1270a39–b6). In addition, older men with younger wives were permitted, and probably encouraged, to bring in younger men for the purpose of procreation (Xen. *Lak. Pol.* 1.8; Plut. *Lyk.* 15.7). Even the practice of wife-borrowing may have originated as a device to ensure that when a couple had decided to have no more children the woman's remaining fertile years should not be wasted.

It is extremely likely that these changes were introduced during the mid- or late-fifth century alongside other reforms intended to combat the growing threat of declining citizen numbers, such as the brigading of *perioikoi* within the Spartiate ranks and the creation of the new military force of the *neodamōdeis* (freed helots). The problem was that these changes attacked only the symptoms of the malaise and ultimately failed. The incentives for fathers of several sons were, as Aristotle pointed out, positively harmful, since they led to still greater division of holdings and consequent impoverishment. The practice of wife-borrowing could, as we have seen, be turned into an instrument of family limitation and property concentration. Even the sanctions against failure to marry could be ignored by a leading citizen like Derkylidas without his forfeiting his prestigious overseas commands.[67]

The one cardinal aspect of Sparta's decline which requires explanation is the failure of Sparta's leaders from the mid-fifth century onwards to tackle not just the symptoms but the roots of the malaise — namely, the economic difficulties facing poorer families. The problem required radical solutions such as a redistribution of land or a restructuring of the economic basis of the common messes and the link between mess membership and citizenship. Such solutions were never embraced and Sparta's leaders chose, whether consciously or not, to take instead the soft options which led to the destruction of her hegemony.

This striking failure is of course partly explicable by the developments already discussed (particularly the concentration of landed property and its increased importance as a determinant of social status, with the associated patterns of attitudes and behaviour to which these gave rise), all of which gave rich, leading Spartiates a vested interest in maintaining the *status quo*. Their importance was still further increased by the impact of the Peloponnesian War and the resulting Spartan empire, especially from *c.* 412 when harmostships and other foreign posts became available in significant numbers for the first time. Continuous tenure of these commands became the ambition of leading Spartiates, according to Xenophon (*Lak. Pol.* 14.4). They were open to men drawn from a much wider age range than the traditional goal of leading citizens, membership of the *gerousia* at age 60 or above; and unlike the *gerousia*, which was an elected body, these commands were usually gained by appointment or nomination.[68] Competition for these attractive positions is likely to have strengthened still further the influence of status-defining wealth and the pressures towards its concentration.

Quite apart from these developments, however, there were two further factors, closely connected with the themes of inheritance and marriage, which merit consideration in explaining the failure of leading citizens to tackle the roots of Sparta's problems. The first was the influence of women, which has been the subject of increasing debate in recent years with different scholars adopting minimalist or maximalist interpretations of the independent role of women within Spartan society.[69] The Spartan *polis* was of course a male club which excluded women from most of its public institutions. Their primary role was, as Plato (*Laws* 805E) observed, to be active in running the home and managing the household. Plato was referring to *married* women, whose personal influence within the household may often have been significant owing to their husbands' frequent absence performing their many compulsory and time-consuming public duties, such as residence in the barracks until age 30, daily commitments in the *gymnasion* and common messes and periodic absence on campaign.

This influence will have been augmented considerably by female ownership of a not insignificant proportion of the property belonging to the household. The woman's position was further enhanced by several of the marriage practices considered above, especially those whose significance increased during the fifth century. Her comparatively late age of marriage combined with the lowering of the male age at marriage made her less unequal in terms of seniority to her husband. Furthermore, not only was she secure from the possibility of the importation of additional wives owing to the practice of male monogamy, but there were circumstances in which *she* could legitimately take on additional partners. When describing the custom of wife-borrowing, the first motive which Xenophon (*Lak. Pol.* 1.9) stresses is that 'the women want to take charge of two households'. Similarly, polyandry should be seen as a practice by which the status of the woman was *underlined*, not undermined. The background to polyandrous marriages must usually have been that the woman was wealthier than any of her male partners and that the sons of the marriage were dependent upon the inheritance of *her* property for the maintenance of *their* status. The development of these marriage practices in the later fifth century, therefore, probably meant an increase in the influence of married women.[70] Studies of classical Athens where women were less advantaged than in Sparta have, nevertheless, noted several examples of female initiative and influence in the affairs of their households.[71] One would expect such initiatives in Sparta to be both more frequent and more effective. Redfield has indeed pointed to the reputation of the women as fierce enforcers of their menfolk's observance of the Spartiate code.[72] The rationale for this was that the public performance of its male members influenced the prestige of the household, and thereby the status of its women-folk, not least because it affected the capacity of the household to contract advantageous marriages for its daughters.

Traditionally, therefore, there was an identity of purpose between the *polis* and the female-influenced household which reinforced official codes of conduct. During the later fifth century, however, this identity of purpose between women and the *polis* may have been seriously weakened by the increasing importance of wealth rather than adherence to the Spartiate code as a determinant of status. This happened precisely at the time when the influence of women was increasing. The two developments were in fact closely linked, since it was greater economic differentiation which led to the changes in marriage practices which increased female influence; and for the benefit of their children women probably supported these new practices which themselves fuelled the growth of economic differentiation. Aristotle was obviously aware of this link when he pointed to the connection between female influence in Sparta and the esteem given to wealth (*Pol.* 1269b23–4). Wealthy women now had both the motive for promoting the interests of their own households to the detriment of poorer families and also the authority to make their wishes effective through their influence upon the behaviour of their husbands. This is precisely what Aristotle complained about in his rhetorical question: 'in the time of their empire many things were controlled by the women; and indeed what difference does it make whether the women rule or the rulers are ruled by women?' (*Pol.* 1269b31–4). In the long run it was the wealthy female descendants of these women who were among the chief beneficiaries of the breakdown of the Spartiate code which followed the decline of Sparta's hegemony. This is vividly illustrated in the description of life in mid-third-century Sparta in Plutarch's biography of King Agis IV (4; 6.4; 7.3–5), in which we see them holding great wealth and wielding considerable informal public influence in obstructing Agis' proposed redistribution of land which would have robbed them of their status and power. In explanations of Sparta's failure to make fundamental reforms in the late fifth and early fourth centuries the role of wealthy women should similarly not be overlooked.

Secondly, I would draw attention to the direct social implications of the new marriage patterns themselves, and in particular the emphasis upon homogamy and the exchange of sons and daughters in the context of wife-sharing and uterine half-sibling marriage. Here we can contrast the situation in modern Greece, as analysed by Ernestine Friedl.[73] As in ancient Sparta, children of both sexes inherit from both father and mother, and daughters typically receive their portion at marriage. But the rules of the Greek Orthodox church and the Civil Code of the Greek state prohibit exchange marriages; and this prohibition 'prevents the transfer of property at marriage from resulting in either a series of equal exchanges between two sets of kin groups or in a regular pattern of circulation through several generations among particular sets of such groups'. In Sparta, which lacked such restrictions, I suspect that the opposite may have occurred, with huge landholdings circulating among networks of wealthy families who became closely associated through exchange marriages. In this way, I suggest, an elite was maintained and the social hierarchy hardened.

The net effect, I submit, was the formation of separate interest groups within Spartiate society. This is our final clue to the failure of Sparta's leaders to remedy the economic problems facing poorer families. The social distance between rich and poor, firmly entrenched by the patterns of marriage which arose out of the need to cope with inheritance by diverging devolution, particularly in the changed conditions from the mid-fifth century onwards, sowed the seeds for the development of two *poleis*, a *polis* of the rich and a *polis* of the poor, as Plato (*Republic* 551D) expressed it in his account of the degeneration of the timocratic state into oligarchy — a description influenced, as we saw earlier, by his perception of contemporary Sparta. As in Plato's idealised state, so also in classical Sparta, the first *polis* had no interest in alleviating the distress of the second. As with the influence of women, we can see these two *poleis* clearly differentiated in the mid-third century, when of the 700 remaining Spartiates there were only 100 with large estates,[74] who throughout Agis' brief reign were implacably opposed to the reforms desired by the other 600 poorer citizens.

Retrospect: Sparta's success and decline

For these reasons, therefore, leading Spartiates ignored the economic problems of poorer citizens, and the unity and identity of purpose among the *homoioi* created by the seventh-century compromise over landownership finally broke down. The rich became richer, while poorer families lost their citizen status and Spartiate numbers continued their rapid decline. After her defeat at Leuktra Sparta had insufficient manpower to prevent the Thebans from liberating Messenia or to regain it afterwards. From being the leading power in sixth-century Greece, a position created and sustained by her large population among whom land was shared with a modicum of fairness such that each family possessed at least an adequate sufficiency, Sparta declined by the second quarter of the fourth century to the level of a second-rate *polis* with a minute citizen body rent by socio-economic divisions. The pattern was set for the abandonment or decay over the following century and a quarter of the key social institutions (the *agōgē*, or upbringing, the common meals and the *diaita*, the simple and austere life)[75] which had been integral to the maintenance of a united body of *homoioi* and had given the classical Spartan state a structure unique in the Greek world. In this long-term transformation of her society we have seen that the roles of the inheritance system and of changing marriage patterns were critically important. In these ways the subjects of inheritance, marriage and demography can be seen to shed light upon both the reasons for Sparta's long-standing success and the problem of her ultimate decline.

Notes

1. E. David, *Sparta between empire and revolution 404–243 BC* (New York, 1981); G.L. Cawkwell, 'The decline of Sparta', *CQ* 33 (1983) 385ff.; T.J.

Figueira, 'Population patterns in late archaic and classical Sparta', *TAPA* 116 (1986) 165ff.; P. Cartledge, *Agesilaos and the crisis of Sparta* (London, 1987), esp. ch. 21, with a convenient analytical summary of the most important ancient and modern interpretations of the Spartan crisis.

2. S. Hodkinson, 'Social order and the conflict of values in classical Sparta', *Chiron* 13 (1983) 239ff.

3. On leading Spartiates' participation in chariot racing, G.E.M. de Ste Croix, *The origins of the Peloponnesian War* (London, 1972), Appendix XXVII; see pp. 96ff., above.

4. Barley is a more reliable crop than wheat, and was consequently the staple cereal for much of Greek antiquity, because it can tolerate a greater degree of drought. The critical minimum amount of precipitation during the growing season (roughly October—May) is around 200 mm for barley, 300 mm for wheat: P.L.J. Halstead, *Strategies for survival: an ecological approach to social and economic change in the early farming communities of Thessaly, N. Greece* (Diss. Cambridge, 1984), Section 2.8.

5. S. Hodkinson, 'Land tenure and inheritance in classical Sparta', *CQ* 36 (1986) 378ff. My views have not been substantially altered by the discussion of landholding and inheritance in D.M. MacDowell, *Spartan law* (Edinburgh, 1986), ch. V for a brief critique of which see my review in *JHS* 107 (1987) p. 231f.

6. See esp. Plut. *Lyk.* 8.3–6; 16.1; *Agis* 5.2–3; also Plb. 6.45.1–3; Justin 3.3.3.

7. E.g. H. Michell, *Sparta* (Cambridge, 1964), 205ff.; P. Oliva, *Sparta and her social problems* (Prague, 1971), 36ff.

8. E.g. J.T. Hooker, *The ancient Spartans* (London, 1980) 116ff.; David (n. 1), 46ff.

9. Herakleides Lembos 373.12 = Aristotelian *Lak. Pol.* fr. 611.12 (Rose): text and translation in M.R. Dilts, *Heraklidis Lembi Excerpta Politiarum* (*GRBS Monographs* 5, 1971).

10. Cf. the case of Lysander's daughters (Plut. *Lys.* 30.6; *Mor.* 230A; Aelian, *Varia Historia* 6.4; 10.15) in which it was not expected that the men to whom they were betrothed would give way to the next of kin.

11. Gortyn Gode 4.37–5.9; 6.9–12: text and translation in R.F. Willetts, *The law code of Gortyn, Kadmos Suppl.* I (Berlin, 1967); Ephorus, *FGrH* 70F149, *apud* Strabo 10.4.20. Note also that the division of inheritance originally privately agreed by the claimants to the estate of Dikaiogenes II in late-fifth-century Athens entailed the same 2:1 ratio of male:female inheritance, since the adopted son Dikaiogenes III was given one-third of the estate and the four sisters shared the remaining two-thirds (Isaios 5.6).

12. The cases referred to are the marriages of (i) Anaxandridas II to his sister's daughter: Hdt. 5.39; (ii) Archidamos II to his step-aunt Lampito: Hdt. 6.71; (iii) Eudamidas II to his aunt Agesistrata: A.S. Bradford, *A prosopography of Lakedaimonians from the death of Alexander the Great, 323 BC, to the sack of Sparta by Alaric* (Munich, 1977), Appendix 6; *id.*, 'Gynaikokratoumenoi: did Spartan women rule Spartan men?', *Ancient World* 14 (1986) 13ff., with a variant genealogy at p. 16. For more detailed discussion of these cases, Hodkinson (n. 5), 400ff.

13. R. Lane Fox, 'Aspects of inheritance in the Greek world', in *Crux*.

Essays presented to G.E.M. de Ste. Croix, eds P. Cartledge & F.D. Harvey (Exeter, 1985), 208ff., esp. 211ff. & 216. Even the property rights of Spartiate women are paralleled elsewhere in Greece: R. Van Bremen, 'Women and wealth', in A. Cameron & A. Kuhrt (eds), *Images of women in antiquity* (London & Canberra, 1983), 223ff., at 231.

14. Hodkinson (n. 2), 254.

15. For example, at funerals, MacDowell (n. 5), 120ff.

16. On uniform equipment, P. Cartledge, 'Hoplites and heroes: Sparta's contribution to the technique of ancient warfare', *JHS* 97 (1977) 11ff., esp. 13, 15 & 27.

17. This initial equal distribution of land is of course an entirely fictional construct whose sole purpose is to depict in sharper relief the different degrees of inequality generated by the two inheritance systems. The figure of 10,000 couples is simply a convenient round number of the approximate order of magnitude for the size of the Spartiate citizen body at its apogee, being the factor of ten closest to the figure of 8,000 *homoioi* put by Herodotus (7.234) into the mouth of King Damaratos in 480. It does not imply belief in the veracity of the figure of 10,000 Spartiates which some fourth-century writers mentioned with reference to former times (Arist. *Pol.* 1270a36–7).

18. The distribution used in this study derives from the work of Professor E.A. Wrigley and Dr R.M. Smith, who have produced a number of distribution tables employing varying assumptions regarding fertility and mortality rates and rising, stationary and declining populations: cf. E.A. Wrigley, 'Fertility strategy for the individual and the group', in C. Tilly (ed.), *Historical studies of changing fertility* (Princeton, 1978), 135ff. = Wrigley, *People, cities and revolt: the transformation of traditional society* (Oxford, 1987), 197ff., Tables 3.1–3.3; R.M. Smith (ed.), *Land, kinship and life cycle* (Cambridge, 1984), 44ff., Tables 1.2–1.7. Table 4.1 represents my own extrapolation from these published tables, which I have extended to cover combinations of surviving daughters as well as sons. This extrapolation has been cross-checked against similar, unpublished calculations made by Dr Smith, then subjected to minor adjustments to ensure complete population stability. The assumptions behind the table have deliberately been kept as simple as possible, since my purpose is to compare the two systems of inheritance, not to construct a hypothetical Spartan reality.

19. It seems unlikely that a system of dowries or marriage-settlements, in which the amount and type of property given to a daughter were not linked to any universal inheritance right, would have produced these effects. In most Greek *poleis* which operated on this basis dowries were not normally given in land: A.R.W. Harrison, *The law of Athens* I (Oxford, 1968), 46f., n. 3; D.M. Schaps, *Economic rights of women in ancient Greece* (Edinburgh, 1979), ch. 6. & App. I. Even if landed dowries had become universal, the consequence would have been increased property differentiation, since the allocation of dowries would not have been as random in its incidence as the variable forces of fertility and mortality which directly determine the inheritance prospects of daughters under the system I have advocated.

20. J. Goody, 'Inheritance, property and women: some comparative

considerations', in J. Goody, J. Thirsk and E.P. Thompson (eds), *Family and inheritance: rural society in western Europe 1200–1800* (Cambridge, 1976), 10.

21. Hodkinson (n. 5), 395ff.

22. J.L. Rowlandson, *Landholding in the Oxyrhynchite nome 30 BC–c. 300 AD* (Diss. Oxford, 1983), chs. 2–3, esp. 155, where she notes that the Egyptians' reputation for casualness about their numbers of offspring may stem from the availability of public land. Contrast the incentives Sparta had to offer to fathers of several sons (Arist. *Pol.* 1270b3–4). The lack of public land in Sparta is evident from Aristotle's contrast (*Pol.* 1272a13–21) between the Spartan and Cretan methods of supporting the public messes.

23. Rowlandson, ibid. 176ff; *id.*, 'Sales of land in their social context', *Proceedings of the XVI International Congress of Papyrology* (Chico, 1981), 371ff., at 377.

24. J. Goody, *Production and reproduction* (Cambridge, 1976), ch. 2, esp. 13ff.

25. *Polyandry* occurs when a woman has more than one husband; *polygyny* when a man has several wives. On the association of polyandry with 'systems in which women as well as men are the bearers of property-rights', cf. E.R. Leach, 'Polyandry, inheritance and the definition of marriage', *Man* 55 (1955) 182 ff., at 185 = *Kinship*, ed. J. Goody (Harmondsworth, 1971), 151ff.

26. Plut. *Lyk.* 15.4; P. Cartledge, 'Spartan wives: liberation or licence?' *CQ* 31 (1981) 84ff., at 94f. Note, however, that a delay in marriage can sometimes have beneficial effects on fertility, since 'women who marry young . . . will be particularly at risk because of the strains already made on their resources during puberty': V. Higgins, in R. Hodges & J. Mitchell (eds), *San Vincenzo al Volturno, BAR Int. Ser.* 252 (Oxford, 1985), 115.

27. On the *kyrieia* at Sparta, Cartledge, ibid. 99f., with references to earlier studies.

28. Cartledge, ibid.; MacDowell (n. 5) 77ff.

29. The account which brings out most clearly the many complexities involved in this controversy is the judicious discussion of Andrewes, *HCT* IV. 111ff., who ultimately reaches his own conclusion only 'with misgiving'.

30. P.A. Cartledge, *Sparta and Lakonia: a regional history 1300–362 BC* (London, 1979) ch. 14; cf. also (n. 1) 409 where he emphasises his view that '*oliganthrōpia* was ultimately a function of the Spartan class struggle'.

31. A.J. Toynbee, *Some problems of Greek history* (London, 1969), ch. 4; Lane Fox (n. 13), 220ff.; Figueira (n. 1), esp. 177ff.

32. E.g. David (n. 1).

33. For my rejection of the historicity of the law of Epitadeus and, more generally, of explanations which place the main decline in numbers only after the Peloponnesian War, see Hodkinson (n. 5), 386 & 389ff.

34. Goody (n. 24), chs. 1–4; cf. I. Morris, 'The use and abuse of Homer', *Classical Antiquity* 5 (1986) 81ff., at 112.

35. Hodkinson (n. 2).

36. Ibid. 243 n. 14.

37. (n. 24) 13.
38. Cf. the references collected by J.K. Davies, *Athenian propertied families 600–300 BC* (Oxford, 1971), xxv–xxvi, esp. n. 7.
39. J.K. Davies, *Wealth and the power of wealth in classical Athens* (New York, 1981), ch. 6, esp. 98ff.
40. This table is based upon the catalogue of Olympic victors by L. Moretti, *Olympionikai, i vincitori negli antichi agoni olympici (Atti della Accad. Naz. dei Lincei, Classe di Scienze morali, stor. e filol.*, Ser. 8, Vol. 8, fasc. 2, Rome, 1959), 53ff.; *id.*, 'Supplemento al catalogo degli Olympionikai', *Klio* 52 (1970) 295ff.; cf. A. Hönle, *Olympia in der Politik der griechischen Staatenwelt von 776 bis zum Ende des 5. Jahrhunderts* (Bebenhausen, 1972), ch. 5, esp. 129f. I have omitted the victory of Diaktoridas in 456 (Moretti no. 278). Moretti suggests that he may have been Spartiate owing to the identity of his name with that of the father of King Leotychidas' second wife. His state of origin, however, is not known and the name is also found in Thessaly and elsewhere.
41. There is some doubt about the date of Lykinos' victory, since Pausanias (5.8.10) states that he won the chariot race for full-grown horses only after one of his animals had been disqualified from entering the race for teams of foals. This race was not introduced until 384. Since most scholars, however, have disputed the authenticity of this story and decided in favour of a fifth-century date for Lykinos' victory, I have adhered to this dating for the purposes of this exposition. For the arguments, cf. J.G. Frazer, *Pausanias's Description of Greece* (London, 1898), I 588; IV 4; W.W. Hyde, *Olympic victor monuments and Greek athletic art* (Washington, 1921), 24 & 259f.
42. I have retained Moretti's original dating for Xenarches' victory. In his 'Supplemento . . .' (n. 40) he subsequently acknowledged the doubts concerning this dating raised by Hönle (n. 40), 154 n. 3. She argued that an earlier date would better suit the context of Pausanias' reference to Xenarches and that, since Pausanias does not state which equestrian event he won, it could have been another contest, such as the horse race, in 428. It is more likely, however, that Xenarches achieved his success in the four-horse chariot race than in any other event because his name stands at the head of a list of known chariot-race victors.
43. Davies (n. 39), 103f.; only for the Olympic games, however, do we possess a usable number of names of chariot-race victors.
44. J.D. Beazley, *Attic black-figure vase-painters* (Oxford, 1956), 369, 'Leagros group' no. 112.
45. *IG* V.1.213; I know of no published translation of this important inscription. I have calculated the minimum period of 12 years by adding the eight victories at the festivals of Poseidon at Thouria and of Ariontia mentioned in ll.18–19 & 24–5 to the four different ephoral years specified in ll.66, 73–4, 81 & 90. One aspect of the uniqueness of the Damonon inscription deserves emphasis. Although L.H. Jeffery, *The local scripts of archaic Greece* (Oxford, 1961), 196 claims that it is 'the crowning example' of a type of local Lakonian inscription of which there are many incomplete examples from the mid-sixth century onwards, it should be noted that none of the victory lists or dedications in her catalogue (198ff.) definitely relates to chariot racing. A number seem to concern

athletic events and of a further ten whose event is unknown (nos. 30, 41–48, 50) only four certainly come from Sparta itself. Evidence that chariot racing elicited forerunners of Damonon's dedication in Lakonia in the period before 450 is at present lacking.

46. For the earlier date, Jeffery, ibid., 196, 201 n. 52, with refs to earlier studies; the lower date is mentioned briefly in *JHS* 101 (1981) 191 and was subsequently argued in more detail in an unpublished paper, 'Lakonian lettering of the late 5th century BC: a reconsideration', which I have been able to consult through the kindness of Professor D.M. Lewis.

47. Chariot dedications of Euagoras and Polypeithes (Paus. 6.10.8; 16.6); statue dedications of Anaxandros and Polykles (6.1.7), Xenarches, Lykinos, Arkesilaos and Lichas (6.2.1–3); Leon (Polemon Periegetes, Müller, *FHG*, p. 122 *apud* scholion on Euripides, *Hippolytos* 231 & Eustathius, *Iliad* 2.852).

48. 25 examples out of *c.* 285 names of Spartiates datable with reasonable certainty in the period 432–362; three out of 110 in the period *c.* 600–433. Statistics from P. Poralla, *Prosopographie der Lakedaimonier bis auf die Zeit Alexanders des Grössen,* 2nd edn, revised by A.S. Bradford (Chicago, 1985).

49. E.g. J. Burckhardt, *Griechische Kulturgeschichte* (Berlin, 1898–1902), IV 102; G. Busolt & H. Swoboda, *Griechische Staatskunde* (Munich, 1920–6) II 662.

50. Figueira (n. 1), 172ff.

51. Wrigley (n. 18), 149.

52. A similar combination of 'raisons accidentales' and 'raisons permanentes' has already been suggested by A. Andreades, 'La mort de Sparte et ses causes démographiques', *Metron* 9 (1931) 99ff.

53. Figueira (n. 1), 178; Toynbee (n. 31), 343ff., esp. 351.

54. A.J. Coale & P. Demeny, *Regional model life tables and stable populations,* 2nd edn (New York & London, 1983), 399 & 449. The South model life tables are extracted from Mediterranean populations, mainly in the late 19th and early 20th centuries (ibid. 12); under mortality level 3 the expectation of life at birth is 25 years for females, 24.66 for males.

55. Despite considerable variations in overall levels of marital fertility, its relative age pattern has been found to be remarkably consistent between widely differing populations: J. Bongaarts & R.G. Potter, *Fertility, biology and behavior* (New York & London, 1983), 22f. The relative marital fertility of women aged 20–44 amounts to roughly 98.7% of that of all women above age 20. In addition there are fewer women in each year class after age 44 than before, thus yielding a figure of over 99%.

56. H. Rosenfeld, 'Social and economic factors in explanation of the increased rate of patrilineal endogamy in the Arab village in Israel', in J. Peristiany (ed.), *Mediterranean family structures* (Cambridge, 1976), 115ff., at 126; J. Okely, *The traveller-gypsies* (Cambridge, 1983), esp. 175ff.

57. M.T. Smith & H. Challands, 'Mortality, marriage and inheritance in Crosthwaite parish, Cumbria, 1550–1660', unpublished paper.

58. Figueira (n. 1), 177 & 180 f. One reason for Figueira's view is the importance he attaches to a putative change in the inheritance system in the late fifth century. According to him (184ff. & 193ff.), the supposedly

traditional life tenancy of a *klēros* was abandoned in favour of partible inheritance and rights of alienation over one's land. For the spurious historicity of life tenancy, however, and the existence of rights of inheritance and of alienation throughout the classical period, see pp. 80ff. and Hodkinson (n. 5).

59. Wrigley (n. 18), 149.

60. N.E. Morton, J.E. Crow & H.J. Muller, 'An estimate of the mutational damage in men from data on consanguineous marriages', *Proc. Nat. Acad. Sci. U.S.A.* 42 (1956) 855ff. I am heavily indebted to Dr David de Pomerai of the University of Nottingham for advice concerning the points in this and the following paragraph.

61. For an explanation of the coefficient of inbreeding, and how to calculate it, intelligible to non-geneticists, C. Stern, *Principles of human genetics*, 3rd edn (San Francisco, 1973), 476ff.

62. N.E. Morton, 'Morbidity of children from consanguineous marriages', *Progress in medical genetics* I (1961) 261ff., at 274. His Table 6 summarises the results of earlier studies.

63. V.A. McKusick *et al.*, *Cold Spring Harbor symposia in quantitative biology* 29 (1964) 99ff.

64. Morton (n. 62), 281.

65. I have suggested elsewhere that the testimony of Aristotle (*Pol.* 1270a26–9) should not be interpreted as evidence for a decrease in such marriages of heiresses in the fourth century: Hodkinson (n. 5), 396f.

66. The magnitude of these risks in conditions of high child mortality is briefly calculated by Wrigley (n. 18), 145.

67. Plut. *Lyk.* 15.7; for Derkylidas' illustrious military career, Poralla (n. 48), no. 228.

68. On the age of holders of foreign posts and the methods of selection, cf. Hodkinson (n. 2), 251 n. 28 & 262f.

69. Minimalist interpretation: Cartledge (n. 26); maximalist: B.L. Kunstler, *Women and the development of the Spartan polis* (Diss. Boston, 1983); Bradford, 'Gynaikokratoumenoi . . .' (n. 12).

70. The position of married women should be contrasted with that of unmarried girls whose marriages may have been subjected to increasing control in the same period as the trends towards homogamous and close-kin marriages developed. This contrast is a common phenomenon in societies with female property ownership; as Goody (n. 24), 21 notes, 'where they are more propertied they are initially less free as far as marital arrangements go, though the unions into which they enter are more likely to be monogamous (or even polyandrous)'.

71. J. Gould, 'Law, custom and myth: aspects of the social position of women in classical Athens', *JHS* 100 (1980) 35ff., at 49f.; Schaps (n. 19), 76f.; L. Foxhall, 'Ownership, property and the household in classical Athens', *CQ*, forthcoming.

72. J. Redfield, 'The women of Sparta', *CJ* 73 (1977/78) 146ff.

73. E. Friedl, *Vasilika: a village in modern Greece* (New York, 1962), 64f.

74. Plut. *Agis* 5.4, following the interpretation of this passage by A. Fuks, 'The Spartan citizen-body in the mid-third century BC and its enlargement proposed by Agis IV', *Athenaeum* 40 (1962) 244ff. = *Social conflict in ancient Greece* (Leiden, 1984), 230ff. Limits of space exclude

discussion of Spartiate demographic history between the loss of Messenia in 370/69 and the time of Agis' reforms.

75. The essential sources are Phylarchos, *FGrH* 31F44 *apud* Athen. 141F–142B; Plut. *Agis* 3.5–6; 4; 6.2; 7.4; 8.2; 10.2–7; *Kleom.* 2.1; 3.1–2; 6.1; 10.4.

5

Spartan Propaganda

J.T. Hooker

Only in a state of very small size and very simple structure could we imagine that 'propaganda' emanated only from the dominant regime and always served precisely the interests of that regime. At Sparta, as in any other society of reasonable complexity, two types of propaganda co-existed and sometimes tended to different, or even opposing, ends. These may be called respectively 'state' and 'non-state' varieties of propaganda. 'State' propaganda was concerned with the well-being and security of the Spartiate class as a whole: the *perioikoi* who lived in the territory of the Spartan state and under its subjection may also have been the beneficiaries of such propaganda, although it was not framed with them principally in mind.

At the heart of this 'state' propaganda lay the Spartan teaching about the origin of the city: specifically the connection of the royal houses with the sons of Heracles. In seeking distinguished founders, close to a god or a famous hero, the Spartans of course resembled other Greeks; their uniqueness consisted in the survival not of one but of two dynasties, occupying no mystical or purely honorific position but performing essential public functions in peace and war. I shall return later to the Spartan kings as projections of 'state' propaganda. Meanwhile it can be observed that the very institution of the double monarchy was productive of 'non-state' propaganda; also that this type of propaganda served the cause of various organs in their conflict with one another.

Although Cleomenes was clearly the most important individual in Sparta between about 520 and 490, we are not well placed to write a connected account of his reign or to analyse his

122

personality with any confidence. Upon Herodotus the character of Cleomenes seems to have made a deep impression, but the many relevant remarks contained in Books V and VI leave us uncertain about the motives of the participants, even when the results of their actions are undisputed. In his lucid paper, Lenschau sets out the principal episodes as follows:[1]

V 39–51   Cleomenes and Dorieus; Cleomenes and Aristagoras.

V 55–77   Cleomenes' part in suppressing the Athenian tyranny.

VI 49–50, 61–64 Cleomenes' involvement in Aegina and his conflict with Demaratus; his disgrace, exile, insanity, and death; a long coda dealing with his war against Argos.

Basing himself in part on Herodotus' own words, Lenschau takes the view that the first and third of these elements are derived from a Spartan source, and one hostile to Cleomenes, while the second is more likely to have originated in Athens, and so *ipso facto* to have been concerned to traduce the Spartan invader. Deeply involved in the third sequence of episodes is Lenschau's so-called 'Demaratus-source', which contributes yet another anti-Cleomenes vein.

Lenschau acknowledges that on occasion Herodotus departs from his sources, and then he is quite capable of uttering a comment wholly favourable to the King; for example when he refers to 'Cleomenes being present in Aegina and toiling for the common good of Greece' (VI 61.1). But I think the truth is more complex than this. Despite the opinion of many modern authors, Herodotus' portrait of Cleomenes as a whole is by no means unflattering; and this would not have been the effect if Herodotus had relied throughout upon anti-Cleomenes sources, only inserting his own comments here and there. In the Dorieus affair, it is Dorieus and not Cleomenes who receives the blame.[2] In his interviews with Aristagoras, Cleomenes is seen in the role of a prudent and far-sighted statesman — and an incorruptible one. And, while of course it is true that Cleomenes resorted to illegal means in ridding himself of Demaratus, we cannot help concluding from Herodotus' narrative that Demaratus contributed greatly to his own downfall. When Cleomenes was away in Aegina, Demaratus stayed at home and 'kept uttering slanders against him' (VI 51); this he did, as Herodotus later remarks, 'not out of love for the Aeginetans but from jealousy' (VI 61.1). Even more irresponsible was Demaratus' desertion of the Peloponnesian army at Eleusis (V 75.1), an act which according to Herodotus led directly to the rise of Athenian power (V 76–77). All the same, as Herodotus is careful to emphasise, Demaratus was a man of parts. He distinguished himself both in thought and in action: above all he had won the chariot-race at Olympia, the only Spartan king to do so (VI 70.3).

The reign of Cleomenes gave Herodotus the opportunity of composing just such a narrative as he chiefly favoured. It began controversially, with Dorieus disputing the right of succession, and ended in madness and suicide, the only events mentioned by Herodotus which corroborate his estimate of Cleomenes as 'insane'. Between that beginning and that end there stretched a career in which success greatly outweighed failure and which saw the prestige of Sparta brought to a very high point.

An arresting story, then; but is any deeper moral to be drawn from it, with regard to the internal history of Sparta? Surely not, as Dickins and others have held, that the reign of Cleomenes was marked by bitter conflicts between the royal power and that of the ephors.[3] Herodotus gives no explicit testimony that this was so; what he does say is that Cleomenes was brought to trial 'by his enemies' *before* the ephors, *and was acquitted by them*! (VI 82.1) If the ephors were convinced by such a far-fetched tale as Cleomenes spun on that occasion, they could not have been anti-royalist on principle. The vital hint is conveyed by Herodotus' allusion to 'the enemies of Cleomenes'. We have heard of no such enemies except Demaratus and his party, and we may fairly interpret Cleomenes' trial as another manifestation of the hostility which kept simmering between the two kings. Herodotus holds that such hostility was bound up with the very existence of the double monarchy (VI 52.8). Possibly so; at least we may be sure that this is the situation in which two mutually-opposed parties, each served by its attendant propaganda, are likely to thrive. And, as we have seen, the propaganda of both the Cleomenes-party and the Demaratus-party has influenced the narrative of Herodotus; it is for this reason that we cannot simply say he followed a 'Spartan source' and leave it at that. Herodotus says enough to make it clear that the two kings differed in their attitude towards public policy, especially foreign policy, but also that there was an antipathy between them. Demaratus had some personal distinctions to his credit, but he could not match the brilliance of Cleomenes on the public stage. Hence the 'jealousy' of which Herodotus speaks; hence also Cleomenes' determination to depose him, once he was strong enough.[4] It seems to me likely that Cleomenes achieved his dominant position partly by the strength of his personality, partly by his actual exploits, but partly through an audacious use of propaganda. It is this propaganda, naturally of the 'non-state' variety, that has left its traces in Herodotus; the propaganda of the pro-Demaratus faction proved less successful, failing to discredit Cleomenes even at his most vulnerable point, his inexplicable failure to capture Argos.[5]

When Thucydides relates the strange career of the regent Pausanias after the battle of Plataea, his account raises a series of notorious historical, and also historiographical, problems (I 128–134). It is a pity that such problems cannot be pursued here, since they go to the root of Thucydides' personality and his methods. Are the accounts of Pausanias and Themistocles biographical 'novellas' in the Herodotean manner? Can their presence be explained purely in terms of the 'structure' of the whole work? Or has Thucydides deliberately selected and manipulated the facts so as to confront a villainous Pausanias and a wise and good Themistocles?[6]

Whatever his motives, Thucydides has constructed a narrative of a man driven by ambition to intrigue with Xerxes and thereby to gain the mastery of Greece. But, although much was reported at Sparta to Pausanias' discredit, no clear proof of his guilt was available 'either to his private enemies or to the city as a whole' (I 132.1). By his use of this phrase, Thucydides introduces the theme of personal animosity which we found to bulk large in Cleomenes' struggles. What is remarkable in Thucydides' account, and what should seem particularly so to those who envisage a permanent state of tension between the ephorate on the one hand and the royal families on the other, is the extreme reluctance of the ephors to proceed against Pausanias.[7] Not even the revelation of some helots that Pausanias had intrigued with them moved the ephors to take action (I 132.4–5). And what Spartiate did not fear the helots more than the Persians? Nevertheless it was only after hearing Pausanias with his own lips indicate his treachery that the ephors decided to arrest him. The very arrest was thwarted by a warning given to Pausanias by a friendly ephor (I 134.1).

But in the end Pausanias was walled up and starved to death, and the oracle told the Spartans to erect two statues where he had died. These statues were seen standing in that very place by the traveller and antiquary centuries later (Pausanias III 17.7). 'It is clear', comments Gomme, 'that the Regent was honoured after his death, and, therefore, that he had strong supporters at Sparta.' One could go still farther and, on the strength of Thucydides' narrative, assume the existence of mutually-opposed parties, even among the ephors; it was only late and with difficulty that the propaganda of the anti-Pausanias party came to prevail.[8]

Two events in the early years of Agesilaus' reign may be cited to show the use of 'non-state' propaganda in the service of individuals, or of competing interests: these are respectively the conspiracy of Cinadon and the conflict between King Pausanias and his enemies. Aristotle mentions both episodes as evidence of the troubles which ensue when political power is concentrated in a few hands and unprivileged persons of ability feel themselves excluded (*Politics* 1306b 31–36). The case of Cinadon is easily brought within the terms of Aristotle's definition, that of Pausanias less so.

Xenophon vividly describes the course of Cinadon's conspiracy (*Hellenica* III 3.4–11): the length of his description may be due to the serious nature of the affair or, equally well, to its providing the material of a readable narrative. As is often the case with conspiracies, the sources have to be scrutinised with special care, because any regime can draw benefit from crying 'conspiracy', from magnifying the danger to the public, and from congratulating itself when the danger has been removed.[9] These propagandistic attitudes on the part of established authority may be matched by seductive slogans coined by the conspirator. Cinadon's slogan as recorded by Xenophon was 'not to be inferior to anybody at Lacedaemon' (III 3.11). These words, in themselves, might point to the personal ambition of a man who followed Lysander's example in desiring to usurp political power. But that is not quite the impression one gets from reading Xenophon. He presents Cinadon as a spokesman for all those classes in the Spartan state which did not share in the political privileges of the *homoioi*: the classes which, in Finley's phrase, formed 'an undigested lump within the system'.[10] Did Cinadon's slogan, then, simply give expression to a point of view held by the immense majority of the inhabitants, constantly frustrated at the inferior status they were compelled to accept? That is how Cinadon himself saw it, and he set himself to exploit the deep enmity which he found already to exist between *homoioi* and non-*homoioi*.[11] On this occasion, the authorities acted quickly and decisively to arrest Cinadon and his associates. Xenophon does not record any riposte the ephors made to Cinadon's slogan; the reason for their success (and it was a complete success) lay in their ability to convince the *homoioi* of a serious danger, which called for a united response.

Two years after the suppression of the conspiracy, Spartan forces suffered a humiliating reverse in the Boeotian campaign, during which Lysander lost his life. When Pausanias the King returned home from the expedition he was made a scapegoat, and was tried on capital charges. He was condemned to death in his absence, and spent the remainder of his life in exile at Tegea (*Hellenica* III 5.25). No doubt David is right to see the trial and sentence as the culmination of the long-standing hostility between the conservative faction represented by Pausanias and the new imperialism of Lysander.[12] (The sympathies of Agesilaus of course lay with the latter, despite the personal differences which arose between him and Lysander.)

Our special interest is aroused by a detail which Xenophon fails to mention. Strabo VIII 8.8 quotes Ephorus to the effect that during his exile Pausanias 'composed a *logos* concerning the laws of Lycurgus'.[13] The word *logos* causes some perplexity. It is commonly rendered 'pamphlet', as if Pausanias wrote a kind of political tract which was taken to Sparta (perhaps after his death) and passed from hand to hand. But *logos* might just as well refer to a 'disquisition' or 'discourse' which was never put into written form. Either explanation raises intriguing possibilities about the nature of political dispute among the Spartiates. The first has a bearing upon the question of Spartan literacy: is it likely that the small, and dwindling, number of citizens ever contemplated, or had need of, such a method of intercommunication? The second implies that persons sympathetic to Pausanias' viewpoint went at least once to Tegea to hear his conversation. But the very composition of the *logos*, whatever form it took, and in particular Ephorus' allusion to it imply that the downfall of Pausanias did not spell the end of the pro-Pausanias faction, despite the ascendancy of the expansionist King Agesilaus and his policies. What, then, did the *logos* contain? Not, we may be sure, a simple apologia, setting out Pausanias' justification for his actions such as he might have presented at his trial. The context in which Strabo mentions the *logos* shows that Pausanias was here concerned with more fundamental issues, particularly the rights of the Kings *vis-à-vis* the ephors. It has been surmised that Pausanias tried to cast doubt on the legitimacy of the ephorate, by questioning whether that institution formed part of the Lycurgan *kosmos*.[14] If that is a correct account of the matter, it finds an interesting parallel in the method adopted by the reforming Kings Agis IV and Cleomenes III in the third century (see below).

In considering the themes of 'state' propaganda at Sparta, we find that these are of two sorts. One was sustained by slogans, which emerged in respect of a particular situation and fell into disuse once the situation had changed. Then there was another, more permanent, type: this enshrined convictions, deeply held by the regime in power and probably by the Spartiate class as a whole, about the image of Sparta which it was thought desirable to project.

The first, more ephemeral, kind of state propaganda may be seen at work in the era of Spartan expansion and again during the Peloponnesian War.

When the Spartans were extending their power in the seventh and sixth centuries, they employed a combination of military force and diplomacy. In the case of states at some distance from their own borders, they needed some more or less plausible pretext for intervention, and this lay ready to hand. Many of the leading states came under the rule of tyrants: a fact which made it expedient for Sparta to pursue an anti-tyrannical policy, justifying her intervention under the pretext of restoring legitimate government. Thucydides gives Sparta the credit for suppressing most of the Greek tyrannies outside Sicily (I 18.1). In writing as he did, Thucydides was perhaps seduced by a seemingly elegant polarity: Sparta, the city which had never known a tyrant, versus the tyrant-ridden cities in the rest of Greece. Sparta's lack of tyrants over a long period was brought by Thucydides into a causal connection with her political stability over a long period; and the latter must be accounted one of the most potent elements in the entire Spartiate legend.

But was Sparta really 'the enemy of tyrants', or did Thucydides mistake a mere creation of propaganda for some underlying truth? Little is known, in general, about Spartan operations designed to put down tyrannical regimes; but Herodotus describes in sufficient detail the intervention in Samos and in Athens to reveal the rationale of Spartan policy. Herodotus' account of the Samian adventure speaks of two possible motives: one political (to help disaffected subjects of Polycrates), one commercial (to avenge the robbery by Samians of valuable gifts) (III 47). No high-minded reasons are adduced for the Spartan action; and we may suspect that whenever the Spartans took steps to suppress a tyrant they were trying to gain advantage from a particular situation rather than giving effect to a settled policy. Suspicion becomes certainty in the case of the Spartan intervention at Athens. Herodotus states that the Spartans first went to depose the Pisistratids in compliance with the Delphic oracle which had been bribed by the exiled Alcmaeonids; and the Spartans themselves professed reluctance, on the ground that ancestral friendship linked them with the Pisistratid house (V 63.1–2). When after some reverses the Spartans at last drove out the tyrants, they found the new regime less to their liking than the old, and proposed to their allies the restoration of the Pisistratid Hippias (V 90–91). So, while it is true that Sparta had never been ruled by a tyrant, it cannot be true that she hated tyranny on principle.

In the eighth year of the Peloponnesian War Brasidas appeared before the city of Acanthus in Chalcidice, in the hope of detaching it from the Athenian alliance. His speech on that occasion helped to attain this end, partly through his attractive personality, partly because 'as a manifesto of professed Lacedae-monian policy'[15] his words fell pleasantly on the ear. The Spartans had sent him, he stated, to substantiate their claim that they were going to war for the liberation of Greece (Thucydides IV 85.1; Brasidas' words echo the motive Thucydides had attributed to the Spartans at II 8.4). The Spartan slogan was not only persuasive in itself (it implicitly ranged the Athenians with Xerxes, 'who attacked Greece with the object of enslaving it', Thucydides I 18.2); it could also be successful in practical terms, as Brasidas proved at Acanthus. It was Sparta's misfortune that after her victory in the war she failed to find an equally convincing slogan to help consolidate the empire she had won from the Athenians.[16]

'State' propaganda of a more permanent kind promulgated three great images of Sparta which had pervasive influence among the other Greeks. The first image is that of Sparta as the leading Dorian city, entitled by right to the hegemony of the Peloponnese. Second we see Sparta as a city where stable government prevailed in surroundings of selflessness and austerity and where nicely-balanced institutions permitted the despatch of public business in a mature and deliberate manner. Third is the image of military prowess: to their training as effective hoplites much of the time and energy of the Spartiates was devoted, and (at least in theory) the habit of obedience acquired in civil life ensured victory in war. Each of these images was made all the more persuasive by the invocation of legend. And 'legend' here must be understood as something alive: not merely an unchanging collection of inherited tales but an organism constantly being reshaped and capable of incorporating fresh elements in response to new situations in which Sparta found herself as her power expanded.

The three images just mentioned are projected forcefully in the poetry of Tyrtaeus and in the legends which accrued about the name and achievements of Lycurgus. These are of crucial importance for the growth of state propaganda, since it was during the archaic period that the main themes of propaganda emerged in a definitive manner. It is also true that the legends cherished at Sparta allowed room for development and enrichment: I suppose that the organic growth of legends continued there until the death of Leonidas in 480, if not later.

Our sources make occasional mention of Tyrtaeus' Athenian origin, but Tyrtaeus in his extant poems conveys no hint of this. On the contrary, he refers to himself as a member of that Dorian race which migrated to the Peloponnese along with the descendants of Heracles: 'Cronus' son himself, Zeus the husband of Hera of the beautiful crown, gave this city to the Heraclids: with whom we left wind-swept Erineos and came to the broad island of Pelops . . . grey-eyed . . . ' (fr. 2.12–16 West). This is the earliest reference we have to Sparta as a city given by Zeus to the Heraclids and Dorians: the word 'grey-eyed' (*glaukopidos*) in line 16 clearly associates Athena in some way with the divinely-appointed migration. The modern term for this migration, the 'Dorian invasion', over-simplifies the ancient belief, since it leaves out of account two vital features: namely that the Dorians came as associates of the Heraclids, and that the latter *returned* to take possession of their rightful domain.[17]

It is interesting to notice that the inventors of state propaganda at Sparta faced two ways at once: they cultivated both the Dorian and the Achaean strain in their inheritance. By their claim that Sparta was the chief Dorian city, they prepared for themselves a title to the high place they occupied among the Dorians from the sixth century onwards. By their insistence on the Heraclid link, they were able to trace back their ancestry, or at least the ancestry of their royal houses, directly to the heroic age. Two well-known episodes attest the continuing importance of the Achaean connection.

According to Herodotus, the attempt to subdue the Arcadian city of Tegea in the early sixth century went seriously wrong; it did not succeed until the Spartans followed the oracle's advice and removed the bones of Orestes from Tegea to their own city. This tale of Herodotus (I 67–8) is a brilliant one; but it cannot be only a tale. On two points he may be misinformed: the reason for the transfer of the bones and the circumstances in which these were brought to Sparta. But we cannot doubt that *some* bones were exhibited at Sparta as being the relics of Orestes, since the Spartan desire to possess them coheres too well with the propagandist movement at Sparta, which sought to base territorial claims on the heroic, 'Achaean' past.[18]

The Spartans' tendency to annex the Achaean past for their own purposes was well understood by Herodotus himself. This fact is demonstrated by his story of Cleomenes who, on approaching Athena's temple on the Athenian acropolis, was told by the priestess that no Dorian might enter there; 'I am no Dorian', he retorted, 'but an Achaean' (V 72.3). The question at issue here is not whether the King ever attempted to enter the shrine, nor whether he uttered such a *mot* as Herodotus relates (of course he was known for his un-Spartan adroitness in speech), but why Herodotus should have formulated his reply in the way he did. The most plausible answer is that his formulation was made under the influence of current Spartan propaganda, which emphasised the 'Achaean' ancestry of the kings of Sparta more than their 'Dorian' affinities. So much is well expounded by J.H.M. Alty; but when Alty speaks of 'the artificial and temporary character of this piece of Spartan propaganda',[19] I must part company with him. For does not the assertion of 'Achaean' ancestry, involving both the recovery of the relics of Achaean heroes and the distinction between Achaean and Dorian drawn by Cleomenes, arise directly from the Spartans' view of themselves which goes back to Tyrtaeus in the seventh century?

An aspect of the Spartan legend which fascinated writers in the fifth and fourth centuries was the long period of stable government which Sparta had reputedly enjoyed. This is not surprising in view of the political discord, or *stasis,* which was endemic in many Greek states; nor is it surprising that in the passage from Thucydides already mentioned (I 18.1) *stasis* is opposed to *eunomia.* The latter term denotes a harmonious way of living rather than a soundly-based political system;[20] but of course Sparta was credited with both these advantages. It is true, as Andrewes remarks,[21] that Thucydides speaks of the political system, not necessarily of a state of *eunomia*, as being very ancient. With this in mind, we may think that the facts upon which Thucydides drew did not differ essentially from those used by Herodotus in constructing his wonderful muddle about the Lycurgan reforms (I 65–66). The difference between the two authors is one of emphasis. Thucydides is not (or is not here) concerned with the details of Spartan political or military organisation or the peculiar way of life of the Spartiates. But such things are of the greatest interest to Herodotus. He, like Plutarch, Xenophon, and most other Greek writers on the subject, attributes many of the distinctive features of Sparta to a lawgiver of genius whom Thucydides, for his part, never names: Lycurgus.

At the beginning of his *Life of Lycurgus* (the fullest source of our information), Plutarch states the difficulties facing anyone who sets out to describe Lycurgus' career. Nearly every aspect of this subject, complains Plutarch, is involved in controversy: not least the time at which Lycurgus is supposed to have lived.

Plutarch, like most other authors, makes Lycurgus travel abroad, especially to Crete, in search of the best laws and customs, and to obtain oracular approval for his reforms. Lycurgus is credited by Plutarch with the redistribution of land and also with the introduction of that austerity for which Sparta was renowned later: he proposed the abolition of distinctions based on difference of wealth. But it is a political reform that Plutarch considers the most important of Lycurgus' achievements: the institution of the *gerousia* of 28 members, to take decisions along with the kings (*Lycurgus* V 6–8). The so-called Rhetra, which Lycurgus received from the oracle, laid it down that the sovereign power should lie with the citizens, who were to be organised according to *phylai* and *obai*; but the citizen body was not to initiate legislation, having the right merely of approving or rejecting what was proposed by kings and *gerontes*.

Plutarch goes on to speak of two refinements of the Lycurgan constitution made by Theopompus: first the introduction of the ephorate, second the insertion of a clause in the Rhetra, empowering kings and *gerontes* to adjourn the assembly if it adopted a crooked motion (*skolian*). Theopompus together with the other king, Polydorus, persuaded the city that this insertion had divine sanction (*Lycurgus* VI).

It is evident that Herodotus did not follow the source used by Plutarch. Despite certain elements shared by them, for example Lycurgus' visit to Crete and the ratification of his reforms by an oracle, they diverge when speaking of the scope of the reforms. Whereas Plutarch regards Lycurgus as one who set the course of Spartan history on the right lines, particularly by his adjustment of the relationship between the assembly on the one hand and the kings and *gerontes* on the other, Herodotus believes him to be a thorough-going reformer, a veritable 'Neugründer des Staates', to borrow Ehrenberg's term. Herodotus emphasises the far-reaching nature of Lycurgus' activity by attributing to him not a *politeia* ('constitution') but a *kosmos*, that is to say the entire way of life, both public and private, to be followed by the Spartiates. And it is true that the Sparta which achieved the brilliant successes of the sixth and fifth centuries was unique among Greek states. Some of her institutions she of course shared with one city or another, but the aggregate of her institutions and customs (what Herodotus meant by her *kosmos*) remained peculiar to herself. We may judge from this fact that there existed an overwhelming reason for those who created propaganda at Sparta to ascribe the instruments of such excellence to the deliberate policy of a gifted individual. Otherwise it would have been necessary to believe that the admired Spartiate *kosmos* had evolved in some haphazard fashion, quite alien to the Spartans' view of themselves.

The *military* aspect of the Spartan legend is naturally of crucial importance, if only because the 'Lycurgan' system was framed with the specific purpose of making the Spartiates efficient in war. 'Efficient' here seems the correct term. No longer was there to be reliance on exhortation, as in the days of Tyrtaeus. Emphasis was placed on rigorous training, physical fitness, and competence in hoplite-combat. Courage and obedience were to be the supreme virtues: the quest for military glory did not occupy an important place.[22]

These attributes of the Spartiate caste were not, of course, wholly the creation of propaganda. It was to celebrate and exploit the most magnificent exhibition of obedience and courage in Spartan history that the arts of propaganda were chiefly deployed. No matter that the occasion was a resounding defeat: the Spartan *system* was fully vindicated by a Spartan army, and a Spartan king, at Thermopylae. We cannot judge from the pages of Herodotus whether Leonidas had mature judgment or was simply obstinate; on the face of it, there seems to be little *military* justification for his decision to hold the pass with his attenuated force.[23] But for the makers of legend the shining deed itself sufficed,[24] and this was fittingly celebrated at Sparta by Simonides, a poet of panhellenic reputation. The surviving fragment of his poem (fr. 531 Page) concentrates upon the person of the King; and his *areta* ('valour, heroic courage') is especially emphasised. The other great Spartiate virtue, obedience, comes to the fore in the famous epitaph on the Spartiate dead quoted by Herodotus: 'Stranger, report to the Lacedaemonians that here we lie, obedient to their commands' (VIII 228.2). Courage and obedience were not only displayed at Thermopylae, but (perhaps even more important from the propagandists' point of view) were commemorated in verse of high quality. It was as well that the makers of propaganda had before them the example of Leonidas and his band, since succeeding events in the fifth century did not always show the Spartan warrior in such a flattering light.

Our sources speak of two occasions on which the traditional Spartan discipline was found wanting. The first of these concerned the Greek manoeuvres preliminary to the battle of Plataea. On giving orders for the army to move by night to a ridge nearer Cithaeron, Pausanias and Euryanax found that one of their officers, Amompharetus, refused to 'flee from the foreigners or willingly to bring shame upon Sparta'; in the end, after a violent quarrel, the rest of the Spartans moved off, leaving Amompharetus to follow — as he presently did (Herodotus IX 53–57).[25] Some 60 years later, when King Agis was leading a Spartan force into Arcadia, a sudden attack by Mantineans led him to order a re-arrangement of the line. Two of his officers failed to obey the order and so put the army into a dangerous situation (Thucydides V 71–72). Thucydides is careful to say that, despite this lapse from the professional standards expected of Spartan officers, there was no shortcoming so far as courage (*andreia*) was concerned (V 72.2). Only once, so far as we know, had that legendary *andreia* failed. When the Athenians made their devastating attack on Sphacteria and accounted for many Spartan hoplites, the remainder declined to die fighting but surrendered, so providing valuable hostages to the enemy (Thucydides IV 31–40). Trenchant comments are made by Thucydides on this event. One is his own, when he compares the plight of the beleaguered men with that of Leonidas (IV 36.3). Thucydides is content to draw the parallel: he refrains from contrasting the devoted bravery of the one force with the cowardice shown by the other. Later he records the astonishment of the Greek world that Spartiate warriors should give up their arms (IV 40.1).[26]

So it was that, partly at least on the basis of propaganda, Sparta acquired her prestige and influence in the Hellenic world. In the mid-sixth century she proclaimed herself the enemy of tyrants, and seems to have been accepted as such. Towards the end of the century she assumed the hegemony of an alliance of states, formed not with an immediate military objective but for political purposes. In 491 her standing was recognised when Athens invited her to arbitrate in the Aeginetan affair. She became the natural choice to lead the allied armies against Xerxes. And when she was at last moved to declare war upon Athens she did so under a new slogan, 'liberator of Greece' — a slogan made all the more credible by the Athenians' conduct towards *their* allies both before and during the Peloponnesian War.

Until the end of the war, the Spartan legend never intolerably outpaced the achievements of Sparta. These achievements were in truth so palpable that (so it was thought) only a city of unique type with unique institutions could have brought them about. In this way, legend and fact gave each other mutual support; legend grew so as to underpin the increasing power of Sparta, while new exploits (such as those of Leonidas and Lysander) nourished the legend. It may seem to us remarkable that the Spartans, and other Greeks too, were so ready to ascribe the Spartan *kosmos* to the inspiration of a single legislator; but this is explained by the predilection of Greek writers for seeing the history of states as a series of interventions by influential persons, not in terms of a gradual progression. But the Spartan legend presents a more surprising feature than this, to which it would not be easy to find an adequate parallel. The propagandists had done their work so well that after 404 the legend took on a life of its own and survived

135

for many years, even when the current behaviour of the Spartans flagrantly contradicted the 'Lycurgan' ideal. The legend operated in two distinct stages. The first stage belonged to the period between 404 and 323, when the Spartan legend captured the imagination of some of the most influential men at Athens. At the next stage, in the third century, the Spartans themselves fell victim to their own propaganda.

It is a commonplace observation that Spartan propaganda was, to a large extent, disseminated at Athens. And the Spartan 'ideal' once had a more practical effect. When the Thirty came to power in 404, they seem to have re-shaped Athenian society, so far as they could, on the Spartan model.[27] The argument in favour of such re-shaping is built up from a number of different observations, ranging from simple imitation of Spartan habits to the outright admiration of Spartan institutions, and even their adoption, when this was feasible. According to this reasoning, not only the five Athenian 'ephors' but the Thirty themselves were constituted on the Spartan model (i.e. 28 *gerontes* + two kings).

Some Athenian authors of the fourth century reveal all too clearly the dichotomy between the earlier, idealised Sparta and the later, debased entity: these include Isocrates, whose bias was violently anti-Spartan, and the pro-Spartan Xenophon.

The attitude of Plato is ambiguous; but he resembles other writers in seeking to dissociate the 'pure' Lycurgan *kosmos* from its regrettable accretions. The ideal city adumbrated by Socrates in the *Republic* has so many points in common with 'Lycurgan' Sparta that the one must have been modelled on the other. But for Socrates Sparta serves as not only a model but a warning. In Book VIII the ideal state is envisaged as suffering a fate very similar to that of Sparta in the early fourth century: the outward forms of the constitution are preserved, but there comes about an inner moral decay which can be traced back to the neglect of 'the true Muse' and the cultivation of gymnastics at the expense of *mousike* (548b–c). In the *Laws* too the Spartan constitution is praised for the balance it holds between despotism and unrestrained democracy; yet the society of the Spartiates as a whole lies open to the criticism made of it in the *Republic,* namely that it is an armed camp, not a community of citizens (666e).

Aristotle is less prone than Plato to believe that there ever was a 'pure' Lycurgan *kosmos.* Only for one reason does the activity of Lycurgus win his approval: that the lawgiver did after all make extensive provision for the citizens' education. Aristotle teaches that a person becomes good as a result of proper training and that such training can be imparted only by the state. Sparta is practically the only city known to Aristotle which imposes such a regimen as a matter of policy (*Nicomachean Ethics* 1180a, *Politics* 1337a); and to this extent it is praiseworthy. But as a result of the long analysis of the Spartan constitution he conducts in the *Politics* (1269a–1271b), Aristotle concludes that the customs which have grown up at Sparta are inimical to good government. He sees the Spartan decline of the fourth century as the direct and necessary outcome of Lycurgus' legislation, particularly that relating to the ownership and alienation of land. And in organising the state along certain lines with the sole intention of creating an efficient war-machine, the lawgiver certainly enabled Sparta to win battles, but left her unfitted to exercise her hegemony in a manner both just and beneficial to herself.[28]

It would be difficult to find two authors more dissimilar than Isocrates and Xenophon. Yet from their opposing points of view they both attest the abiding strength of the Spartan legend. Xenophon makes no secret of his partiality towards Sparta, but he is not the uncritical admirer of everything Spartan that his biography of Agesilaus might lead one to suppose. It is rather that he cannot help contrasting the present actions of Sparta with the ideal she formerly professed. In his narrative in the *Hellenica*, Xenophon regards the year 382 as the turning-point. It was then that the Spartans seized the acropolis at Thebes, contrary to international law as enshrined in the Peace of Antalcidas, and in doing so they committed an act which (in Xenophon's view) led directly to their downfall eleven years later (V 4.1). A similar sense of disillusionment explains the apparent contradiction in Xenophon's *Constitution of the Lacedaemonians*. This work, in fact, has nothing to say about the 'constitution', except incidentally; it is, rather, a paean of praise in 13 chapters for the whole Lycurgan system. The harsh indictment in chapter 14 is all the more telling. 'It is evident', says Xenophon, that the Spartans 'obey neither the god nor the laws of Lycurgus': their departure from the Lycurgan way is shown principally by the corruption and avarice of the Spartan harmosts in the years following Lysander's victory.

The case of Isocrates is more curious and more complex. There would be no difficulty if the *Panegyricus* were the only political discourse of his to have survived. In this work, two of the leading motifs of Isocrates' thinking, *eunoia* ('good will') and *homonoia*

137

('concord'),[29] are deployed to a single end: the winning of support for a panhellenic expedition against Persia. Athens is the only possible leader of such an expedition. Her mirror-image is Sparta, whose deeds do not match her reputation, although she *is* to be commended for having expelled the tyrants. But the ignoble use to which she has recently put her power makes her unworthy to share with Athens the leadership of the Greeks. Isocrates devotes as much space to *exempla* drawn from the mythical past as to contemporary events. The Athenian legend, no less potent than the Spartan, was founded on autochthony and drew its strength from her early reputation as a city of refuge and from her achievements under Theseus. When the same Isocrates later wrote his *Archidamus*, purporting to be a speech by Agesilaus' son, he again demonstrated the persuasiveness of legend. *This* time the legend which recounted the partition of the Peloponnese was invoked to validate Sparta's claim on Messenia. I see no reason to doubt Isocrates' sincerity either when he wrote the *Panegyricus* or when he wrote the *Archidamus*; between the two occasions, the Spartan power had been broken, and the principal enemy in the Athenians' eyes was now Thebes. But our concern here is not with the shifting alliances of the fourth century but with the strength of propaganda. Only by admitting the hold which *ta mythode* had taken on Isocrates' mind can we explain the volte-face at the end of his last discourse, the *Panathenaicus*.[30] No doubt it was a clumsy device to introduce a pro-Spartan pupil to puncture some of the more pretentious claims advanced earlier on behalf of Athens; but Isocrates would hardly have resorted to the device at all unless the Spartan legend had entered deeply into his consciousness. It is worth noting that one of the Spartan virtues extolled by the pupil (ch. 217) is *homonoia*: the 'concord' within a state, which propagandists attributed (unjustifiably) to Sparta.

The Spartans themselves, or at least some of them, appealed to the Lycurgan system during the revolutions of the third century. The first of these comprised two closely-linked reforming movements initiated respectively by King Agis IV and, after his death, by Cleomenes III. Assuming that a broadly accurate account can be elicited from Plutarch's *réchauffé* of Phylarchus,[31] we can see to how great an extent the Lycurgan legend persisted in Hellenistic Sparta. The reforms of Agis promised nothing new but, so far as they went, marked a reversion to the Lycurgan system. His chief opponent was the other king, Leonidas II; and, according to Plutarch, both kings appealed to the institutions of Lycurgus, Agis contending that they favoured his reforms, Leonidas that they did not (*Agis* X 1–3). After Agis had been put to death by his enemies before he could put his reforms fully into effect, Leonidas' son Cleomenes III prescribed different remedies from those laid down by Agis. Above all he maintained that the power of the ephors had increased intolerably. He took the view that the Lycurgan *agoge* must be restored and the ephorate abolished. Since there were two theories about the origin of the ephorate, some attributing it to Lycurgus, others to a king who reigned subsequently, it was imperative for Cleomenes to adopt and justify the latter view. In the event, Cleomenes forcibly suppressed the ephorate, brought back Lycurgus' physical training and common messes, and imposed a redistribution of wealth and of land (*Cleomenes* XI 1–2). Plutarch remarks that the brilliant military victories shortly afterwards won by Cleomenes were ascribed to the resumption of the old virtues of bravery and obedience in conformity with the restored Lycurgan system (*Cleomenes* XVIII 4).[32]

The other revolution in the history of independent Sparta, which was now coming to an end, was fomented by the enigmatic figure of Nabis. It is hard to form a coherent picture of his activity because of the hostile and fragmentary nature of the sources; but he seems to have followed in Cleomenes' footsteps by proclaiming, in his turn, adherence to the Lycurgan system.[33]

The extinction of the city as an autonomous entity in the second century by no means marked the last gasp of the Spartan legend. The outward *forms* of the ancestral way of life were preserved with enthusiasm and elaboration in the Roman period; and, as for the *spirit* of the Lycurgan system, this may not even now be completely dead.

Notes

1. T. Lenschau, *Klio* 31 (1938), 412–29.

2. As R.W. Macan points out, *Herodotus: the fourth, fifth, and sixth books* II (London, 1895), 85. But he should not have added, 'the desire to blacken Kleomenes has led to a *non sequitur*: the person who comes worst out of this story is Dorieus'. There is no such desire, and the *non sequitur* is imaginary. The web of motives underlying Dorieus' expeditions is

examined by A. Schenk von Stauffenberg, *Historia* 9 (1960), 181–215, esp. 182–84.

3. E.g. G. Dickins, *JHS* 32 (1912), 1–42, esp. 27.

4. I accept the arguments presented in P. Carlier's paper, *Ktema* 2 (1977), 65–84. We all know that Herodotus carefully set out the privileges of Spartan kings (VI 56–60), and a valuable list it is; but to appreciate the influence of any particular king we have to consider his personality and (as I would hold) the strength of his propaganda, as well as his theoretical rights: cf. P. Cloché, *LEC* 17 (1949), 113–38, 343–81; C.G. Thomas, *Historia* 23 (1974), 257–70; G.E.M. de Ste Croix, *The origins of the Peloponnesian War* (London, 1972), 149–51.

5. So it is wrong to speak of a sweeping *damnatio memoriae* received by Cleomenes, as P. Cartledge does, *Sparta and Lakonia* (London, 1979), 151. The Spartans exculpated Cleomenes, attributing his delirium to strong drink: is this consistent with a 'sweeping *damnatio memoriae*'? (True to his own beliefs, Herodotus sees a divine hand at work, punishing Cleomenes for his treatment of Demaratus, VI 84.3.)

6. Sound arguments in favour of the last supposition are advanced by H. Konishi, *AJP* 91 (1970), 52–69. See also A. Lippold, *RhM* 108 (1965), 320–41 and P.J. Rhodes, *Historia* 19 (1970), 387–400.

7. It is mainly for this reason that I cannot follow certain authors in seeing Pausanias' later career in the light of a conflict of political ideologies: e.g. H. Landwehr, *Philologus* 49 (1890), 493–506; J. Wolski, *Eos* 47 (1954), 75–94; A.Ye. Parshikov, *VDI* 103 (1968), 126–38; A.S. Schieber, *SCI* 4 (1978), 1–9.

8. Among powerful instruments of such propaganda must be reckoned the letters which Thucydides quotes as having passed between Pausanias and the Persians. That would hold true whether the letters were genuine or not: on the question of their authenticity cf. Lippold (n. 6), 321–34.

9. It is true that the regime in question, namely Agesilaus and (some of) the ephors, could have been confirmed in their assessment of the danger by the perennial fear of a helot rising: R. Vattuone, *RSA* 12 (1982), 19–52, esp. 52. Xenophon's account offers no support for L.G. Pechatnova's contention that the conspiracy marks an advanced stage of social disintegration at Sparta: *VDI* 168 (1984), 133–40.

10. M.I. Finley, *The use and abuse of history* (London, 1975), 171.

11. E. David, *Athenaeum* n.s. 57 (1979), 239–59, esp. 252.

12. E. David, *PP* 34 (1979), 94–116.

13. 'Concerning' (*peri*), not 'against' (*kata*), must be the correct reading for the reasons put forward by David (n. 12), 95–8.

14. David (n. 12), 112–15.

15. G. Grote, *A history of Greece* VI (London, 1884), 179.

16. Cf. M. Clauss, *Sparta* (Munich, 1983), 62–3.

17. In my own view, the insistence on the theme of a 'return' is one of the factors which show the entire migration to have been created and sustained by propaganda.

18. Cf. G.L. Huxley, *GRBS* 20 (1979), 145–8. The parallel tradition concerning Orestes' son Tisamenus is examined by D.M. Leahy, *Historia* 4 (1955), 26–38.

19. *JHS* 102 (1982), 1–14 (p. 13). On this episode see also D. Musti in *Le origini dei Greci: Dori e mondo egeo* (ed. Musti) (1985), 66–7 (n. 12).

20. A. Andrewes, *CQ* 32 (1938), 89–102.

21. Andrewes (n. 20), 102.

22. Cf. Finley (n. 10), 172.

23. In seeking a motive for Leonidas' decision, it seems we have to choose between (i) simple incompetence, (ii) good military sense, and (iii) deliberate sacrifice of a small number for the Spartan and allied good; of course neither (i) nor (ii) is, by itself, incompatible with (iii). Cf. A. Dascalakis, *SC* 6 (1964), 57–82 and J.A.S. Evans, *GRBS* 5 (1964), 231–7.

24. Cf. Clauss (n. 16), 37.

25. How and Wells explain the narrative in a different way, as follows. 'The story of Amompharetus reads like a camp tale. It is no doubt a fact that he remained behind with a detachment; it is very possible that in a council of war he opposed the plan of retreat. But the whole scene here described is opposed to the high repute of Spartan discipline, and the maxim that it is a disgrace to retreat before the enemy is as mythical as "the Guard dies but never surrenders". Probably he was left behind with a rear-guard to cover the delayed retreat.' But the powerful motive impelling Herodotus to describe the events in such detail was exactly this: that you did not *expect* a Spartan officer to disobey his superior — hence the bewildered astonishment of Pausanias! And, strangely enough, 'maxims' and 'myths' do play a large part in determining human behaviour: a point which Herodotus understood better than some of his critics.

26. On the 'belle mort spartiate' see especially N. Loraux, *Ktema* 2 (1977), 105–20.

27. D. Whitehead, *AS* 13–14 (1982–3), 105–30.

28. On Aristotle's treatment of Sparta the good paper of E. David, *AS* 13–14 (1982–3), 67–103 should now be consulted.

29. J. de Romilly, *JHS* 78 (1958), 92–101.

30. Cf. F. Zucker, *VSAW* 101 (1954), 13–17.

31. T.W. Africa, *Phylarchus and the Spartan revolution* (Berkeley, 1961); nor, of course, is Phylarchus the sole source, cf. A. Fuks, *CQ* n.s. 12 (1962), 118–21.

32. On Spartan propaganda and the redistribution of land, cf. G. Marasco, *Prometheus* 4 (1978), 114–27.

33. Cf. J.G. Texier, *Nabis* (Paris, 1975), 33.

6

Spartan Religion[1]

Robert Parker

'Those who honour the gods most finely with choruses
are best in war' ('Socrates' fr. 3 West).

Does an essay on 'Spartan religion' deserve a place in a volume
devoted to the 'success of Sparta'? One needs first to show that
there was something distinctive about Spartan religious beliefs
and practices. Of course, the cults of any one Greek state differed
in countless particulars from those of any other, but superficial
divergences may cover similarity at a deeper level. How
significant is it that when a Spartan spoke of 'the two gods' he
meant Castor and Pollux, whereas an Athenian was referring to
Demeter and Persephone? The Dioscuri lived close to Sparta at
Therapne, while Demeter's chief contact with life on earth had
been a few miles from Athens at Eleusis: so both the Athenian
and the Spartan were appealing to the same implicit concept of
privileged local access to Olympus.

Even at a more superficial level, more in Spartan religion
appears as Greek than as distinctively Spartan. It emerges, for
instance, from a famous inscription, in which one Damonon lists
his own and his son's many victories, that in the fifth century
there were nine distinct festivals in Laconia and Messenia that
included competitions in athletics and horse-racing. Laconia had
evidently been deeply affected by the panhellenic movement of
muscular paganism.[2] Again, one of the three great festivals of
Sparta itself, the Carneia, was one shared by most Dorian states;
and it can come as a surprise to realise that Athena, the familiar
'city-holding' goddess of the Athenians, performed the same
office from the acropolis of Sparta. It seems that the most we can

hope to discover is a distinctive set of Spartan emphases within the religion common to all Greece.

How is the Spartan mark to be identified? It is almost inevitable, explicitly or implicitly, to draw a contrast with the other state that we know best. Of course, Spartan religion may differ from that of Athens without being unique in the Greek world. But we cannot hope to discover absolutely unique features, when so little is known of the religion of most of the 158 Greek states recognised by Aristotle. It is scarcely possible to make a systematic comparison between Spartan religion, seen as a connected body of beliefs and practices, and that of, for instance, another Dorian or Cretan state. But it is still worth showing that Sparta differed in certain respects from Athens even if we may suspect that it differed much less from, as it might be, Lyttos.

A regional study should start from the organisation of religious life in the city. What is most conspicuous in Sparta is the old-fashioned predominance of the kings. According to Xenophon, Lycurgus prescribed that the king 'should make all the public sacrifices on behalf of the city, as being descended from a god', and should act on campaign as 'priest towards the gods'. Aristotle confirms that 'dealings with the gods are assigned to the kings'. At Athens too, the 'king-archon' organised 'almost all the ancestral sacrifices'; but while the king-archon had become no more than an annually elected functionary, the ritual responsibility of the Spartan kings was still associated with political power. (But we can only guess whether, in consequence, the kings had any special authority in religious interpretation or jurisdiction.) Much of Herodotus' account of the kingship is taken up by their religious privileges: he mentions tenure of two appropriate priesthoods, of Zeus Lakedaimon and Zeus Ouranios (sovereignty in Sparta and sovereignty at large, we might gloss these titles); unlimited rights of sacrifice on campaign; places of honour, precedence and double portions at all public sacrifices and competitions; free victims to offer to Apollo twice monthly (as personal offerings, no doubt, distinct from the public sacrifices); perquisites of real value, the skins and (on campaign) backs of all animals sacrificed; and a special relationship with Apollo of Delphi. It is clear from this meticulous enumeration that religious privilege was one of the most important expressions of royal prestige.[3]

There must have been other priests too, even though none is certainly attested before the Roman period. The kings could not have conducted the day-to-day business of a great sanctuary such as the Amyclaeum, and by specifying the two priesthoods that the kings held Herodotus clearly implies that others existed too. There is some, very questionable, evidence that Spartan priests received unusual honours in death,[4] none that they exercised special powers in life. At least one competition, the Gymnopaediae, seems to have been under the administration of the ephors, much as in Athens the ancestral sacrifices were supplemented by many popular new festivals not controlled by the king-archon. How far this diffusion of religious responsibility had gone in Sparta it is impossible to tell. The kings retained their privileges at such competitions, even if freed from duties.[5]

Further details of organisation and finance are very uncertain. 'The cicada is a Spartan, eager for a chorus', says Pratinas: everywhere in the sources we hear of competing choruses, but nowhere is it stated explicitly how the competitions were organised. In a fragmentary commentary on the choral poet Alcman we seem to find references to a chorus of 'girls of Pitana' — a division by obe (village) — but also of 'girls of the Dymanes' — a division by Dorian tribe. The great festival of the Carneia was celebrated at least in part by 'phratries'. We cannot, therefore, identify any single typical mode of participation in public rites.[6] Nor do we know how the honourable and demanding duties of organising the choruses were assigned.[7]

Sparta's distinctive social organisation intruded on private religious practice with the requirement that any Spartiate who made a sacrifice should share the meat with his mess-companions.[8] An Athenian would probably have treated relatives and friends of his own choice. With this restriction, though, the Spartiate could make sacrifices in his own home and dedicate offerings to the gods on his own behalf. And it is interesting that though festivals of the obes, tribes and other sub-groups are not attested — perhaps merely by chance — in the classical period,[9] there is some evidence for cults connected with particular families or other hereditary associations. The Talthybiadae, the hereditary guild of heralds, must surely have tended the shrine of Agamemnon's herald Talthybius, and it may possibly have been the similar guild of chefs who served, less gloriously, Matton and Keraon, 'Kneader' and 'Mixer'. Such occupational cults were perhaps special cases, but Herodotus also mentions that the mysterious clan of the Aegeidae had a shrine of the Erinyes of Laius and Oedipus, their ancestors.[10] To this extent religion seems to have resisted that undercutting of kinship ties which the system of shared messes sought to achieve.

What of the other inhabitants of Laconia? One might have predicted that the religious life of agricultural helots would differ significantly from that of slaves in other Greek states. The religion of the chattel-slave, who shared his master's house, was largely conducted on the fringes of his master's. The helot had his own hearth, and lived amid other helots of the same nationality who also had their own hearths. But all that is certainly known is that helots enjoyed certain rights of sanctuary, and that at one festival, the Hyacinthia, masters 'entertained their own slaves'; and both these details have exact parallels in the life of chattel-slaves.[11] We hear nothing of shrines or festivals of the helots, unless it was they who worshipped 'Kneader' and 'Mixer',[12] and (with the possible exception of the wet-nurses involved in the 'Nursling' ceremonies)[13] we do not find them participating actively in the Spartan festivals. If they did take part, it may have been under compulsion and to their shame. According to Plutarch, helots were forced, on what occasions he does not say, to perform 'ignoble and ridiculous songs and dances'.[14]

The *perioikoi*, by contrast, evidently had their own shrines, festivals, competitions and oracles.[15] Interestingly, the gods who dominate Spartan religion — Artemis, the Dioscuri, Poseidon and, above all, Apollo — are also prominent among the *perioikoi*, and 'hero-reliefs' too are widely distributed throughout Laconia. Thus the religious evidence supports the view that the *perioikoi* took their masters as their models, or at least did not rebel from them culturally.[16] A fragment of the distinguished Spartan antiquarian Sosibius perhaps shows them participating in one procession in Sparta itself. At the Promacheia, an otherwise unknown festival, 'the people from the countryside are garlanded with reeds or reed-crowns, while the boys undergoing Spartan training follow ungarlanded'.[17] A sharp distinction is drawn, by the difference in garlands, between the 'people from the country', probably *perioikoi* rather than helots, and the future Spartiates. In just the same way the Athenian metics participated in the Panathenaic procession, conspicuous in purple amid the white-clad citizens. The inferior outsider is both temporarily admitted, and at the same time marked off as distinct. If this interpretation is sound, the *perioikoi* will have shared Spartan rites only occasionally, and on sufferance. They were probably admitted to the Promacheia, a war-festival to judge from its name, in acknowledgement of their contribution to the Spartan army.

If we turn from religious organisation to the cults themselves, wholly distinctive phenomena remain elusive. One can point to several features that are thoroughly in place in Spartan society, but would not be inconceivable elsewhere. Spartan gods tended to be armed. The Spartiate who looked up at the colossal archaic statue of Apollo at Amyclae, 45 feet high and doubtless the most sacred object in all Laconia, saw there the image of a supernatural warrior, with bow in one hand, spear truculently raised in the other. This statue had a twin at Thornax, just north of the city. And the 'armed Aphrodite' of the Spartans was notorious. But early Greek cult-statues often bore weapons, as did their oriental models, and it was perhaps conservatism as much as militarism that made the Spartans slow to disarm their gods.[18] Even in Athens, in the fifth century, Phidias designed a giant warrior Athena for the Acropolis: the tip of her spear and the crest of her helmet were visible as one sailed in from Sunium.[19]

The military-sounding Promacheia ('before battle' festival? festival of 'front-line fighters'?) has already been mentioned. We hear too of a procession to the temple of Athena by warriors under arms; and the great festival of the Carneia evoked the myth of the return of the Heraclidae, the Dorian 'great trek', and was described by Demetrius of Scepsis in the second century BC as an 'imitation of military life'.[20] But the same festival of the Carneia included a musical and athletic competition of familiar pan-hellenic type; and the ethos of many Spartan festivals seems to have been closer to a *fête champêtre* than to the parade of tanks in Red Square. 'The *kopis* is a special form of dinner' (in Sparta):

> When they hold a *kopis*, they make tents beside the god's temple; in these they put coverings (*stibades*) of wood, and on these they lay rugs. They feast their guests as they lie on these, not just people from Laconia but strangers who are visiting.

There follow details of the menu at a *kopis*, which formed a part of several festivals. At the Hyacinthia, 'the whole city is full of movement and delight at the spectacle'.[21] Some of the predictable ritual concomitants of militarism are absent from Sparta. Ares has no unusual prominence,[22] Heracles, the Dorians' warlike ancestor, is astonishingly obscure in cult, and it was the

Athenians and not the Spartans who honoured their war-dead with elaborate public rites.[23]

Two forms of cult are prominent in the archaeological remains of Laconia; and yet it proves difficult to associate them closely with any distinctive feature of Spartan society. Dedications to the Dioscuri are extremely common; they have their own characteristic iconography and symbols. There is, too, abundant literary evidence for the popularity of these 'stewards of spacious Sparta'.[24] On comparative grounds, scholars have often associated the twin sons of Zeus with the two Zeus-descended kings of Sparta. A detail given by Herodotus confirms that such a symbolic connection was sometimes made: if only one king went to war, only one son of Zeus accompanied the army (in effigy, we presume). And the Spartans believed that their dual kingship had its origin in a pair of twins.[25] But there is no reason to seek the basis of the cult's appeal in this occasional association. When sacrificing to the Dioscuri, Spartans are much more likely to have thought of their excellence in young men's pursuits, athletics, horsemanship, warfare and, of course, rape.[26] Even to make the Dioscuri gods of the young Spartiates is perhaps too narrow. Miraculously, they still lived in Therapne on alternate days,[27] and any inhabitant of Laconia might turn to powers who were so great and yet so close to hand.

The 'hero reliefs' have long been among the most conspicuous and most enigmatic Laconian artifacts, as well as among the ugliest works of Greek art.[28] The indispensable element is a seated male, who holds a wine-cup. A snake, sometimes bearded, may be present, and a female is often seated by the male or stands before him. Minuscule worshippers sometimes approach the heroic couple. A long-standing dispute about their function was, it seems, finally resolved when about a thousand terracottas of related type were discovered in the 1950s at a shrine in Amyclae.[29] This fine abundance proves that they are not funerary reliefs marking the graves of the 'heroised dead', but votive offerings dedicated in the shrines of heroes, like the 'heroic meal' reliefs found in the rest of Greece. The same excavation showed for the first time what kind of hero might receive such gifts: the Amyclaean shrine almost certainly belonged to none other than Agamemnon and his Spartan consort Alexandra/Cassandra. The Spartans also worshipped historical figures, such as Chilon the ephor, Alpheios and Maron, the two bravest victims at Thermopylae, and from the more distant past their pseudo-historical lawgiver Lycurgus. Such heroisation for patriotic service is perhaps something distinctively Spartan, at least in its extent.[30] But the new find proves that the hero-reliefs could equally honour heroes of the mythological period, as they were worshipped in Attica and the rest of the Greek world. One may remember that the Spartans 'brought home the bones of Orestes', and of Tisamenus, tended a shrine of Agamemnon's herald Talthybius, and worshipped Menelaus and Helen in a large precinct with honours not heroic but divine.[31] Possibly they were distinctive in the degree to which they picked out their own local heroes for high honour, and even adopted as Spartans figures such as Agamemnon and Orestes who were originally domiciled elsewhere. Spartan hegemony was thus seen to have begun early, and gloriously. But few Greek states ever neglected a chance of emphasising or creating a local association with prestigious panhellenic myth.

None the less, certain features of Spartan ritual life do perhaps reflect the distinctive Spartan ethos. The first has been much discussed,[32] and can only be touched on here. Sparta was the only city of mainland Greece in which an elaborate initiatory system survived, adapted to new needs, and adolescents of both sexes accordingly had a particularly prominent role in the city's rites. The public festivals could become, as it were, public examinations at which the rising generation were tested in their rough skills. The Spartan ephebe was expected in everyday life to steal food, at the risk of a whipping if caught. Periodically, therefore, a display of such 'theft amid blows' was given at the altar of Artemis Orthia. Such was the simple origin of the infamous 'competition in endurance' of the Roman period, at which boys allowed themselves to be whipped to death, 'proudly and cheerfully competing for victory', to the admiration of the assembled tourists.[33] The original 'stealing amid blows' is the only early-attested rite at this hugely popular shrine, repository of over 100,000 small votives; it seems to have been the centrepiece of a festival of civic importance. Boys also played important parts in the three greatest festivals, as runners at the Carneia, and as choir-members at the Gymnopaediae and Hyacinthia. Indeed at the Hyacinthia the performances in the theatre by 'very many choirs of youths' were the highlight of the second day (and at this festival girls too sang and danced): again the ephebes displayed their skills, gentler in this case, before a large audience. A main ground for the popularity of Helen and such lesser figures as the

Leucippides must have been their care for young girls.[34] Of course, youths and maidens had important ritual roles in every Greek state, Athens not least, but the extent of their involvement in central cults and festivals at Sparta is perhaps exceptional. It reflects intense public concern with the training of the future Spartiates. This must be a main reason why Artemis and Apollo, gods of the young, are so prominent in the Spartan pantheon. The three principal festivals all honour Apollo, the model youth.

A far larger proportion of young Spartans were probably engaged in these rites than of young Athenians in their equivalents. And Spartiates perhaps continued to participate directly in public ritual throughout their lives. By the fifth century, many Athenians probably attended the public festivals merely as spectators of the performances and recipients of cuts of meat from the public victims. Less free meat was available at Spartan sacrifices, but there are hints that some measure of active participation at least on some occasions may have been almost universal. It is said for instance that cowards were given the most humiliating positions in the choruses. One wonders why they were not excluded altogether, unless it was the norm for all Spartiates to take part. We even find King Agesilaus 'taking the place the choirmaster gave him' at the Hyacinthia. On campaigns, according to Xenophon, the army-divisions sang paeans together each evening.[35] The chorus was perhaps a place where the status of the 'equals' was defined and displayed. All Spartiates participated, subject to the same discipline of the choirmaster. It was also, of course, a place where the ambiguities of the ideal were displayed, since, as we have seen, unequal honour attached to different positions in the choir of equals. And since festivals were above all occasions of public display, they could be exploited as opportunities for certain of those humiliations in which Spartan life was so rich. Though we may doubt Clearchus' account of how women dragged bachelors around an altar, whipping them the while, Plutarch very credibly describes ceremonies at which the girls mocked the youths before their elders.[36] One can still feel through Plutarch's account the young men's anguish.

Another phenomenon that we may suspect is the 'laconising' of familiar elements of Greek religion. In one case we can observe it clearly. The Gymnopaidiai was probably by derivation the festival not of 'naked boys' (*paides*), as most ancient etymologists thought, nor of 'jokes' (*paidiai*), 'made by those with no clothes

149

on', which was perhaps a view known to Plutarch, nor of course of 'bare feet' as the Roman translator who coined *Nudipedalia* supposed, but of dancing (*paidia/paizo*) 'unclad' or perhaps 'unarmed'. We know that competitive dancing by choirs of adults as well as boys formed the main content of the festival.[37] Such choral dancing is surely one of the most joyous forms of devotion that can be imagined. But a passage in Plato mentions 'terrific endurance' at the Gymnopaidiai 'as they fight in' (or 'against') 'the baking heat'.[38] Unless the reference is to an otherwise unattested athletic competition, it looks as if the Spartans had transformed even choral dancing into a test of endurance and an ordeal, by making the choirs perform, perhaps for hours on end, in the hottest month of the year in one of the hottest places in Greece. Appropriately, the Gymnopaidiai was also a commemoration of the Champions who won the celebrated battle against the Argives in the sixth century, and so set the standard that every Spartan youth sought to emulate.[39]

Plutarch saw the Spartan attitude to the dead as a distinctive trait. He lists Lycurgus' various unusual funerary regulations: he permitted intra-mural burial (to accustom the young to death), banned grave-gifts except the very simplest, forbade inscribed grave-monuments except for men dead in battle and, probably, women dead in childbirth, and set strict limits on periods of mourning. As the only undeniable inscribed grave-markers of Spartans bear men's names followed by 'in war' or women's names with 'in childbirth', Plutarch's ban seems to have been observed.[40] One wonders whether the relatives of those who died peacefully can have brought continuing commemorative offerings to such unmarked, unhonoured graves. If they did not, a half of what an ordinary Athenian understood by piety was foreclosed to a Spartan. Perhaps his devotions were diverted towards the heroes of Laconia, a class which as we have seen included great Spartan patriots of the more recent and more distant past.

The divergent development of the festival calendars at Athens and Sparta is a final and most important distinction. By the fifth century, rites of Demeter and Dionysus occupied much of the Attic sacred calendars, in deme and city alike. Neither god was neglected in Sparta; both had shrines, and Demeter was patroness of an athletic and musical competition at which Damonon competed.[41] But we would not expect the cults to have their Attic form or importance, given that classical Sparta was deeply hostile to public drunkenness, and Spartiates ostentatiously shunned all involvement in the tilling of the fields from which they lived. A speaker in Plato's *Laws* claims that drunken Dionysiac festivals open to the population at large, of the type so popular in Attica, were unknown in Laconia;[42] and nothing proves him wrong. Dramatic festivals of the Athenian type were also unknown. Spartans assembled in the theatre to watch dancing choirs of boys, and were thus free from the national demoralisation that, according to Plato, is the consequence of mimetic art. Of the three concerns of the Attic Demeter, the agricultural year, the afterlife,[43] and the life of women, Spartan Demeter perhaps cared chiefly for the third: her cult at the Eleusinion south of Sparta, the one we know best, was apparently confined to women, like the Athenian Thesmophoria. Hephaestus, another god of rising popularity in Athens, had no place at all in Sparta, where citizens shunned manual work. An outsider in the fifth century, asked to list the most important Spartan gods, might have named Apollo of Amyclae, Apollo Karneios, Athena Chalkioikos, the Dioscuri, Artemis Orthia, Helen (and Menelaus), Poseidon of Taenarum, the Leucippides and Lycurgus.[44] As we have seen, the god who dominated Spartan festivals was lucid, disciplined Apollo.

Were there then no rituals of earthy, orgiastic kind at Sparta? Was licensed disorder unknown? The evidence leads in two directions. On the one hand, to judge from Aristophanes' *Lysistrata*, one of the features of Spartan life that most struck outsiders was the zest for odd and vigorous dances. The maidens run like bacchants, the women do the 'back-kick to the buttocks', and even the ambassador takes the floor in a 'two-step'. Excited dancing was certainly performed by women in cults of Artemis and Dionysus; for as a women's god rather than a god of wine Dionysus did have a place in liberated Laconia, by a neat symmetrical reversal of the situation in Attica where he was predominantly a god of the drinking man. Obscure lexicographical glosses even speak of obscene dances performed in honour of Artemis Dereatis, though they do not say who the performers were or what the circumstances.[45] On the other hand, one of the ways in which Spartiates marked their difference from helots was, as we have seen, by forcing them to perform 'ridiculous and humiliating' songs and dances. The Spartiates' own dances ought, therefore, to have been seemly, however vigorous.

A particularly intriguing problem is raised by the famous clay masks found in large numbers in the shrine of Artemis Orthia,

and dating mostly from the sixth century.[46] As they have eye-
holes, they seem to be replicas of masks that were actually worn.
The two commonest types are the 'old woman', an ugly,
wrinkled, aged face, taken to be female because it lacks a beard,
and the 'hoplite'. Given the civic importance of the shrine, the
rite to which they relate must surely have been performed by
members of the Spartiate class. We hear from lexicographers of
brullicha (?), ugly female masks worn 'to be ridiculous and base' in
Spartan rites of Artemis and Apollo;[47] about the sex of the
wearers our sources differ, but the form of the name designating
them, *brullichistai*, suggests that they were men. If the *brullichistai*
were male Spartiates, an obvious further possibility is that they
were ephebes, ever close to Artemis Orthia in whose shrine the
masks were found. It has been suggested, accordingly, that the
ephebes were, so to speak, inoculated against the 'ridiculous and
base' by being required occasionally to embody it. Decked in
shameful masks, they trod the lumpish capers of a helot, and so
came truly to understand baseness by experience, and to despise
it. On other occasions, by contrast, they would imitate the
exemplary models suggested by the hoplite masks.[48] This is
speculation; but it is perhaps more plausible to associate the
masks with the ephebes than with any other group.[49] Rituals of
reversal and disorder would therefore be a stage in becoming a
Spartiate, not a relief from being one.

From ritual we turn to the role of religion in public life. Every
state had cults that served as a focus of national identity, but
Sparta was unusual in worshipping the founder of its constitution
as a god.[50] Could one eat meat from the annual sacrifice to
Lycurgus, and then with a good conscience express dissatisfaction
with the Spartan way of life? What most impressed other Greeks,
though, was the semi-divinity that hedged the Spartan kings.
Herodotus looked to barbarian lands for parallels, and Xenophon
spoke of the 'more than mortal honours' of a Spartan royal
funeral. The funerals indeed reveal that the laws of Lycurgus
'honour the kings not as mortals but as heroes'.[51] Both kings
could trace their descent straight back step by step to Heracles
and thus to Zeus himself. They are the only historical Greeks who
enter the pages of Herodotus to such a genealogical fanfare.[52] The
Pythia in 427 urged the Spartans to 'bring home the seed of the
semi-divine son of Zeus' by restoring the exiled Pleistoanax, and
Xenophon in the *Cyropaedia* is no doubt echoing Spartan ideology
when he emphasises how heartening it is to follow a king

descended from a god. Not surprisingly, the kings held priesthoods of their royal ancestor, and were associated symbolically with his twin sons the Dioscuri.[53] The controversies that surrounded the exile and recall of King Pleistoanax, and the accession of Agesilaus, are instructive: at a certain level of belief, the whole well-being of Sparta depended on the king, and if an unentitled person occupied the royal seat military disaster and famine might follow. Conversely, a good king by his death could save the state, as did Leonidas at Thermopylae. There were strong inhibitions against doing violence to such sacred persons.[54]

As we have seen, the kings had a central ceremonial role in the conduct of public rites. Regular rituals relating to their royal office were therefore unnecessary; but the installation of a king could be accompanied by elaborate ceremonial — Pleistoanax was brought back 'amid the same choruses and sacrifices as when they first founded Lacedaemon and established the kings'[55] — and royal funerals were surely among the most spectacular pageants that the Peloponnese ever saw.[56] Fixed numbers of *perioikoi* and helots from all Laconia converged on Sparta to join a man and a woman from every Spartiate household; and, says Herodotus, 'when they are all assembled, many thousands of them with the women too, they beat their brows enthusiastically and lament without ceasing'. Subsequently all public business remained suspended for ten days. Nothing brings out the realities of hierarchy and power as well as a funeral. The royal corpse became a symbol of regal authority for the Spartiates, of Spartan authority for the subject classes; representatives of every class, including helots and *perioikoi* who perhaps never normally visited the capital, were summoned to Sparta to do it forced homage. Such pomp was, obviously, in sharp and deliberate contrast to the simple exequies of ordinary Spartans.

The welfare of the king was of public concern. Demaratus received his name, 'prayed for by the people', because the Spartiates *en masse* had prayed for a child to be born to his father King Ariston. By an obvious corollary, there were religious sanctions against opposition to the royal authority. Any Spartiate who resisted the king's right to lead out the army wherever he wished was 'to be held in the curse', says Herodotus. Public curses against subversive crimes were a commonplace in Greek states, but usually it was the authority of the laws or the magistrates that they protected rather than of a king. It is tantalising to know so little of an institution that must have given expression to central Spartan values. Just one further possible provision is mentioned: Plutarch's Lycurgus made it 'accursed' for a master to exact from a helot more than a fixed due of agricultural produce.[57]

Because of their central ceremonial role, the kings were also closely involved with public divination. The gods spoke to the Spartans through the public sacrifices. Thus did Talthybius indicate his anger at the murder of Xerxes' heralds, and set in train the quest for two Spartiates willing to 'die for their fatherland' to appease him; later the first warning of the conspiracy of Cinadon was given by the same means.[58] It is surely significant that no comparable incident can be cited in Athenian history, even though omens were taken at all the very numerous public sacrifices. At Sparta, the first recipients of these divine messages, apart from the seers themselves, were of course the kings.

They were not, however, the only Spartans who could engage in influential divination. The power to consult the gods was diffused among the decision-making bodies of the state, just as power itself was. Spartans loved oracles, more perhaps than did the citizens of any other Greek state, and granted them an unusual importance in political debate. Had not their own constitution been prescribed by Apollo of Delphi himself? And had not Lycurgus learnt to rely on Apollo from the example of King Minos, who ruled Crete through the prophetic advice that he received as a 'communer with mighty Zeus'? The dual kingship too had received the sanction of the Pythia.[59] Oracles of every kind — fresh Delphic responses, 'sleepers' and 'floaters' — all on occasion had their influence. Demaratus was deposed and Pleistoanax was recalled in consequence of advice from Delphi; the debate surrounding the accession of a third king, Agesilaus, centred on a floating oracle which warned against a 'lame kingship'; and according to Herodotus it was in obedience to an unwelcome Delphic command that the Spartans expelled their good friend Hippias from Athens, since they 'put the god above human considerations'.[60] And these are only the most spectacular examples.[61]

Delphic Apollo was closely associated with the kings. The *Pythioi*, permanent officials whose job it was to consult Delphi on public business — a post known only from Sparta — were royal appointees and shared the kings' tent, and the kings kept official archives of past responses into which they could dip at need. This does not necessarily mean, though, that the kings could consult the oracle on their own initiative about matters of public importance, and then expect the ephors and assembly to bow to the god's will. On the contrary, the many references to questions put by 'the Spartans' suggest that the decision to dispatch the *Pythioi* about a public question was normally taken publicly.[62] And the ephors had means of divination of their own. Once every nine years, they observed the heavens on a clear night. If a shooting star appeared, it was a sign that the king had committed a religious offence and should be deposed. A similar ritual of observing the heavens is attested for Athens: the issue there, however, was whether a religious mission should be dispatched to Delphi.[63]

If this star-gazing could only occasionally have influence, the ephors appear also to have frequented *ex officio* the incubation-oracle of Pasiphae at Thalamae. A dream sent to an ephor who was sleeping on official business will have had weight; but it is obvious how liable an ephor's dreams were to reflect his own daytime sense of what was good for the state. We see from Plutarch's *Agis and Cleomenes* that both these modes of divination had their importance in the revolutionary crisis of the third century BC. A fine inscription from Pasiphae's shrine seems to record a dedication made by a Spartan elder, in consequence of a prophecy given by the goddess to an ephor. It is true that in the fourth century the Athenian state patronised the incubation-oracle of Amphiaraus on issues of some importance — indeed they patronised the god to the extent of awarding him a golden crown for services rendered, as if he had been one of their own demagogues; but it is doubtful whether they would ever have allowed an oracle quite such broad potential for influence over political as well as religious affairs as did the Spartans.[64]

Military divination was even more important.[65] Behind a Spartan army there trotted a mixed herd of sacrificial animals, ready for use to test the will of the gods at any time.[66] The only two foreigners ever to be granted citizenship were the Iamid seer Tisamenus and his brother, says Herodotus, so eager were the Spartans for the advice of this still untried young man. The gamble paid off, and Tisamenus 'helped them to win five great competitions' in battle.[67] Most striking of all, there are the many cases of plans altered and even campaigns abandoned because of the disfavour of the gods. This is not a phenomenon confined to the Spartans — witness the disastrous Athenian response to the eclipse at Syracuse in 413 — and it is very plausible that our impression of Athenian attitudes would be very different if they had conducted more campaigns on land, under generals of the same cast of mind as Nicias and Xenophon. But as it is the Spartan evidence is uniquely abundant, and they alone seem to have had the obstacle of crossing-sacrifices to surmount before leaving their own territory.

Cleomenes in 494 set out to invade the Argolid by land; but the omens at the river Erasinus proved unpropitious, and he was obliged to send his force round to Tiryns by sea. On three separate occasions during the Peloponnesian War invasions of the Argolid were actually abandoned because of unpropitious border-sacrifices, and the troops marched back home.[68] Earth tremors too caused campaigns to be abandoned in mid-course in 426, 414 and ? 402, while in 413/412 the commander of a proposed expedition was changed, and the size of his force reduced by a half.[69]

While a Spartan army was in enemy territory, consultative sacrifices were very regularly performed before undertaking any fresh initiative:[70] Agesilaus was deterred in 396 from marching further inland and later from crossing the Maeander, and Agesipolis in 388/387 abandoned the project of building a fort in the Argolid and returned home.[71] Omens might hold back the day of joining battle or beginning a siege,[72] and even when pitched battle was imminent final sacrifices were performed to determine the right moment for marching out. At Plataea the Spartans supposedly had to stand unresisting under heavy fire from the approaching Persians until, by a desperate prayer to Hera, Pausanias at last secured the omens for an advance.[73]

And finally the extraordinary story of Cleomenes' trial well shows the weight that Spartans were believed to attach to religious factors in warfare. Denounced on a charge of sparing Argos through a bribe, Cleomenes explained with fine precision the divine signs that had convinced him that he could not take the city. Having captured a grove called Argos, he suspected that the Delphic prophecy that he was to 'take Argos' had been already fulfilled. When he sacrificed in the Heraeum to test the matter further, fire blazed from the chest of the goddess' image. Had it come from the head, that would have meant that he would capture the city 'from the top'; fire from the chest indicated that he had achieved all that the god wished. According to Herodotus, 'the Spartiates found this a convincing and plausible defence, and he got off easily'.[74]

Xenophon has a detailed description of the preliminary sacrifices and crossing-sacrifices which finely illustrates the meticulous symbolism of a Spartan ritual:

The king first sacrifices while still at home to Zeus the Leader and the gods associated with him [reading doubtful]. If he gets good omens here, the fire-carrier takes fire from the altar and leads the way to the borders of the land. The king sacrifices there too to Zeus and Athena. When the sacrifices to both these gods produce good omens he crosses the borders of the land. And the fire from these sacrifices leads the way and is never put out, and all kinds of sacrificial animals follow.

Xenophon goes on to explain that the king sacrifices before dawn, 'wishing to forestall the gods' favour', but he emphasises that this is a public ceremonial attended by company commanders, allied generals and two ephors. 'When the rites are completed the king calls them all over and issues instructions.' And he concludes: 'Seeing all this you would think that other peoples are improvisers in soldiering while the Spartans are the only craftsmen in warfare.' Such is Xenophon's unexpected diagnosis of the key point in Spartan military professionalism.[75]
The importance of such rites is manifest from this account. Xenophon seems to take it for granted that they will be performed, and we may assume that a king or general who regularly neglected the crossing-sacrifices would have risked most dangerous unpopularity, even if he remained within the law.[76] It is very striking that only one minor instance of a Spartan commander simply disregarding omens seems to be recorded.[77] And yet, insistent though Xenophon is that this is a truly public examination of entrails, there is no doubt that the dominant figure at the ceremony is the king. In this passage Xenophon simply fails to mention the professional seer who must have provided the formal interpretation of the sacrifice.[78] The rite was in theory public and objective, in practice under the close supervision of the king; the army was assured that its leader was following the guiding hand of the gods, but the whole conduct of the ceremony lessened the likelihood of serious conflict between human and divine will.
Military divination has often puzzled and embarrassed modern historians. Almost every incident of a campaign abandoned or an

attack postponed because of unpromising omens has received a rationalising explanation from one scholar or another.[79] As it happens, allegations that the sacrifices were being manipulated in a particular case were sometimes made by the ancients themselves. Such things were even said by and about the pious Xenophon.[80] No one, however, who reads the whole of his works can seriously doubt this general's committed faith in divination. As he explains in a passage to which many a Spartan king or general might have given assent:

> If anyone is surprised that I have so often prescribed that one should act 'with the gods', it is certain that he will be less surprised if he often comes into danger, and if he realises that in a war enemies plot against one another but seldom know whether these plots are well-laid. It is impossible to find any other advisers in such matters except the gods. They know everything, and give signs to those they wish to through sacrifices, birds of omen, voices and dreams.[81]

Often quite elaborate hypotheses have to be constructed to make the rationalising explanations work. Whose interests could it serve in 419, for instance, to summon the *perioikoi* for a secret expedition, march out 'no one knew whither', disband the army on the borders of Argos on the pretence that the crossing-sacrifices were adverse, and re-assemble a force for a second expedition against Argos later in the year?[82] In recent years, therefore, there has been more willingness to take the ancient sources on these matters at their word.[83]

But if the scepticism of the sceptics has been shown up as dogmatic, there is something simplistic about the faith of the believers. They tend to overestimate the real objectivity of techniques of divination. The king or general decided when the gods should be consulted and what enquiry should be put to them. The gods' message had to be elicited from the voiceless liver through interpretation by a seer; and the seer is likely to have shared the commander's presumptions about the kind of advice that the gods could reasonably be seeking to convey.[84] (Pious Greeks did not 'believe because it was absurd', but expected the gods to show good strategic sense.)[85] Above all, if the omens from a first sacrifice were discouraging, it was the king's decision whether to perform it again in hope of something better or to abandon the enterprise. Unless there were unusually strict restrictions on the repetition of crossing-sacrifices, they would always have come right in the end for a sufficiently determined leader.[86]

Divination, therefore, left room for manoeuvre even to the pious. What mattered above all was the king's strength of will and confidence in his cause. Cleomenes accepted the indication of the omens that he should not cross the Erasinus — but instead of marching home he sent his troops round by sea.[87] There were perhaps certain phenomena, above all earth tremors, that would cow almost any Spartan, but even here an exception can be found. In 388/387 Agesipolis led an army into the Argolid, confident in the support that had been promised him by Zeus and Apollo, in response to a little diplomatic questioning. Xenophon takes up the story:

> While [Agesipolis] was having dinner on the first evening in Argive territory, and the after-dinner libations were being performed, the god shook the earth. The Spartans, starting with the staff of the public mess-tent, all struck up the paean to Poseidon [how much that phrase tells of Spartan piety, discipline and willingness to sing] and the rest of the army expected to depart, because, on a previous occasion when an earth tremor occurred, Agis had led the army back from Elis. But Agesipolis said that, if the tremor had occurred while he was still on his way to invade, he would have believed that the god was seeking to prevent him; but since it came after he had invaded he thought the god was encouraging him. And so on the next day he sacrificed to Poseidon and led them not far into the country.[88]

This fine distinction had escaped previous Spartan kings, who in similar circumstances had led an invading army home; but having received the approval of Apollo and his father Zeus for his expedition, Agesipolis perhaps felt unusual confidence as to what Apollo's uncle Poseidon must intend.[89] However that may be, he succeeded in defusing a most explosive omen by a religious interpretation that was apparently accepted by pious contemporaries.

If, therefore, a plan or expedition was abandoned because of the lesser obstacle of discouraging sacrifices, the king must either have been unusually timorous, or have felt genuine doubt whether the proposed action was wise. In 396 Agesilaus abandoned a plan to march further inland because the 'offering was lobeless', and returned to the sea; he realised, Xenophon adds without a hint of irony, that he could not campaign successfully in the plain without cavalry support.[90] It is striking that during the Peloponnesian War not one of the many invasions of Attica was prevented by crossing-sacrifices — one yielded to an earth-tremor — while three of the much less frequent expeditions against the Argolid turned back at the borders.[91] Were there factors that made aggression against the Dorian neighbour Argos more controversial than against Attica?

Divination was doubtless under control in Sparta, as it normally is wherever it is practised. Pious Spartans manipulated it without realising that this was what they were doing. (The important correlate is that no Spartan explicitly rejected its validity.) Perhaps we should see the relation of, say, Agesilaus to his seers as much like that of a modern politician to his economic advisers. Politicians believe profoundly in economic predictions; politicians are sometimes swayed by economic advice; politicians find ways of carrying through certain favoured policies whatever economic advisers may say. It is not a matter of simple bad faith but of the complexity of the factors that shape any human decision.

The charm of divination for the consultant is that he need never feel that he is acting at random. Spartans liked clear directives; and many of their distinctive religious attitudes reflect the disposition to conduct life according to fixed rules. It is well known how determined they were to hold the traditional festivals at the traditional times, even at the risk of military disadvantage;[92] and they showed notable respect for the festivals of other states.[93] The rules of sanctuary too were taken seriously by the Spartans, and the threatened or exiled king living holed up in a sacred precinct is one of the recurrent figures in Spartan history.[94] A state which before going to war declares ceremonially that its cause is just is insisting on its adherence to certain rules: the practice is familiar from Rome rather than from Greece, but we find King Archidamus in 429 formally calling the 'gods and heroes who occupy the land of Plataea' as witnesses to the justice of the Spartan invasion, and Brasidas using similar language to the Acanthians in 424. Respect for rules can lead to a narrow legalism. Each year the ephors declared war on the helots 'so that killing them might not cause pollution'.[95]

But Spartan religion was not a system designed to justify the conduct of Spartiates in every situation. When they broke their own rules they acknowledged their guilt, and as a state they appear in our sources as almost uniquely willing to ascribe national misfortunes to collective religious guilt. The great earthquake occurred because helots exercising their right of sanctuary in Poseidon's shrine at Taenarum had been lured out with promises and treacherously killed.[96] (The memory of this never-forgotten national catastrophe must have kept the sense of religious danger alive, and largely explains the Spartans' subsequent unease about earthquakes.) The Spartans fared so unexpectedly ill in the Archidamian war because they had entered on it illegally, in violation of oaths, or perhaps because King Pleistoanax had secured his recall by corrupting the Pythia. Agamemnon's herald Talthybius was enraged at the impious murder of the heralds of Darius, and to appease him two Spartiates were sent up to Susa for punishment, it was said. Ceremonial redress had also to be made for the killing of the regent Pausanias, in partial violation of sanctuary. Perhaps the most awe-inspiring cautionary tale in Herodotus is that of Glaucus, son of Epicydes, whose family was obliterated root and branch because he enquired tentatively of Apollo whether he might retain a deposit by fraud. The hapless Glaucus was a Spartiate, and it must have been in Sparta that the story had its origin.[97]

The Spartans heeded divine signs and obeyed the rules. Even a rogue Spartan such as Lysander, whose disposition to 'treat the gods as enemies' is stigmatised by Plutarch as quite un-Laconian, understood and exploited this tendency of his compatriots.[98] Harsh terms, superstition and religiosity, have accordingly often been applied to their religious outlook. It may be captious to object that superstition had not been invented at the date of most of the events here discussed. *Deisidaimonia* did not acquire its familiar sense until the second half of the fourth century, when traditional religious concepts were being in some measure rethought in response to philosophical criticism. It seems that no single term had existed before this to stigmatise a religious attitude that erred by excess.[99] The real objection is that the so-called Spartan superstitiousness is not a matter of isolated quirks unrelated to the central tenets of Greek religion. The power of prophecy, the sanctity of sanctuaries and festivals, the threat of divine punishment: it is on issues such as these that the distinctiveness of the Spartan attitude emerges. And their eccentricity is merely to believe with unusual seriousness what other Greeks believed too.

It is more helpful to relate Spartan religion to the society that produced it, and in particular to the singular Spartan discipline. Mary Douglas has argued in *Natural symbols*[100] that the forms of social discipline in a society and its conceptions of divine power are related phenomena. The more an individual feels subject as a social being to a set of rules that he must obey without question, the more he is bound within a hierarchical structure of power, the more likely he is to understand religion too as a matter of fixed and formal observance, of strict obedience to rules. Where the conditions of life are, so to speak, more open to negotiation and where persuasion and explanation are valued, there the gods too become less legalistic, and intentions come to count for more than acts. Any classical scholar who reads *Natural symbols* must be put in mind of the contrast often made in Thucydides between Spartan and Athenian society.[101] This is particularly so since Douglas makes a connection between forms of social discipline and linguistic practices: a tightly controlled society is reflected in the 'restricted code', full of orders not backed by explanations, while more open social forms have their equivalent in the more discursive and explanatory 'elaborated code'. Pericles in Thucydides praises the Athenians' belief in the power of rational discussion;[102] the English word 'laconism' bears witness that the Spartans invented the 'restricted code'.

The gods were at the top of the chain of command that ran down through Spartan society.[103] Their traditional rules, about festivals and sanctuary and the like, were there to be obeyed without question; and amid life's contingencies it was constantly necessary to seek further specific instructions through divination supervised by the humans just below them in the chain of command. Fear of the gods, *deisidaimonia*, was a particular form of that 'fear' which in Greek thought was the foundation of social discipline.[104] Spartan religion was Spartan more in its insistence on orderliness and obedience than in any particular military emphasis it may have had. For the gods of disorder, imagination and individualism it had little place. Thus it contributed to the 'success of Sparta' by supporting the dominant norms of Spartan society. Its ethos is perhaps caught best in a happy comment by Xenophon, after he has described the military and athletic competitions with which Agesilaus trained his army at Ephesus:

Anyone would have been heartened who saw first Agesilaus

and then the rest of the troops going away garlanded from
the exercise-grounds and then dedicating their garlands to
Artemis. When men were honouring the gods, training for
war, and learning to be obedient, was not everything there
bound to inspire cheerful hopes?[105]

Notes

1. For recent surveys see J.T. Hooker, *The ancient Spartans* (London,
1980), 47–70; M. Clauss, *Sparta* (Munich, 1983), 169–79. Hooker's
account of shrines and festivals well complements the present study.
These works contain extensive bibliographies; some subsequent works
will be cited below, and note too C. Calame, 'Spartan Genealogies', in J.
Bremmer (ed.), *Interpretations of Greek mythology* (London, 1987), 153–86.
The basic collections of evidence remain S. Wide, *Lakonische Kulte*
(Leipzig, 1893); L. Ziehen, *PW* 3A (1929) s.v. *Sparta (Kulte)*, 1453–1525.
Evidence from the Roman period, much exploited by Wide and Ziehen,
needs very careful handling, for reasons suggested by the title of a paper
by A.J.S. Spawforth, 'Roman Sparta and the "Invention of Tradition"'
(delivered at the conference *Hollow Lakedaimon* at the University of
Newcastle-upon-Tyne, 8 Feb. 1986). Abbreviations are those of the
Oxford Classical Dictionary, 2nd edition, or are easily recognisable.

2. *IG* 5.1.213, E. Schwyzer, *Dialectorum Graecarum exempla epigraphica
potiora* (Leipzig, 1923), no. 12. For further evidence see L.H. Jeffery, *The
local scripts of archaic Greece* (Oxford, 1961), 185.

3. Xen. *Rep. Lac.* 15.2, 13.11 (I speak of this work as Xenophon's,
without wishing to express any commitment on its authorship); Arist.
Pol. 1285 a 6; *Ath. Pol.* 57.1 (king-archon); Hdt. 6.56–7. The kings' sacral
functions on campaigns will be discussed below; instances at home are
mentioned in Xen. *Hell.* 3.3.4, Plut. *Lyc.* 12.5. Cf. in general P. Carlier,
La royauté en Grèce avant Alexandre (Strasbourg, 1984), 256–69.

4. They were separately buried after Plataea, according to the ms.
text of Hdt. 9.85 — which is however defensible only if we delete with
Sitzler (see R.W. Macan's edition) the reference to the four bravest
Spartiates, since it would be an incredible coincidence that these should
all have chanced to be priests. The most that can be got from the ms. text
of Plut. *Lyc.* 27.3, associated with the Herodotus passage by W. den Boer,
Laconian studies (Amsterdam, 1954), 288–300, is a claim that 'sacred
women' (not priests or priestesses) were entitled to an inscribed grave-
marker: see D.H. Kelly, *Greek, Roman and Byzantine studies* 22 (1981), 33;
W.K. Pritchett, *The Greek state at war* (Berkeley, 1971–1985), vol. 4, 244 n.
430. More probably Latte's conjecture 'women dead in childbirth',
which has epigraphical support (see Pritchett), should be accepted.
Inscribed grave-markers (?) for mysterious 'sacred men' and 'sacred
women' (*hieroi* and *hierai*) are, however, known from Laconia and
Messenia (see C. Le Roy, *BCH* 85, 1961, 228–32); some from the Gerenia
region, on the Laconia/Messenia border, appear to date from the fifth/
fourth c.: *IG* 5.1.1338, ? 1367, *SEG* 11.951. No clear epigraphic example

of an epitaph from the relevant period for a priest or priestess survives: M.B. Wallace does not explain his dating (*Phoenix* 24, 1970, 99 n. 11) of *IG* 5.1.1329 (Leuctra), undated in *IG*, to the fifth century, and it is not necessarily an epitaph; *IG* 5.1.711 is Roman.

5. Gymnopaediae: Xen. *Hell.* 6.4.16. Privileges retained: Hdt. 6.57 (front seats), which perhaps gives the story of Leutychidas' jibe to the deposed Demaratus at the Gymnopaediae its bite (Hdt. 6.67). For other festivals clear evidence is lacking. The role of the ephors in Polyb. 4.35.2–4 is irrelevant, since at the date of the incident (late in 220) Sparta was kingless (Polyb. 4.34.5). The ephors perhaps organised the Hyacinthia; a king could participate in a humble role (Xen. *Ages.* 2.17).

6. Pratinas fr. 2 Page (*Poet. Mel. Gr.* 709) *ap.* Ath. 633a; *P. Oxy.* 2389 fr. 35 = Alcman fr. 11 Page: cf. C. Calame, *Les chœurs de jeunes filles en Grèce archaïque* (Rome, 1977), 381–5 (and, on the apparent association of Dymainai with the cult at Caryae, 273–6). Carneia: Demetrius of Scepsis *ap.* Ath. 141e. Hesych s.v. *karneatai* gives further information, marred by a lacuna: five unmarried youths from each [   ] were selected for a four-year period for the *leitourgia* of Apollo Karneios. The new inscription *SEG* 28.404 (important for Spartan institutionalised homosexuality) perhaps reveals a similar group of Hyakinthioi, unless it is rather a dedication to [Apollo] Hyakinthios by a group of *aitai* (*eromenoi*). About the *Tainaristai* (Hesych.; cf. *IG* 5.1.210–2) (if any) of the classical period nothing is known. The competitions of the *sphaireis* were fought in the Roman period between the obes: see F. Bölte in *PW* 3A (1929), 1362–3; L. Ziehen, ibid., 1491.

7. Hesych. s.v. *karneatai* (see previous note) does not prove that there was a liturgical system like that of Athens: *leitourgia* often refers to performance of rites, not the financing of them (cf. P. Roesch, *Études Béotiennes*, Paris 1982, 149–51).

8. Plut. *Lyc.* 12.4.

9. Obe cults are perhaps implied for the second/first c. BC by *IG* 5.1.26 = Dittenberger *SIG* 932. The Amyclaeans had a special place within the Hyacinthia (Xen. *Hell.* 4.5.11), but the festival was open to all Spartans.

10. Talthybiadae: Hdt. 7.134.1, cf. 6.60; Matton and Keraon: Demetrius of Scepsis *ap.* Ath. 173f. (cf. Polemon *ap.* Ath. 39c), who says that they were worshipped by the attendants (*diakonoi*) at the messes, possibly an uncomprehending reference to the hereditary *mageiroi* of Hdt. 6.60. But G. Berthiaume, *Les rôles du mageiros* (Leiden, 1982), 24–7, 41–3, is more probably right to distinguish between Herodotus' guild, honourable Spartiate amateurs chiefly employed at sacrifices, and helot *diakonoi* (cf. Plut. *Comp. Lyc. Num.* 2.6) who did the day-to-day serving. Aegeidae: Hdt. 4.149.

11. Sanctuary: Thuc. 1.128.1 (cf. 1.133.1, 103.1–2); for slaves' rights of sanctuary at the Theseum in Athens see R.E. Wycherley, *The Athenian agora*, 3 (Princeton, 1957), 114–9, and for elsewhere see e.g. Plut. *Alex.* 42.9. (Such 'protest-supplication' is a neglected aspect of supplication: it could also be performed by the free, as e.g. in Thuc. 3.70.5, Isaeus 5.39.) Hyacinthia: Polycrates *FGrH* 588 fr. 1 *ap.* Ath. 139f.; for parallels see H.S. Versnel in Bremmer, *Interpretations* (above, n. 1), 130.

12. Cf. n. 10 above. If so, the Spartans must have tolerated the cult because it reminded the helots of their degrading functions.

13. Athenaeus 139a: the wet-nurses perhaps performed (?orgiastic) dances, cf. Hesych s.v. *koruthalistriai*, Calame, *Les chœurs*, 297–302. Their status is unclear; at Athens, only poverty would force a citizen-woman to act as a wet-nurse (Dem. 57.35): the Spartan nurses bought by members of other states (Plut. *Lyc.* 16.5) must have been slaves.

14. *Lyc.* 28.8–9.

15. Pausanias 3, *passim*; for festivals see e.g. 22.2, 22.7, 23.8, 24.5, 24.9, for an oracle 26.1, for competitions the inscription of Damonon (above n. 2). For the archaic period we are dependent on archaeological and epigraphic evidence, but this in broad outline confirms the picture of Pausanias: cf. P. Cartledge, *Sparta and Lakonia* (London, 1979), 185–93. Spartans often used and may in some cases have controlled sanctuaries in perioecic territory: the details of ownership, rights of access and administrative responsibility are wholly unknown.

16. Cf. Cartledge, *Sparta and Lakonia*, 98; A.J. Holladay, *CQ* 27 (1977), 123–4; G.L. Cawkwell, *CQ* 33 (1983), 390–5, esp. 391: 'The mirage spartiate dazzled all classes alike.'

17. *FGrH* 595 fr. 4, from Ath. 674a–b. Jacoby *ad loc.* thinks of a festival of master-slave reversal, of Saturnalia type; thus 'those from the country' would be helots. Neither the name 'Promacheia' nor the solemn procession suits this view.

18. Amyclaean Apollo: Paus. 3.19.2–3; cf. I.B. Romano, *Early Greek cult images* (diss. Pennsylvania, 1980), 99–114 (I owe a copy to the kindness of the author); and for probable illustrations of the image *Lexicon iconographicum mythologiae classicae* 2.1 (1984), 196 nos. 55ff. Thornax: Paus. 3.10.8. Armed Aphrodite: in Sparta, Paus. 3.15.10 and many further references (Wide, *Lakonische Kulte*, 137–8); in Corinth and — significantly — on Cythera, Paus. 2.5.1, 3.23.1; cf. *Lexicon iconographicum* 2.1, s.v. *Aphrodite*, 36, nos. 243–5; F. Graf, *Zeitschrift f. Papyrologie u. Epigraphik* 55 (1984), 250–1, and for oriental armed gods and goddesses W. Burkert, *Greek religion*, tr. J. Raffan (Oxford, 1985), 140, 153. (On Aphrodite Areia see n. 22 below.) Plut. *Apophth. Lac.* 239a, 232c unreliably claims that all Spartan gods and goddesses were armed; Macrobius *Sat.* 1.19.1–2 mentions a spear-carrying Dionysus. Laconian religious conservatism is suggested by the frequent references to *xoana* in Pausanias 3, as Holladay notes, *CQ* 27 (1977), 120.

19. Paus. 1.28.2. The Athena in the Parthenon was also armed, 1.24.7.

20. Procession: Polyb. 4.35.2–4. Carneia and Heraclidae: see in particular W.F. Otto, *Paideuma* 7 (1959–60), 25–30 = *Das Wort der Antike* (Stuttgart, 1962), 76–84. Much else was also involved (cf. Burkert, *Greek religion*, 234–6), but the interrelation of the details that we know about this long and complex festival is too uncertain for interpretation to be at all secure. Demetrius: *ap.* Ath. 141e.

21. Ath. 138f, 139f (Polycrates, *FGrH* 588 fr. 1). Hyacinthia as play: Hdt. 9.11.1. On the relaxed, rustic associations of *stibades* see A. Henrichs in B.F. Meyer and E.P. Sanders (eds), *Jewish and Christian self-definition*, 3

(London, 1982), 217 n. 44. Spartan festivals attracted tourists: e.g. Plut. *Ages.* 29.3.

22. Compare for instance the entries for Attica (to which add *SEG* 21.519) and Laconia in L.R. Farnell, *The cults of the Greek states*, 5 (Oxford, 1909), 409–412. The Aphrodite Areia (Paus. 3.17.5., ? *SEG* 11.671) of Sparta was probably envisaged as warlike, as 'armed Aphrodite' (above, n. 18) must have been, even though the cult-pairing of Ares and Aphrodite elsewhere perhaps rather expresses the polarity of war and peace (Burkert, *Greek religion*, 220); but, if so, this virago finds more than her match in the Athena Areia of Athens. The pre-battle sacrifices to Eros (Ath. 561e) probably reflect the well-known Greek association between courage and homosexual affection: cf. Ath. 561e, who offers this explanation and quotes a Cretan parallel, and K.J. Dover, *Greek homosexuality* (London, 1978), 191–4. Did the Spartans interpret their military Aphrodite similarly? (For a different solution see Graf, n. 18 above).

23. Heracles: Wide, *Lakonische Kulte*, 302. War-dead: see Pritchett, *Greek state at war*, 4, 243–6. M.I. Finley, 'Sparta and Spartan society', printed most recently in *Economy and society in ancient Greece* (London, 1981), 24–40, well characterises Spartan society as military rather than militaristic.

24. Pind. *Nem.* 10.51: cf. Wide, *Lakonische Kulte*, 304–15, and for the reliefs M.N. Tod and A.J.B. Wace, *A catalogue of the Sparta museum* (Oxford, 1906), 113–18; *Lexicon iconographicum mythologiae classicae* 3.1 (1986), 573, 586–7, 589–90.

25. Hdt. 5.75, 6.52; cf. the works cited by Burkert, *Greek religion*, 433 nn. 6 and 7, and now Carlier, *La royauté*, 298–301. I have not seen M. Hatzopoulos, *Le culte des Dioscures et la double royauté à Sparte*, (thèse dact., Paris, 1970).

26. Cf. C. Calame, edition of *Alcman* (Rome, 1983), 310: 'les Dioscures incarnent à Sparte la figure même du *néos*, du jeune citoyen récemment initié'. The few specific details about the cults point in this direction: the Dioscuri are associated with athletics (Paus. 3.14.7), ephebes (Paus. 3.20.2), armed dances (Pl. *Leg.* 796b), and a battle-song (Plut. *Mus.* 1140c); the army on campaign celebrates festivals in their honour (Paus. 4.27.2). In Sparta as elsewhere the Dioscuri were evidently entertained as 'divine guests' (cf. Paus. 4.27.2, 3.16.2–3, and perhaps *IG* 5.1.206–9): one would like to know where (in the messes?). For a sober discussion of the Dioscuri see M.P. Nilsson, *Geschichte der griechischen Religion*, 1, 3rd edn (Munich, 1967), 408–9.

27. Alcman *ap.* schol. Eur. *Tro.* 210 (cf. fr. 7 Page); Pind. *Pyth.* 11.61–4, *Nem.* 10.55–6, *Isthm.* 1.31; Theog. 1087–8 — evidently a potent myth.

28. For examples see e.g. L.F. Fitzhardinge, *The Spartans* (London, 1980), 80–1, 85. For discussion see especially M. Andronikos, *Peloponnesiaka* 1 (1956), 253–314, whose interpretation has been vindicated; also R.N. Thönges-Stringaris, *Athenische Mitteilungen* 80 (1965), 60, with references. For three new specimens see *BCH* 102 (1978), 675.

29. See C.A. Christou, *Praktika* 1956, 211–12; 1960, 228–31 (graffiti); 1961, 177–8; cf. *BCH* 81 (1957), 548–51; Hooker, *The ancient Spartans*, 66–8.

30. Paus. 3.12.9; 3.16.4 (which mentions also a further heroisation or heroisations, associated with Dorieus' expedition to Sicily; the text is corrupt); Hdt. 1.66. Cf. Jeffery, *Local scripts*, 186, 193. Other states more often worshipped athletes; but even the Spartans had a *heroon* of Kyniska, the horse-rearing daughter of Archidamus (Paus. 3.15.1).

31. Hdt. 1.67–8; Paus. 7.1.8; Hdt. 7.134.1; H.W. Catling and H. Cavanagh, *Kadmos* 15 (1976), 145–57. These cults contained idiosyncratic traits not derivable from panhellenic myth (Helen's divinity; her tree; her care for young girls; Agamemnon's consort Alexandra . . .); but the myths must none the less have contributed hugely to their prestige and appeal.

32. By H. Jeanmaire, *Couroi et courètes* (Lille, 1939), Ch. 7, esp. 524–40; A. Brelich, *Paides e parthenoi* (Rome, 1969), 113–207; Calame, *Les chœurs*, 251–357, esp. 350–7. But for a warning against treating ephebes as the sole or principal participants in cults and festivals in which they were, admittedly, important, see C. Sourvinou-Inwood, *JHS* 91 (1971), 174 (on Artemis Orthia): at both the Gymnopaediae and Hyacinthia there were choirs of adults (Xen. *Hell.* 6.4.16, 4.5.11) as well as of boys.

33. See most recently F. Graf, *Nordionische Kulte* (Rome, 1985), 86–90, with extensive bibliography. Daily stealing: Xen. *Rep. Lac.* 2.7–8. Ceremonial stealing: ibid. 2.9, probably Pl. *Leg.* 633b, Plut. *Aristid.* 17.10. 'Cheerfully competing': Plut. *Inst. Lac.* 239c. The ceremonial stealing, which was performed publicly by a group (Plut. *Aristid.* 17.10), differed from the daily stealing, the stealthy work of an individual; whipping was in the latter case a punishment for failure, in the former a necessary ordeal (Vernant n. 48 below, 20). But stealthy individual theft could not be enacted ritually in just that form; and a participant cannot have been unaware of the resemblance between the two forms. There was a similar ceremonial of food-stealing on Samos, but whipping is not mentioned (Hdt. 3.48).

34. For details see the works cited in n. 32. 'Very many choirs': Polycrates, *FGrH* 588 fr. 1 *ap.* Ath. 139e. Note too the lurid ritual preliminaries to the brutal ephebic mock-battle described in Paus. 3.14.8–10 (but I suspect pseudo-archaism here).

35. Xen. *Rep. Lac.* 9.5 (on such humiliating positions in a Spartan chorus cf. Plut. *Reg. Apophth.* 191e, with Nachstädt's parallels in the Teubner); Xen. *Ages.* 2.17; *Rep. Lac.* 12.7. Less free meat: Plut. *Lyc.* 19.8 (cf. Pl. *Alc.* 2.149a), the Lycurgan sacrifices were 'small and cheap'.

36. Clearchus of Soli fr. 73 Wehrli *ap.* Ath. 555c (cf. Wehrli's note); Plut. *Lyc* 14.3–6.

37. See for details F. Bölte, *Rh. Mus.* 78 (1929), 124–30; H.T. Wade-Gery, *CQ* 43 (1949), 79–81; Jacoby's note on *FGrH* 595 fr. 5. Plutarch: *Lyc.* 14.4–6.

38. Plato *Leg.* 633c. On the heat in Sparta, and the date of the festival, see Bölte, cited in n. 37.

39. Sosibius *FGrH* 595 fr. 5. Possibly though (cf. Jacoby *ad loc.*) this association only arose after 370/69, by amalgamation with the Parparonia, another festival commemorating the same event.

40. Plut. *Lyc.* 27.1–5 (cf. *Inst. Lac.* 238d): cf. n. 4 above. Spartan tombs are 'cheap and the same for all', according to Heraclides (=Aristotle fr.

611.13 Rose). On the archaeological evidence see the works of Wallace, Kelly and Pritchett cited above, n. 4; on the Spartan attitude to death see C. Sourvinou-Inwood in R. Hägg (ed.), *The Greek renaissance of the eighth century BC* (Stockholm, 1983), 44.

41. For details see 'Demeter, Dionysus and the Spartan Pantheon', in R. Hägg and N. Marinatos (eds), *Early Greek cult practices* (Stockholm, forthcoming). On the cult at the Eleusinion see J.M. Cook, *BSA* 45 (1950), 261–81.

42. 637a-b.

43. About Spartan attitudes to the afterlife we know almost nothing. 'Collecting priests', of the kind who spread Orphism at Athens (Pl. *Resp.* 364b–365a), were supposedly banned (Plut. *Lyc.* 9.5). 'What the Spartan said to the mystery-priest' was a popular form of story (Plut. *Apophth. Lac.* 217c, Antalcidas 1; 224e, 2 and 3; 235e, 57 (with Nachstädt's parallels in the Teubner), from which we can learn nothing reliable. Iamblichus, *Vit. Pyth.* 267, knows of female Spartan Pythagoreans.

44. See e.g. Ar. *Lys.* 1297–1321; Eur. *Hel.* 1465–74; Eur. *Alc.* 448; Ar. *Ach.* 510; Xen. *Rep. Lac.* 2.9; Hdt. 1.65 (only a selection of the early attestations, in most cases). Other cults attested in literary sources by the fourth century are of Zeus the Leader (Xen. *Rep. Lac.* 13.2), Zeus Lakedaimon and Zeus Ouranios (Hdt. 6.56), Zeus Syllanios and Athena Syllania (rhetra *apud* Plut. *Lyc.* 6.2), Hera (Hom. *Il.* 4.52, Alcman fr. 60 Page), Poseidon Earth-Holder (Xen. *Hell.* 6.5.30), Artemis Agrotera (Xen. *Hell.* 4.2.20), the heroes Orestes, Laius and Oedipus, Talthybius, Astrabakos (Hdt. 1.67–8, 4.149, 7.134, 6.69), the Graces Phaenna and Kleta (Alcman fr. 62).

45. Ar. *Lys.* 1309–13, 82, 1243. Spartan dance-names are very numerous; Vernant (below, n. 48), 15, assembles a rather too comprehensive list, not all of which are certainly Laconian. Cf. in general K. Latte, *De saltationibus Graecorum* (Giessen, 1913), 17–26. Artemis and Dionysus: see e.g. Calame, *Les chœurs*, 241–5, 253–64. Artemis Dereatis: see M.P. Nilsson, *Geschichte der griechischen Religion*, 1, 3rd edn (Munich, 1967), 161 nn. 9, 12; and for phallic dances in honour of an unspecified Laconian Artemis see Hesych. s.v. *lombai* (ibid. 162 n. 3) with Pollux 4.105 (*lombroteron*). For the possibility that Dionysiac dances were performed by men in archaic Laconia see 'Demeter, Dionysus' (above, n. 41), n. 13. The evidence is sociologically too imprecise for discussion to be very profitable.

46. See G. Dickins, in R.M. Dawkins (ed.), *The sanctuary of Artemis Orthia* (London, 1929), 163–86; cf. J. Boardman, *BSA* 58 (1963), 6 (chronology).

47. See e.g. A.W. Pickard-Cambridge, *Dithyramb, tragedy and comedy* (Oxford, 1927), 257–8 (the link with Artemis and Apollo comes from Pollux 4.104). Other suggested connections, with the *kurittoi* (Hesych. s.v.), or (Wilamowitz, *Glaube der Hellenen*, 1, Berlin, 1931, 200–1) with the *deikelistai* (Ath. 621d–e) or (Graf, *Nordionische Kulte*, 88, cf. *Zeitschrift f. Papyrologie u. Epigraphik* 62, 1986, 43–4) with the Lydiasts, are less close.

48. See J.P. Vernant, 'Une divinité des marges: Artémis Orthia', in *Recherches sur les cultes grecs et l'occident*, 2 (Cahiers du centre J. Bérard 9, Naples, 1984), 13–28.

49. As does Graf (n. 47 above), by a slightly different route. Cf. Jeanmaire, *Couroi et courètes*, 519–22. There is an obvious though not of course probative parallel in the masked bands of youths of the European Middle Ages or later, often associated with carnival: see e.g. W. Mannhardt, *Wald und Feldkulte 1, Der Baumkultus* (Berlin, 1875), 540–8; K. Meuli, *Gesammelte Schriften* (Basle, 1975), 1, part 1, 'Zum Maskenwesen', *passim*, e.g. 133–9. Masks could be worn in *komoi*, Dem. 19.287. Groups of young men ('countrymen', *agroikoi*: ? = ephebes, cf. perhaps *SEG* 28.404) are also associated with Artemis in the legends (one set in Laconia) about the origins of pastoral poetry, though masking is not explicitly mentioned: cf. F. Frontisi-Ducroux, 'Artémis Bucolique', *Rev. Hist. Rel.* 198 (1981), 29–56, and on Lydiasts/Bucoliasts Graf. (n. 47 above).

50. See Hdt. 1.65–6, Aristotle fr. 534 Rose *ap.* Plut. *Lyc.* 30.4, Wide, *Lakonische Kulte*, 281–3.

51. Hdt. 6.58.2, 59; Xen. *Hell.* 3.3.1; Xen. *Rep. Lac.* 15.9 (this last text does not necessarily mean, as is often assumed, that the kings received continuing heroic cult *post mortem*: cf. *Liverpool Classical Monthly* 13.1, Jan. 1988, 9–10; answered ibid. 13.3, March 1988).

52. 7.204, 8.131.2. In a poem apparently written for a Spartan symposium, Ion of Chios (fr. 27 West *ap.* Ath. 463a) calls for libations to be poured to the kings' heroic ancestors 'starting from Zeus', and probably speaks of one of the kings with striking fulsomeness as 'our saviour and father': cf. M.L. West, *Bulletin of the Institute of Classical Studies* 32 (1985), 74 (though West believes the 'saviour and father' to be Dionysus). This is why sterility and illegitimacy were so feared: see especially Hdt. 5.39.2, Carlier, *La royauté*, 296.

53. Thuc. 5.16.2 (Pleistoanax); Xen. *Cyr.* 4.1.24, 7.2.24, cf. *Rep. Lac.* 15.2; Hdt. 6.56 (priesthoods); n. 25 above (Dioscuri). Cf. P. Cartledge, *Agesilaos* (London, 1987), 100–10, who endorses Max Weber's designation of the Spartan kingship as 'family-charismatic'.

54. See Thuc. 5.16.1–2 (Pleistoanax: note the Pythia's threat); Xen. *Hell.* 3.3.1–4, Plut. *Ages.* 30.1 (Agesilaus); Hdt. 7.220.4 (Leonidas); Plut. *Cleom.* 19.9, 21 (inhibitions): see the excellent discussion by Carlier, *La royauté*, 292–301; and, on the prestige of the kingship, G.E.M. de Ste. Croix, *The origins of the Peloponnesian war* (London, 1972), 139. Similar attitudes to leaders are found in myth, and persisted in diluted form in other parts of historical Greece: cf. R. Parker, *Miasma* (Oxford, 1983), 265–9.

55. Thuc. 5.16.2.

56. Hdt. 6.58, cf. Tyrtaeus fr. 7 West, Xen. *Hell.* 3.3.1, *Rep. Lac.* 15.9; Cartledge, *Agesilaos*, 331–43 (who cites modern sociological studies of the symbolic significance of royal funerals).

57. Demaratus: Hdt. 6.63.3; curse: Hdt. 6.56 (details are problematic — cf. most recently Carlier, *La royauté*, 257–60 — but there is no reason to doubt that the king's authority on campaign was supported by a curse); Plut. *Apophth. Lac.* 239e (helots). On public curses in general see the references in Parker, *Miasma*, 193–4.

58. Hdt. 7.133–4; Xen. *Hell.* 3.3.4. I owe this point to S. Hodkinson, 'Social order and the conflict of values in classical Sparta', *Chiron* 13

(1983), 239–81, esp. 273–6, where the role of divination in Spartan life is well emphasised.

59. Tyrtaeus fr. 4 West; Strabo 10.4.19 (482) = Ephorus *FGrH* 70 fr. 149 (cf. Hom. *Od.* 19.179); Hdt. 6.52.

60. Hdt. 6.66.1; Thuc. 5.16.2; Xen. *Hell.* 3.3.2–4; Hdt. 5.63. The plots of Lysander are also very revealing: Ephorus *FGrH* 70 frs. 206–7, with Jacoby.

61. See further 'Greek states and Greek oracles', in *Crux, Essays presented to G.E.M. de Ste. Croix*, ed. P. Cartledge and F.D. Harvey (London, 1985 = *History of political thought*, 6), 298–326, esp. 306–9, 318–19. Add Hdt. 5.90.2 (influence of oracles brought from Athens by Cleomenes); Thuc. 1.103.2 (influence of an old Pythian response); Steph. Byz. s.v. *Anthana* (oracles written by Cleomenes). Paus. 3.18.3 comments too on the Spartans' special interest in Ammon.

62. *Pythioi*: Hdt. 6.57.2–4, Xen. *Rep. Lac.* 15.5. On the right of consultation (for the point at issue cf. Xen. *Anab.* 5.6.27) see Ph.E. Legrand, *Quo animo Graeci divinationem adhibuerint* (Paris, 1898), 72–3; Carlier, *La royauté*, 268. Two military questions are assigned to kings (Hdt. 6.76.1, Xen. *Hell.* 4.7.2), perhaps loosely; otherwise 'the Spartans' consult.

63. Star-watching: Plut. *Cleom.* 11.3–6, cf. *Crux*, 319–20 with n. 75; Carlier, *La royauté*, 293–6 (sceptical of its importance). Athens: Strabo 9.2.11 (404), cf. L. Deubner, *Attische Feste* (Berlin, 1932), 203.

64. Pasiphae; Plut. *Cleom.* 28.3, cf. 9.1–4; Cic. *Div.* 1.96; *IG* 5.1.1317, on which see D.W. Prakken in *Studies presented to D.M..Robinson*, 2, (St. Louis, Missouri, 1953), 340–8; cf. Jacoby on *FGrH* 596 (*Anonymoi*) fr. 46. Amphiaraus: *IG* 7.4252 (cf. 4253–4). For a consultation on an important issue, but still a religious one relating to the god himself, see Hyperides, *Euxen.* 14–17.

65. Cf. H. Popp, *Die Einwirkung von Vorzeichen, Opfern und Festen auf die Kriegführung der Griechen* (Erlangen, 1957); Pritchett, *Greek state at war*, 1, 109–15; 3, 47–153, esp. 67–71; R. Lonis, *Guerre et religion en Grèce à l'époque classique* (Paris, 1979), 43–67, 95–115; A.J. Holladay, *CQ* 36 (1986), 152–60.

66. Paus. 9.13.4, Xen. *Rep. Lac.* 13.3 (cf. 15.5).

67. Hdt. 9.33–5.

68. Hdt. 6.76; Thuc. 5.54.1, 55.3, 116.1.

69. Thuc. 3.89.1, 6.95.1; Xen. *Hell.* 3.2.24; Thuc. 8.6.5. Similarly in 480 an eclipse encouraged Cleombrotus to lead the Spartan army home from the Isthmus (Hdt. 9.10.3).

70. Cf. Lonis, *Guerre et religion*, 97.

71. Xen. *Hell.* 3.4.15; *Hell. Oxy.* 7.4; Xen. *Hell.* 4.7.7. Thunderbolts too deterred Agesipolis' force; but, significantly, his main work was done (cf. Popp, *Die Einwirkung*, 58).

72. Hdt. 9.36 (cf. Popp, *Die Einwirkung*, 49), Xen. *Hell.* 3.1.17–19.

73. Hdt. 9.61–2. Cf. Xen. *Hell.* 4.6.10 (Agesilaus).

74. Hdt. 6.81–2; cf. de Ste. Croix, *The origins of the Peloponnesian war*, 351.

75. Xen. *Rep. Lac.* 13.2–5.

76. Pritchett, *Greek state at war*, 3, 139, appears to go beyond the

evidence in saying that the king was 'compelled by law to act in accordance with the sacrifice'.

77. Xen. *Hell.* 4.8.36, Anaxibius, 389. A consequence of casualness, not irreligion, according to Xenophon.

78. Cf. Pritchett, *Greek state at war*, 3, 67–8.

79. Popp and Pritchett (above n. 65) assemble and criticise many such rationalisations.

80. Xen. *Hell.* 4.2.18, *Anab.* 6.4.14

81. *Hipparchicus*, 9.8–9.

82. Thuc. 5.54–5.

83. See the works cited above, n. 65.

84. Pritchett has shown that in education, background and interests seers often differed little from commanders, and might even control rather than increase their religious scruples (*Greek state at war*, 3, 47–72, 110–11: note especially Plut. *Nic.* 23.7 on Stilbides, *Dion* 22.6 on Miltas). Even Tisamenus was an outsider only in nationality; as an Olympic competitor (Hdt. 9.33.2) he was very much 'one of us'.

85. Xen. *Anab.* 2.2.3 (cf. Popp, *Die Einwirkung*, 61) is instructive; cf. too e.g. Hdt. 8.60, last sentence, Philochorus *FGrH* 328 fr. 135.

86. Rules governing repetition are not recorded, for any form of military divination. Pritchett notes (*Greek state at war*, 3, 77) that Xenophon twice abandoned for the day a proposed march after three failures to secure omens (*Anab.* 6.4.16, 19). Before battle, sacrifices could presumably be repeated *ad infinitum*.

87. Hdt. 6.76.

88. Xen. *Hell.* 4.7.2–4. The diplomatic questioning in 2 — cf. Arist. *Rhet.* 2.1398b 33–5 — shows a similarly opportunist but not necessarily irreligious attitude.

89. So G. Grote, *A history of Greece* (edition in 12 volumes, London, 1883), vol. 9, 183. Similar circumstances: above, n.69.

90. *Hell.* 3.4.15.

91. See p. 156 above. Was Agis soft on Argos (cf. Thuc. 5.60)?

92. For a balanced recent survey see A.J. Holladay, *CQ* 36 (1986), 157–60, who notes that the principle was not absolute and remarks 'her piety, though remarkable, was not total and suicidal'.

93. For references see Parker, *Miasma*, 155–6.

94. Thuc. 5.16.3, Plut. *Lys.* 30.1, Plut. *Cleom.* 16.6, 18–19. For Spartan respect for supplication cf. further e.g. Thuc. 1.103.2, Xen. *Hell.* 4.3.20 (contrast Hdt. 6.79). Of course violations also occurred (see below).

95. Thuc. 2.74.2, 4.87.2; Aristotle fr. 538 Rose *ap.* Plut. *Lyc.* 28.7.

96. Thuc. 1.128.1; cf. P. Cartledge, 'Seismicity and Spartan Society', *Liverpool Classical Monthly* 1 (1976), 25–8, who points out that Laconia suffered far more from earthquakes than Attica did.

97. Thuc. 7.18.2; 5.16.1; Hdt. 7.133–7; Thuc. 1.134.4; Hdt. 6.86. Religious explanations were also available for the Spartans' 4th c. reverses at Theban hands (Xen. *Hell.* 5.4.1, 6.4.7), but we do not know how seriously they were taken in Sparta.

98. Plut. *Lys.* 8.4; for other instances of alleged religious scheming cf. 20.6–8, 25–6.

99. See Nilsson, *Geschichte der griechischen Religion*, 1, 796, and the works

he cites. Xenophon still applies *deisidaimon* to Agesilaus (*Ages.* 11.8) in its old favourable sense of 'god-fearing'. The extent to which the re-valuation of the term (in the Peripatos? — cf. e.g. Theophrastus *ap.* Porph. *Abst.* 2.7.p.138.10 — 139.19 Nauck with Plut. *De Superst.* 164e–65c) signalled a real alteration in religious values needs to be clarified. It had always been possible in other ways to criticise supposedly religious behaviour as misguided (see e.g. Hom. *Od.* 2.178–86, Thuc. 7.50.4, Hippoc. *de Morbo Sacro* p.144.16–20 Jones, 28 Grensemann).

100. Revised edition, London, 1973. But the supposed distinction between 'restricted' and 'elaborated' codes, derived from Basil Bernstein, has been much criticised: see e.g. M. Coulthard, 'A discussion of restricted and elaborated codes', *Educational review* 22.1 (1969), 38–50; M. Stubbs, *Educational linguistics* (Oxford, 1986), 235–6.

101. Most obviously in the speech of the Corinthians, 1.68–71, and by implication in Pericles' Funeral Oration. On the contrasting character of political debate see e.g. P.A. Cartledge, *JHS* 98 (1978), 34–7.

102. 2.40.2.

103. Cf. Thuc. 5.66.2–4: on campaign almost every Spartan is a 'commander of a commander'.

104. Aesch. *Eum.* 517–19, 696–9: cf. C.W. Macleod, *JHS* 102 (1982), 135–6 = *Collected essays* (Oxford, 1983), 31–2. 'The Spartans have a shrine of Fear . . . they honour fear not like the powers they seek to avert, considering it harmful, but thinking that the constitution is chiefly held together by fear': Plut. *Cleom.* 30. Cf. Hodkinson, above n. 58, rather than P. Epps, 'Fear in Spartan Character', *CPhil* 28 (1933), 12–29.

105. *Hell.* 3.4.18. I have delivered a part of this paper to a seminar organised by Oswyn Murray in Oxford, as well as to the London Classical Society. I am grateful to the participants on both occasions for helpful observations, to Paul Cartledge for expert written comments, and to Anton Powell for the invitation to study this subject.

7

Mendacity and Sparta's
Use of the Visual[1]

Anton Powell

Modern critics of the Spartans have tended to fall into one of two schools, each perhaps somewhat inhibited in looking for signs of intelligence. On the one hand, those of us deeply influenced by de Ste. Croix's *The Origins of the Peloponnesian War* recall the comparison of the Spartans with Fafner, who became a dragon to guard his treasure and lived a nasty life in a cave.[2] The suggestion of profound irrationality may be potent; the Spartans, it may be thought, threw out the baby with the bathwater when they gave up the relaxed life of Greek gentlemen to guard their treasure, the southern Peloponnese and its population of helots.

The best-known case of Spartan nastiness (and mendacity) shows with special clarity how dragon-like behaviour may discourage us from the search for intelligence. During the Ten Years' War the Spartans, in fear of 'the intractability and sheer number' of the helots, made a proclamation to the latter, calling on them

> to select whoever of them claimed to have proved outstanding in Sparta's interest in war, as they [the Spartans] were going to free them. They did this as a test, thinking that the men with the spirit to think themselves worthy of being freed first were the ones likeliest to attack them. Having made the selection to the number of 2,000 or thereabouts, the helots for their part put on celebratory garments and went round the temples, as men who had gained their freedom; but the Spartans not long afterwards did away with them, leaving it mysterious how each of them was killed.[3]

Since it is in the nature of scholars to value intelligence, if we are offended by behaviour such as this we may well be disinclined to look for, or to mention, associated intelligence in the Spartans — if only for fear of giving to our audience the false idea that we are praising. And yet Sparta performed a considerable feat in first deceiving then cowing an enormously superior number of helots. The numbers of the helots were evidently judged to be so great that some 2,000 of the most impressive could be killed without crippling the economy. By this period the total of Spartiate warriors may itself not greatly have exceeded 2,000. The organisation and secrecy, with which the Spartans were able to kill something approaching their own number of vigorous men, are noteworthy. The facts in outline of course emerged with time. What skills were then involved in persuading the remaining, outraged, helots, that they should still refrain from trying to 'eat the Spartans raw'?[4] Without inviting an audience to diabolism, we should strive to confront the intelligence which must lie behind wickedness accomplished on the grand scale.

Moral repulsion concerning Sparta has grown in recent years. Another, perhaps older, school of thought tends to admiration of the Spartans for their physical courage, their military discipline and the general subordination at Sparta of the individual to the group. It is worthwhile to glance at an article published in 1934, entitled 'The Public School of Sparta', which draws an extensive analogy between Sparta and the classic English boarding school, the deliberately isolated training camp for the administrative elite of an empire.[5] We may not wish to follow its author in his approval for the system of physical training organised in his day by Signor Mussolini. But the article has the virtue of making explicit and memorable an analogy which, in a submerged and perhaps sometimes barely conscious form, may have been highly influential. It is not difficult to conflate the products of the *agōgē* with those of the English Public School. Each group had undergone intensive physical training in an institution stratified by age and policed by whip-bearing prefects. Each institution inculcated reverence for 'pluck' and contempt for 'funk'. Each emphasised corporate self-interest ('team spirit'), combining social homogeneity with an acute sense of hierarchy and competition. Both institutions taught a respect for their carefully preserved, or contrived, traditions, and their products tended to share a towering self-esteem. An effect of this conflation is probably to emphasise moral rectitude and to play down brains, unrealistically in the case of both groups. The idea of Spartan simplicity and virtue is, we shall suggest, a result of steady propaganda from the Spartans themselves. It must not be claimed that the Spartans were secret intellectuals, as was done, if playfully, on at least one occasion in antiquity.[6] But we shall look for signs of communal wisdom in Sparta, if sometimes of a rather formulaic kind.[7]

For whatever reasons, scholars have written dismissively of Spartan intelligence. Sparta is accused of 'folly',[8] 'arrogant stupidity',[9] disastrous ineptitude,[10] 'characteristic selfishness and lack of foresight'.[11] Her commanders were 'rather dull-witted and stubborn'.[12] Even Grote could write of the 'slackness and stupidity' of Sparta.[13] In this matter a strong lead was given by Thucydides. He wrote of Brasidas as 'an able speaker — for a Spartan'.[14] Elsewhere he stated emphatically that, with their slowness and lack of (strategic) daring, the Spartans 'proved, as on many other occasions, the most convenient people in the world for the Athenians to oppose in war'.[15] As with other reports of his on Spartan history,[16] Thucydides' comments on the mental capacity of Spartans are interestingly close to Sparta's own propaganda, as known or reconstructible. Herodotos records the making of a long speech by Samians at Sparta, to which the Spartan authorities replied that they had forgotten the start of it and did not understand the rest.[17] Thucydides represents King Arkhidamos as boasting of the way in which the sound judgement of his people rested on ignorance.[18] The occasion of this claim was a private one, for Spartans only.[19] But if Thucydides reconstructed this section of Arkhidamos' speech in the knowledge that Spartans made such boasts to a wider audience, our suspicions should be aroused. Thucydides' general comment on the secrecy of Sparta's political arrangements should constantly be borne in mind:[20] the Spartans had a lively sense of what it suited non-Spartans to know.

The idea of Spartan stupidity is, in any case, difficult to maintain if we consider the scale and duration of Sparta's ascendancy and the smallness of the citizen population with which that ascendancy was achieved. Personal errors, corruption and ingrained constitutional defects there undoubtedly were.[21] But the more shortcomings we identify, the more obvious should be the need to analyse the ingenuity which allowed the little band of Lakonians to dominate much of Greece.

Xenophon's *Constitution of the Spartans* contains revealing disclaimers. On homosexuality, we read that Lykourgos encouraged association between man and boy, where it was the boy's character that was admired, but decreed that obvious lust for a boy's body should be rejected utterly.[22] Xenophon suggests that the lawgiver was successful in this respect. 'However,' he adds guilelessly, 'I am not surprised that some people do not believe this.' Among those people was Xenophon himself at other times, when the need to praise Sparta was less prominent in his mind.[23] Another telling disclaimer concerns the role of simplicity in Spartan soldiering. Xenophon denies that the Spartan hoplite formation is, 'as most people think', exceedingly complex.[24] But he states that Spartan soldiers perform with great ease manoeuvres which others think very difficult.[25] Xenophon's refusal to admit the existence of complexity in Spartan manoeuvres recalls the apparent propaganda-theme mentioned above: Sparta's alleged simplicity did not apply only to *logoi*. How might Sparta be helped by the dissemination of that theme which, after all, could readily be transformed into an idea similar to that of Thucydides, that Spartans were strikingly incompetent? Xenophon may again prove helpful. He writes that fighting in an unforeseen position, amid confusion, 'is not ... easily learned except by those schooled under the laws of Lykourgos'.[26] Enemies of Sparta might be demoralised by the thought that her military ascendancy was due to the sheer discipline and physical hardness of her men, since in those respects few non-Spartans could expect their cities to make the sacrifice of comfort or of peaceful economic activity needed to match Sparta. On the other hand, skill in strategy and tactics could be assimilated and countered more easily. Spartans may have been eager for their enemies not to understand how much they depended on such skill; they perhaps could not afford to have, in Aristotle's phrase, 'rivals in education'.[27]

Brasidas, we learn, behaved with encouraging rectitude in the Ten Years' War. Greeks conceived a firm hope that other Spartan commanders were like him, writes Thucydides in a passage which *may* be pregnant with paradox.[28] But it is the upright Brasidas rather than later, lesser, Spartans who occupies the memorable position in Thucydides' history, again tending to discourage, at least on a superficial reading, an idea of Spartan deviousness. It may help to examine closely some of the rhetoric employed by Brasidas to win over the obscure statelet of Akanthos. He told the Akanthians that they were 'people with a reputation for intelligence, forming an important city'.[29] Flattery seldom fails completely, appealing as it does to wishful thinking. With consummately smooth impertinence Brasidas used a personal tone of wounded innocence about his reception at Akanthos: 'I am surprised that you have shut the gates against me; I thought you would be glad to see me.'[30] One may see here either conscious posing or the sincere and fruitful vanity of a traditional ruling group, exploiting the widespread human tendency to take others at their apparent self-assessment.

Brasidas also spoke deceptively about the circumstances of his previous success against the Athenians in the Megarid. After reporting Brasidas' speech, Thucydides intervenes to say explicitly that on the subject of the Megarid campaign Brasidas spoke untruth.[31] This is unusual for Thucydides. His speakers are usually represented as following the principle formulated in our own day by the former British Prime Minister, Harold Macmillan — 'You do your best with the facts, but you don't actually lie.' Now, Greeks were given to telling lies. We recall the reported reaction of the Persian Kyros who, irritated by a lordly demand from Sparta, virtually defined the Greeks as men who gathered in a market place and deceived each other under oath.[32] Modern experience suggests that lying flourishes especially in wartime. So we may suspect that the scarcity of clear-cut lies in the reported speeches from the Peloponnesian War is a sign of Thucydides' didactic intervention. Copious lies might mislead readers, or call for tediously frequent editorial rebuttal. On the other hand, speeches in Thucydides often characterise their makers. In characterising Brasidas, did Thucydides see an unusual need to include lying? As we shall see, in a later passage he has Brasidas explicitly commending deceit in wartime.

Sparta's paraded religiosity also discourages thought of under-hand behaviour. Religion among the Spartans was, as Robert Parker helps us to see,[33] far from being a mere cloak, conscious or unconscious, for secular motives. But it did have, on occasion, predictable secular benefit. Xenophon describes Agesilaos in Asia, steadfastly and ostentatiously refusing to break his oath, while knowing that the other party to the agreement, his opponent Tissaphernes, was breaking his.[34] But then hostilities were formally declared. Xenophon writes that Agesilaos there-after 'appeared to have achieved something characteristic of a proper general (*strategikon*): when war was declared and decep-tion as a result became religiously permissible and just, he completely outclassed Tissaphernes in deceit'.[35]

Religiosity might entice opponents into failing to guard against the deceit which Sparta had in store for them following the moral alchemy of a declaration of war. It was a familiar point in antiquity that life at Sparta in many ways resembled that of a military camp.[36] Spartan deceptiveness may be partly understood in this light. To mislead an enemy would be taught as good military practice. (Compare Virgil: *Dolus an virtus, quis in hoste requirat?*[37] In English, if we wish to refer without disapproval to a deceptive arrangement, as of household furniture or shop goods, we may talk of things being 'strategically placed'.) In addition, war and peace alike gave many opportunities of deceiving without oath-breaking or even uttering a direct lie. And the moral distinction between war and peace might be overlooked at times because of the permanent militarism and permanent military threat under which the Spartans lived. Sparta would always be aware that the image she transmitted was an important instrument of war.

Cases of Spartan commanders seeking to deceive a foe are numerous. Lysandros' triumphant outwitting of the Athenians at Aigospotamoi may be the most important.[38] Lysandros' technique, of letting a pattern of Spartan behaviour implant a false prediction in the enemy's mind, recalls the victorious procedure of Kleomenes at Sepeia.[39] In 392 the Spartan Pasimakhos lured men of Argos into battle by equipping his men with shields which bore a sigma, the badge of Sikyon. Contemporary report had Pasimakhos saying 'By the twin gods, these sigmas will deceive you, Argives, into coming to fight us.'[40] Thucydides describes Brasidas as seeking to persuade his (mainly non-Spartan) soldiers of the virtue of a surprise attack, meant to exploit an enemy's mistake: 'These stealthy actions involve the greatest glory when they most deceive the enemy and most benefit one's friends.' The word here translated as 'stealthy actions', *klemmata*, if it was not Brasidas' own, may perhaps have been chosen by Thucydides to illustrate a connection between two Spartan institutions: adult military deceit and juvenile theft.[41]

In two remarkable cases, Spartan commanders applied grand deception to their own troops. After the defeats at Arginousai and Knidos, in 406 and 394 respectively, Eteonikos and Agesilaos each informed his men elsewhere that Sparta had in fact been victorious. In both cases there was an energetic charade of sacrificial thanksgiving. Xenophon's account of the earlier occasion nicely illustrates Sparta's combination of secrecy and

178

deceit. Those who had brought the bad news were ordered to sail away in silence, speaking to no one, and then to return, 'garlanded and shouting that Kallikratidas was victorious in a sea battle, and that all the ships of the Athenians were lost'. Of the second case Xenophon notes that Agesilaos' falsehood had the effect of fortifying his men for war;[42] allies, who formed a large part of his army, might otherwise have proved fickle.

In the Periklean funeral speech it is suggested that Spartan soldiers depended on rehearsed manoeuvres and on deceit.[43] Alkibiades successfully assumed that it was possible to persuade a Spartan delegation to seek to mislead the Athenian assembly.[44] In 373/2 the Athenian general Iphikrates heard that the Spartan commander of an opposing force, Mnasippos, was dead. He reacted by remaining ready for battle. 'For,' in Xenophon's words, 'he had not heard the news about Mnasippos from any eye witness, but was on his guard, suspecting that the statement had been issued to deceive.'[45] Careful source-criticism in Spartan matters was a means of staying alive. In the *Peace* Aristophanes has the bellicose soothsayer Hierokles allude to the Spartans as 'little foxes . . . with treacherous souls, treacherous minds'.[46] The tale recorded in later antiquity, of a Spartan boy who chose to endure in silence while a stolen fox cub fatally wounded him, has traditionally been told as reflecting courage.[47] But it also should be seen as glamorising deception. We are far from the values implied in the story of young George Washington. The Spartan boy is remembered not because he could not tell a lie, but because he would not tell the truth.

We have already begun to touch on Sparta's use of the visual. Indeed, sophistication in the use of visual images might almost be predicted, once there is a recognition of Sparta's interest in deceit and in the use of few words. When an army of the Peloponnesian league contained Spartan hoplites, it might be important to draw attention to them, to let Sparta's reputation do its work on enemy minds. The red cloaks worn by Spartan troops proved distinctive and memorable,[48] as they were surely intended to be. The famous long hair of Sparta's soldiers was meant to be conspicuous and intimidating; according to Xenophon, Lykourgos 'allowed the hair to be grown long, thinking that in this way [Spartans] would appear larger . . . and be more frightening.'[49] (One may compare, with the leonine Spartans, the French grenadiers and British guardsmen of the 19th century, with their large hats.)

Records of visual propaganda cluster around Agesilaos, one of the most closely observed of Sparta's commanders. According to his admirer, Xenophon, he accoutred his army in such a way that 'it gave the impression of consisting entirely of bronze and scarlet'.[50] Believing that contempt for the enemy fortified men for battle, he ordered that enemy prisoners be sold naked. The spectacle of the latter, fat, white, and not hardened by toil, convinced Agesilaos' soldiers, according to Xenophon, that the war would be virtually the same as fighting against women.[51] Xenophon praises the impression created by the sight of Agesilaos' physical arrangements at Ephesos:

> *you could see* the gymnasia full of men exercising, the hippo-drome full of horsemen riding, the javelin-throwers and the archers at target practice . . . The market place was full of armaments and horses for sale, while the bronze-smiths and carpenters, ironworkers, leatherworkers and painters were all preparing military equipment. As a result you would truly have thought the city a workshop of war. *One would also have been fortified to see* first Agesilaos then the other soldiers wearing garlands . . . which they offered up to the goddess Artemis. For wherever men revere the gods, train for war and practise to obey the authorities, there it can be expected that everything will radiate optimism.[52] [Emphasis mine]

There can be little doubt as to where Agesilaos learnt to project the image of a city as a workshop of war, radiating optimism, a showpiece of piety and of obedience to the secular authorities. Elsewhere, Xenophon notes of another scene combining religious and secular order, 'seeing this . . . you would think that the Spartans alone were true craftsmen in matters of war'.[53]

After the battle of Lekhaion in 390, Agesilaos led home through the Peloponnese a Spartan force which had been badly defeated. He did so in a way calculated to conceal the small number of the survivors. Their arrival at Peloponnesian towns was timed to occur at a late hour, and their departure very early in the morning. Mantineia was passed in the hours of darkness.[54] A British scholar has recently suggested that 'the Spartans' practice of starting at night on expeditions out of Lakonia' was due to the high incidence of sunshine in that part of the Peloponnese.[55] This recalls the reason put forward by Meiggs to explain the refusal of the Ionians to abandon their territory after Mykale — the splendid climate of Ionia.[56] Aversion from thoughts of social differences has traditionally been common among classical scholars, inspired partly by a delicate reluctance (which the Spartan oligarchs might well have understood) to introduce divisive conversation into their own group. In the case of Ionia, the weather was surely less important than the unwillingness of rich and influential Ionians to exchange their privileged position for mere promises of land elsewhere. As to Sparta, if armies did generally set out from home by night,[57] the analogy with Agesilaos' furtive march should suggest that the purpose was to deceive. The obvious targets of deception were the helots, who were to be kept in the dark as to how many of their masters were going away. This would make particularly good sense if, as we may suspect, helots were kept under curfew. A curfew would explain why the *krypteia* reportedly involved killing helots caught on the road at night.[58]

Various social lessons for Spartiates themselves were reinforced by visual presentation. Differences in personal wealth were obscured by dress. Aristotle records that rich Spartiates wore clothes 'of a sort that even any poor man could get'.[59] (Compare 'classless denim', and its role in the relatively *stasis*-free United States.) Thucydides comments on the Spartans' moderation in dress, and on the unusual lengths to which the most prosperous of them went in assimilating their style of life to that of ordinary citizens.[60] Among many other functions, the *syssition* served as a show of homogeneity.

The revered Tyrtaios had taught with words the value of a soldierly and patriotic death, in a way reminiscent for us of the slogan of Nationalist troops in the Spanish Civil War: *Viva la Muerte.*[61] The lesson could be imparted in another way. After the defeat at Lekhaion there was much grief in the Spartan army, according to Xenophon, 'except for those whose sons or fathers or brothers had died there. They went about radiant, as if they had won a victory, rejoicing in what had happened to their families.'[62] There was another remarkable exhibition when the Spartans at home received the news of Leuktra; Xenophon again stresses the visual:

> on the following day you could see those who had lost relatives going about in the open, radiant and anointed [or 'sleek' — λιπαροὺς], whereas few were in evidence of those whose relatives had been reported to have survived, and they went about humbled and gloomy.[63]

In the latter case it is clear that there was a conscious manipulation of appearances. The ephors, when the bad news arrived, refused to interrupt the performance by the men's chorus at the Gymnopaidiai, and instructed the women not to cry out, but to bear their lot in silence.[64] The didactic display of rejoicing in soldierly death should be compared with the public demeanour required of those identified as cowards; they, according to Xenophon, were forbidden to walk around anointed.[65]

We have seen one Athenian general guarding against Spartan military deceit. Action ascribed to Theban commanders after their victory at Leuktra suggests that they may have learned something of Sparta's use of the visual. The Thebans apparently caused the very numerous corpses of Spartiates to be displayed on the battlefield separately from the others.[66] Thebes countered Spartan secrecy with a flash of publicity, using Sparta's own technique of the memorable visual image. When the Thebans invaded Lakonia in the aftermath of the battle, the Spartans were forced to make an even clearer demonstration of their small number. Using their utmost numbers to defend their home villages the Spartans, in Xenophon's significant phrase, 'both were very few and were seen to be'.[67] By publicising Spartan numbers and Spartan losses Thebes perhaps did almost as much to undermine the power of her enemy as she did by winning at Leuktra and by freeing the Messenian helots. The illusion of Spartan strength, for long ingeniously sustained, was now at an end.

If the material presented above is judged to establish that Sparta tended to deceive and to use the visual, it may be permissible now to apply our findings briefly and speculatively to a number of other topics, even though none of them can be dealt with thoroughly in this brief way. What was the purpose of the driving-out of foreigners from Sparta, the distinctive *xenēlasia*? As with the Eleusinian Mysteries, speculation on this subject may be the most that can be achieved, precisely because of the measures taken to prevent general access. In the Periklean funeral speech it is stated that Athenians 'never use *xenēlasiai* to prevent anyone from learning or seeing something which . . . it would profit an enemy to see; *we* rely not for the most part on preparation and deceit but rather on spontaneous courage'.[68] It is here suggested that a Spartan sense of the instructive spectacle is put to negative use. Complex manoeuvres might need to be practised in secret, for reasons we have seen. One military process above all might

require the removal of alien witnesses. The Spartans, with their
sense of military opportunity, would almost certainly have had a
mechanism to deal with the fact that Sparta consisted of villages,
which might be attacked in isolation. There was surely a system
of alarm, to be followed by a rapid assembly into one or two
places of the entire Spartiate community, including *gerontes*,
children and women. The system would need to be secret, to
prevent its being exploited by some enemy stratagem. Also, the
assembly of the community would reveal its size, or rather its
smallness. It was in connection with the size of Sparta's army
that Thucydides made his general remark about Spartan secrecy.
We recall Xenophon's emphatic statement that the army was
seen to be small after Leuktra.[69] These considerations may not
fully explain the existence of the *xenēlasia*,[70] but they suggest that,
given Sparta's psychology and military position, something along
the lines of the *xenēlasia* would have been desired.

Why did the Spartans persist in living in villages, a fact which
Thucydides found remarkable?[71] Pride in tradition may be part
of the answer. The centralised *polis* may have come to be
associated with alien *dēmokratia*. But centralisation and a wall
would have given protection against surprise attack. Did Spartans
shun a wall as a visual advertisement of weakness, of the fear of
attack?[72] Also, a population concentrated in a single place would
have been more easily perceived by an enemy as small than one
scattered in villages. Thucydides wrote that Sparta's buildings in
certain circumstances might underrepresent her strength.[73] But
he there had in mind temples, and the lower parts of buildings
which might survive as ruins. Durable, expensive, stone structures
were not the only device for suggesting power to contemporaries.
A host of much flimsier buildings might be sufficient to suggest
human multitudes within.

Since the Spartans conceived of excluding strangers from their
home villages, and indeed had a familiar mechanism for doing it,
why did they not do it all the year round? Strangers might
corrupt, as the exemplary Gorgo observed.[74] Diplomacy could be
conducted a few miles from Sparta, if Spartans *en masse* needed to
hear the arguments, and perhaps much further away when only
officials needed to attend. We hear of Sellasia being used in some
such way during diplomatic exchanges with Athens at the end of
the Peloponnesian War. The ephors dealt with an Athenian
delegation at Sellasia on two occasions; only when the Athenians
were deemed to have come with suitable instructions were they

allowed, it appears, to proceed to Sparta itself.[75] That Sparta at other times could be visited by representatives of rival powers,[76] in effect by spies, is unlikely to have resulted from oversight or lack of imagination on the part of the Spartans. We recall Agesilaos' projection of the image of a city as a workshop of war. Limited access to Sparta was perhaps allowed precisely in order that visitors should take away certain images. The idea of such motivation was certainly known to the Greeks; it is involved in Herodotos' story of Greek spies, captured by the Persians on the eve of Xerxes' invasion, and deliberately set free to report the daunting facts about the scale of the Great King's forces.[77] Xenophon, when explaining the existence of the *syssitia*, imputes to Lykourgos the view that exposure to inspection in public by other Spartans discouraged sloppiness in individuals.[78] Shirking was surely an endemic concern at Sparta, given the severe nature of the required style of life.[79] Was the presence of a few outsiders, even enemy spies, quietly welcomed also as a discipline for the whole community? Sparta's internal arrangements reflect a potent belief in the value of competition for raising standards. In any case, the combination we suggest, of exclusion of foreigners in some circumstances, and of presentation to outsiders in other circumstances of contrived and suggestive military spectacle, has analogues today. There is the May Day parade in Moscow, and Open Day at a NATO air-base.

Three Spartan rulers of the early fifth century disgraced themselves in colourful style: the kings Kleomenes and Leotykhidas, and the regent Pausanias. Leotykhidas' fall has attracted relatively little attention, but for various reasons scholars have often expressed grave reservations about the accounts, in Herodotos and Thucydides respectively, of how Kleomenes and Pausanias ended their lives. Kleomenes, we recall, went mad and killed himself by cutting his flesh into rags.[80] Pausanias is described as revealing his treasonable dealing with Persia to an ex-boyfriend, in a hut of some kind which, unknown to him, contained listening ephors.[81] Leotykhidas' downfall is recounted in the same context as that of Kleomenes: he

> commanded a Spartan campaign against Thessaly, and when he had it in his power to get total control he accepted a large bribe of silver. Caught red-handed there in the camp, sitting on a glove full of silver, he was exiled from

Sparta by the sentence of a court and his property was demolished. He fled to Tegea where he died.[82]

In each of the three cases the alleged act of lunacy or wickedness occurred with very few witnesses. The surviving stories recall modern destructive journalism. They are shocking, simple and memorable. They damn the individual in a way likely to inhibit the growth of a faction loyal to him or his memory. They divert attention from the surviving authorities and from the constitution, which might otherwise be criticised on the principle that rebels are not born but made. They exploit the fact that the deeds of an individual, presented to the visual imagination, claim attention far more effectively than do constitutional abstractions. In our own day, perhaps the most memorable and damning element in the account of Harold Wilson's last Prime Ministerial honours list was the detail that it was drafted by a female aide on lavender-coloured notepaper: 'the lavender list'. Our three Spartan stories appeal strikingly to the visual: Kleomenes with his knife; Pausanias with the lurking ephors; Leotykhidas sitting on his glove of silver. In each case the scene is set; the stocks, a hut, and a military encampment, respectively.

Alan Griffiths shows some remarkable resemblances between Herodotos' details of Kleomenes' misbehaviour and information from the same author on the Persian King Kambyses.[83] He suggests that intercultural folk-tale motifs have influenced Herodotos. We may feel more surprise at Thucydides for his uncharacteristic storytelling on the subject of Pausanias, especially when we contrast the level of detail in his story with the admirable caution expressed at the start of his history (I 1 3). Events before the Peloponnesian War were not strictly knowable, he wrote there, in a passage which has provoked scholarly discomfort to the point of emendation.[84] Yet the fall of Pausanias is recorded in great detail, in spite of its having occurred 30 years or more before the *Kerkyraïka*. This Thucydidean lapse, if so we take it, may be of a piece with another remarkable case of optimism in him. The approximate age of the Spartan constitution, he wrote, was slightly more than 400 years.[85] The approach to precision is hard to square with the caution and agnosticism concerning events in, or shortly preceding, the historian's own lifetime.

The institution of theft by juveniles, described in the classical period by Xenophon, offended — on the face of it — against two ideals of Spartan society: obedience and respect for elders. It may be worth looking for a countervailing benefit. Xenophon states that boys stole in order to become better warriors, and identifies certain elements of military training imparted by the stealing: the young thieves learned to stay awake at night and to deceive by day, to lie in ambush and to set lookouts.[86] Ambush and living off the land by stealth do not sound like elements of warfare for the hoplite phalanx. In another passage Xenophon writes that Spartans on expedition were discouraged from going far from camp to excrete.[87] The aftermath of defeat might require irregular foraging, but the Spartan system did not countenance the survival of defeat. The education in theft may need a different explanation.

The helot revolts of which we hear most were large affairs, which Sparta could not keep secret, if only because she needed help from outside to deal with them. How common were small-scale revolt and brigandage? That we hear little of them is hardly surprising. If the Spartans were masters of deceit, secrecy and military opportunism,[88] we should not expect them to advertise gratuitously their own distractions. In connection with the Athenian seizure of Pylos, Thucydides states that Sparta had previously been inexperienced in regard to brigandage and the kind of fighting which went with it.[89] His opinion cannot be firmly discounted, but we may wonder how he arrived at it. He is in effect putting forward a very large and vulnerable claim — that in a long preceding period the Spartans had always or almost always been uninvolved with brigandage — about a state whose desire to obscure its own circumstances he notes in this very context. Also, he himself records that at the start of the Pylian episode the Athenians got help from Messenian brigands 'who happened to be present'.[90] We may suspect that irregular fighting in Spartan territory had a longer history than Thucydides' Peloponnesian informants could or would make clear. Tegea over the northern border could not harbour runaway helots.[91] Taking to the hills or the coasts, and living by plunder off the rich lands of Lakonia and Messenia, was perhaps the resort of numerous small groups of helots who had lost patience with their masters. Guerrilla war notoriously imposes its own tactics on the opposition. That may have been why young Spartans were taught to live off the land, deprived of food and normal clothing.

There are, then, three Spartan topics on which Thucydides may seem to have been uncharacteristically credulous: the fall of

Pausanias, the age of the constitution, and the scarcity of guerrilla war in Spartan territory. In all three areas Thucydides' account corresponds with what we might guess the Spartan authorities wished to have propagated. In one case, the older the constitution could be made to seem, and the greater its durability, the less hope there might be for any revolutionary spirits within Sparta. In another, Sparta's victory at Plataia was surely a permanent and important prop to the Spartans' extraordinary self-confidence. The commander at that battle was therefore someone whose reputation might need especially destructive attack if it was not to rise from the grave and breed *stasis* from the royal families downwards. The grounds of attack reflected in Thucydides could hardly have been more damaging. The alleged dealings with the Mede poisoned the memory of Pausanias as the victor at Plataia. The treason of the regent with the helots represented probably the ultimate crime for a Spartiate.

In a prefatory remark on his work, Thucydides tells of the difficulties he regularly faced from informants who gave divergent accounts.[92] But in a way the very diversity of those accounts might be of value, in that it obviously called for criticism and a suspension of belief. One may suspect, though only suspect, that Thucydides, through being used to the famous variety of character and freedom of speech at Athens, was at times taken off guard by a unanimity on the part of informants from Sparta, a state so disciplined as to produce virtually a 'party line'. The word *homoioi*, applied to the Spartiates,[93] is commonly translated as 'peers' or 'equals'. These translations may focus too narrowly. The Greek word did more than connote similarity in political status. It meant similarity full stop. We do well to remember the ways in which Sparta lacked perfect homogeneity, as between rich and poor Spartiates, for example.[94] But while Spartan eyes, on the well known cognitive principle, would no doubt become accustomed to perceiving fine differences in character and status beneath the surface of homogeneity, to outsiders homogeneity would often be the main thing noticed, especially since many of the characteristics which Spartiates seemed to share were unusual by general Greek standards. We are of course speculating when we suggest that to a trained Spartiate ear there may have been distinctly different nuances in accounts by different Spartans of sensitive matters from the city's history, whereas to historians trained in the variety of Athens the main impression derivable from different Spartiate informants was one of uniformity, from which it was a short step to assuming reliability.

So far we have deliberately refrained from making much use of post-classical Greek testimony. However, details from Plutarch's *Life of Lykourgos* may gain a new significance in the light of classical (and particularly Xenophontic) evidence for Sparta's use of the visual. There is some slight overlap in detail between Xenophon and Plutarch on this subject. Both refer to the use of long hair to intimidate,[95] though Plutarch is the fuller on the point, and his presentation does not suggest borrowing from Xenophon. Otherwise, several well known passages of the *Lykourgos* concern the role of the visual in instructing Spartans. There was the forced parade of naked bachelors, designed to humiliate them and thus to promote marriage.[96] 'The processions of the maidens, their removal of clothes and their contests where young men could see' were intended, according to Plutarch, to incite men to marry.[97] Plutarch's record of helots being forced to become drunk, as an instructive spectacle for young Spartiates, and to dance and sing absurdly and degradingly, is dealt with by Ephraim David elsewhere in this volume.[98] Plutarch's autopsy of flogging ordeals in which 'many' youths died at the altar of Artemis Orthia testifies not only to the longevity of noble death at Sparta, but also to the Spartans' persistence in using the visual to instruct outsiders.[99]

Less well known is Plutarch's treatment of the progress of the Spartan phalanx into battle, calm and rhythmic to the sound of the pipes, as a terrifying spectacle.[100] He suggests that burials were allowed to take place within the inhabited area of Sparta, and funerary monuments to be placed near shrines, so that constant exposure to the sight of them would make the young calm and unafraid in the face of death.[101] The period set for mourning was short, writes Plutarch, in a way which corresponds pleasingly rather than suspiciously with Xenophon's detail on grief after battle.[102] Plutarch summarises:

> He [Lykourgos] caused the city to be studded with a mass of instructive models for behaviour; the people who came into continual contact with them and were brought up alongside them were bound to be influenced into conforming with what was good.[103]

If there were no particular reason *a priori* for trusting either

Xenophon or Plutarch in this matter of Spartan use of the visual, we might still be impressed by the manner of their convergence. In neither writer is the theme emphasised in such a way as to raise doubt, and the difference of detail makes borrowing from Xenophon by Plutarch an unlikely explanation of the convergence. Since, however, we know that Xenophon had unusually good access to Sparta and to Spartan armed forces, it seems better to make the orthodox assumption that his material on Sparta's use of the visual is likely to be correct in the main. From this it would follow that Plutarch's congruity with Xenophon in this matter has something to tell us about the general usefulness of the *Life of Lykourgos*.[104]

Notes

1. In this paper I have tried to make a full statement of ideas to some extent outlined in my *Athens and Sparta* (London, 1988), some passages have been taken over directly from that book.
2. Op. cit. 91.
3. Thuc. IV 80 3f.
4. Cf. Xen. *Hell.* III 3 6.
5. T. Rutherford Harley, *Greece and Rome* III (1934) 129ff.
6. Plat. *Protag.* 342A–343B.
7. Elsewhere I have tried to demonstrate that Sparta's warlike initiatives against Athens in the fifth century happened virtually to formula; *Antiquité classique* XLIX (1980) 87–114. See also, on obedience to rule in Spartan religion, R. Parker, pp. 160ff. of this volume.
8. W.G. Forrest, *A history of Sparta* (London, 1968), 105, 139, cf. 100.
9. Ibid. 138.
10. A.H.M. Jones, *Sparta* (Oxford, 1967), 59.
11. H. Michell, *Sparta* (Cambridge, 1952), 39f., cf. 335 and P.A. Brunt, *Historia* II (1953–4) 141.
12. R. Meiggs, *The Athenian empire* (Oxford, 1972), 355.
13. *A history of Greece* vol. 8 p. 58 (Everyman edition).
14. IV 84 2. Aristotle, in the passage where he refers to the Spartans as making their boys bestial (*Pol.* 1338b), suggests that Spartan education aimed exclusively or mainly at producing the virtue of physical courage.
15. VIII 96 5.
16. See below, on the age of the Spartan constitution, the downfall of Pausanias, and the incidence of brigandage in Spartan territory.
17. III 46 1, cf. Thuc. I 86 1, 3.
18. I 84 3.
19. Thuc. I 79 1.
20. V 68 2.
21. See especially S. Hodkinson, *Chiron* 13 (1983) 239–81.

22. II 13.

23. *Hell.* V 4 25, cf. IV 1 39f., V 4 57, *Agesilaos* V 4–7. On male homosexuality at Sparta, P.A. Cartledge, *Proc. Camb. Phil. Soc.* 27 (1981) 17–36.

24. *Lak. Pol.* XI 5.

25. Ibid. 8.

26. Ibid. 7.

27. *Pol.* 1338b. Cf. Plut. *Lyk.* XIII where it is stated that there was a *rhetra* of Lykourgos forbidding Spartans to make war repeatedly against any one enemy, so that the enemy 'should not be made warlike through becoming accustomed to defending themselves'. In this context a story is told of Agesilaos' being blamed by Antalkidas for having 'taught the Thebans to fight'.

28. IV 81 3.

29. IV 85 6.

30. IV 85 3.

31. IV 85 7 with 108 5.

32. Hdt. I 153 1f.

33. See pp. 142ff. of this volume.

34. *Agesilaos* I 10ff.

35. Ibid. 17.

36. Isok. VI 81, Plat. *Laws* 666E, Plut. *Lyk.* XXIV 1, cf. Arist. *Pol.* 1324b.

37. *Aeneid* II 390.

38. Xen. *Hell.* II 1 22–8.

39. Hdt. VI 77f.

40. Xen. *Hell.* IV 4 10, cf. Arist. *N.E.* 1117a.

41. V 9 5; cf. Xen. *Lak. Pol.* II 7, where the connection is explicit, and *Anab.* IV 6 13ff.

42. Xen. *Hell.* I 6 36f.; IV 3 13f. One thinks of the photograph from the First World War showing Russian soldiers crowding a train bound for home; it was published in wartime Britain with the encouraging caption, 'Russian troops hurry to the front'. On photographic and other mendacity from the period see A. Ponsonby, *Falsehood in wartime* (London, 1928), ch. XXIV and *passim*.

43. Thuc. II 39 1.

44. Thuc. V 45.

45. Xen. *Hell.* VI 2 31.

46. ll.1067f.

47. Plut. *Lyk.* XVIII 1.

48. Ar. *Lys.* 1138–41, Xen. *Lak. Pol.* XI 3 etc.

49. *Lak. Pol.* XI 3, but cf. Arist. *Rhet.* 1367a.

50. *Agesilaos* II 7.

51. Ibid. I 28. *Hell.* III 4 19 is almost identical.

52. *Agesilaos* I 26f. *Hell.* III 4 16–18 is almost identical.

53. *Lak. Pol.* XIII 5.

54. Xen. *Hell.* IV 5 18.

55. G. Huxley, *Hermathena* 128 (1980) 41.

56. R. Meiggs (n. 12) 34.

57. Cf. Hdt. IX 10. Many other nocturnal military movements by the

Spartans are recorded; e.g. Thuc. IV 103 1 (Brasidas against Amphipolis), VII 4 2 (Gylippos outside Syracuse), Xen. *Hell.* V 4 20–21 (Sphodrias against Periraieus). Cf. *Lak. Pol.* II 7, V 7.

58. Plut. *Lyk.* XXVIII 4.

59. *Pol.* 1294b.

60. I 6 4.

61. For Tyrtaios see, most conveniently, *Elegy and iambus* I (ed. J.M. Edmonds, London, 1931) pp. 68–73. On *Viva la Muerte,* H. Thomas, *The Spanish Civil War* (London, 1961), ch. 29. On Spartan attitudes to death cf. N. Loraux, *Ktema* II (1977), 105–20.

62. *Hell.* IV 5 10.

63. Ibid. VI 4 16.

64. Ibid.

65. *Lak. Pol.* IX 5. Further on the conspicuous treatment of cowards see E. David, pp. 14f. of this volume.

66. Paus. IX 13, Plut. *Mor.* 193B.

67. *Hell.* VI 5 28.

68. Thuc. II 39 1. See Xen. *Lak. Pol.* XIII 5 (and cf. Hdt. VII 211) for the idea that, by comparison with the Spartans, others were mere improvisers (*autoskhediastas*) in matters of war.

69. The conspirator Kinadon, though not one of the *homoioi*, is shown seeking in good Spartan style to demonstrate the weakness of his enemies (the Spartiates) by employing the spectacle of their small number in the *agora*; Xen. *Hell.* III 3 5.

70. Cf. Xen. *Lak. Pol.* XIV 4.

71. I 10 2.

72. Cf. Plut. *Lyk.* XIX 12.

73. I 10 2.

74. Hdt. V 51 2; cf. Xen. *Lak. Pol.* XIV 4.

75. Xen. *Hell.* II 2 13, 19.

76. E.g. Thuc I 72 1, 90 5.

77. VII 146f.

78. *Lak. Pol.* V 2.

79. Xenophon's term for shirking, used repeatedly, is ῥᾳδιουργεῖν, ῥᾳδιουργία; *Lak. Pol.* II 2, IV 4, V 2, XIV 4.

80. Hdt. VI 75.

81. Thuc. I 133.

82. Hdt. VI 72.

83. Pages 58, 60f., 67, 70f. of this volume.

84. See Gomme, *Historical commentary on Thucydides, ad loc.*

85. I 18 1.

86. *Lak. Pol.* II 7.

87. Ibid. XII 4.

88. On opportunism, see the article cited above, n. 7.

89. IV 41 3.

90. IV 9 1, cf. 53 3.

91. Plut. *Mor.* 292B with de Ste. Croix, *The Origins of the Peloponnesian War*, 97.

92. I 22 3.

93. Xen. *Hell.* III 3 5, *Lak. Pol.* XIII 1, 7, Arist. *Pol.* 1306b.

94. See Hodkinson (above, n. 21) and (in this volume) pp. 79ff.

95. *Lyk.* XXII 2.

96. XV 1f.

97. XV 1.

98. XXVIII 8f. with pp. 6f., 9 of this volume.

99. XVIII 2.

100. XXII 5.

101. XXVII 1.

102. XXVII 4.

103. XXVII 5.

104. For a recent contribution to this subject, D.M. MacDowell, *Spartan law* (Edinburgh, 1986), 17–22.

Index

Greek names have been hellenised wherever possible; thus, for example, Karneia, Lykourgos, Tainaron.

The Oklahoma Series in Classical Culture is a publishing venture of the University of Oklahoma Press. The series formalizes the Press's long tradition of publishing books in the classical fields. Series editor A. J. Heisserer (University of Oklahoma) and an advisory board of twelve distinguished scholars from the United States, Canada, and Great Britain work closely with the University of Oklahoma Press to publish books of the highest quality in the following areas:

(1) General studies in ancient culture, including literature, history, and archaeology.

(2) General textbooks in English intended primarily for use in undergraduate courses.

(3) Classroom textbooks intended primarily for use in Greek and Latin courses, such books invariably containing the text in the original language together with helpful notes for students.

(4) Specialized monographs in ancient culture, dealing with such areas as ancient medicine, Ciceronian studies, Latin literature in the Late Empire, and the social and political history of Classical Greece.